THE CAMBRIDGE COMPANION TO
GEORGE ORWELL

George Orwell is regarded as the greatest political writer in English of the twentieth century. The massive critical literature on Orwell has not only become extremely specialised, and therefore somewhat inaccessible to the non-scholar, but it has also contributed to and even created misconceptions about the man, the writer, and his literary legacy. For these reasons, an overview of Orwell's writing and influence is an indispensable resource. Accordingly, this *Companion* serves as both an introduction to Orwell's work and furnishes numerous innovative interpretations and fresh critical perspectives on it. Throughout the *Companion*, which includes chapters dedicated to Orwell's major novels, *Nineteen Eighty-Four* and *Animal Farm*, Orwell's work is placed within the context of the political and social climate of the time. His response to the Depression, British imperialism, Stalinism, the Second World War, and the politics of the British Left are all examined. Chapters also discuss Orwell's status among intellectuals and in the literary academy, and a detailed chronology of Orwell's life and work is included.

John Rodden has taught at the University of Virginia and the University of Texas at Austin. He has authored or edited several books on George Orwell, including *The Politics of Literary Reputation: the Making and Claiming of 'St George' Orwell* (1989), *Understanding* Animal Farm *in Historical Context* (1999), *Scenes from an Afterlife: the Legacy of George Orwell* (2003), *George Orwell Into the Twenty-First Century* (2004), and *Every Intellectual's Big Brother: George Orwell's Literary Siblings* (2006).

D0139506

THE CAMBRIDGE
COMPANION TO
GEORGE ORWELL

EDITED BY
JOHN RODDEN

CAMBRIDGE
UNIVERSITY PRESS

CAMBRIDGE UNIVERSITY PRESS
Cambridge, New York, Melbourne, Madrid, Cape Town, Singapore, São Paulo

Cambridge University Press
The Edinburgh Building, Cambridge CB2 8RU, UK

Published in the United States of America by Cambridge University Press, New York

www.cambridge.org
Information on this title: www.cambridge.org/9780521675079

© Cambridge University Press 2007

First published 2007

Printed in the United Kingdom at the University Press, Cambridge

A catalogue record for this publication is available from the British Library

ISBN 978-0-521-85842-7 hardback
ISBN 978-0-521-67507-9 paperback

CONTENTS

CONTENTS

NOTES ON CONTRIBUTORS

GORDON BOWKER taught at Goldsmith's College, University of London. He now works as a full-time biographer and journalist. His books include *Malcolm Lowry: Under the Volcano: A Casebook* (1987); *Malcolm Lowry Remembered* (1985); *Pursued by Furies: A Life of Malcolm Lowry* (1993); *Through the Dark Labyrinth: A Biography of Lawrence Durrell* (1996); and *George Orwell* [*Inside George Orwell* in the US] (2003). He is now working on a book about literary exile.

WILLIAM E. CAIN is Professor of English at Wellesley College. He is the editor of *A Historical Guide to Henry David Thoreau* (2000) and *American Literature*, a two-volume anthology (2004).

ROBERT CONQUEST is a research fellow at the Hoover Institution, Stanford University. He is the author of some thirty-one books of history, biography, poetry, fiction and criticism, including *The Great Terror*, which has appeared in more than twenty languages, *The Harvest of Sorrow*, *Reflections on a Ravaged Century*, and *The Dragons of Expectation*.

BERNARD CRICK is Professor Emeritus of Birkbeck College, University of London. His prolific writings span both the academic and the popular, a public intellectual in the old sense. His best known books are *In Defence of Politics* (1962 and still in print) and *George Orwell: A Life* (1980); and also four books of essays including *Essays on Politics and Literature, Political Thoughts and Polemics*, and *Essays on Citizenship*. More recently he wrote *Democracy*. In 2002, he was knighted 'for services to citizenship and political studies' after having chaired the advisory group that brought citizenship into the national curriculum for England. He has lived since 1984 in Edinburgh, where he has been active in the Scottish devolution movement.

MORRIS DICKSTEIN is Distinguished Professor of English at the Graduate Center of the City University of New York, where he teaches courses in literature, film and American cultural history. He is a senior fellow of the Center for the Humanities, which he founded in 1993. His books include a study of the 1960s, *Gates of Eden* (1977), which was nominated for the National Book Critics Circle Award in criticism; *Double Agent: The Critic and Society* (1992); and *Leopards in the Temple* (2002), a widely reviewed social history of postwar American fiction. His latest book is a collection of essays, *A Mirror in the Roadway: Literature and the Real World* (2005). He is completing a cultural history of the United States in the 1930s.

ERIKA GOTTLIEB is the author of *Dystopian Fiction East and West: Universe of Terror and Trial* (2001); *The Orwell Conundrum: A Cry of Despair or Faith in the Spirit of Man?* (1992); and *Lost Angels of a Ruined Paradise: Themes of Cosmic Strife in Romantic Tragedy* (1982). Her essays are published in *Contemporary Literary Criticism*, *Shakespearean Criticism*, and *Utopian Studies*. Gottlieb has taught at McGill and Concordia Universities in Montreal, at the faculty of English in Budapest's ELTE University, and in Toronto at Seneca College and Ryerson Polytechnic University.

CHRISTOPHER HITCHENS is among the best known and most controversial figures in contemporary intellectual life. He is a prolific author, journalist, literary critic and public intellectual who is often described as a 'contrarian'. Now living in Washington, DC, he has been a columnist at *Vanity Fair*, *The Nation*, *Slate* and an occasional contributor to many other publications. He is the author of *God Is Not Great: The Case Against Religion* (2007); *Thomas Jefferson: Author of America* (2005); *Love, Poverty, and War: Journeys and Essays* (2004); *A Long Short War: The Postponed Liberation of Iraq* (2003); *Why Orwell Matters* (2002), among other books.

MICHAEL LEVENSON is the William B. Christian Professor of English at the University of Virginia. He is the author of *A Genealogy of Modernism: A Study of English Literary Doctrine, 1908–1922* (1984); *Modernism and The Fate of Individuality: Character and Form in the Modern English Novel* (1991); *The Spectacle of Intimacy: A Public Life for the Victorian Family* (2000; co-author Karen Chase), the forthcoming *Modernism*, and editor of the *Cambridge Companion to Modernism*.

NEIL McLAUGHLIN teaches sociological theory, and works in the broad area of the sociology of culture, knowledge and intellectuals. He is working on the concept of the 'global public intellectual' and is researching the social context of 'academics as public intellectuals' in Canada in two projects funded by the Canadian Federal government's Social Science and Humanities Research Council (SSHRC). He has previously published on the sociology of reputations and critical theory in journals such as *The Sociological Quarterly* and *Sociological Theory*, on the topic of Canadian sociology in *The Canadian Journal of Sociology* and *The American Sociologist* and on political issues in *Dissent*.

JOHN NEWSINGER is senior lecturer at Bath Spa University. He is the author of *Orwell's Politics* and numerous articles on Orwell. His most recent book is *Rebel City: Larkin, Connolly and the Dublin Labour Movement* (London: Merlin Press, 2004.) He is currently working on a history of the British Empire.

JOHN RODDEN has taught at the University of Virginia and the University of Texas at Austin. He has authored or edited several books on George Orwell, including *The Politics of Literary Reputation: the Making and Claiming of 'St. George' Orwell* (1989), *Understanding* Animal Farm *in Historical Context* (1999), *Scenes from an Afterlife: The Legacy of George Orwell* (2003), *George Orwell Into the Twenty-First Century* (with Thomas Cushman, 2004), and *Every Intellectual's Big Brother: George Orwell's Literary Siblings* (2006).

JONATHAN ROSE is Professor of History at Drew University. His books include *The Intellectual Life of the British Working Classes*, *The Holocaust and the Book: Destruction and Preservation*, and *The Revised Orwell*. He recently coedited (with Simon Eliot) *A Companion to the History of the Book*. He was the founding president of the Society for the History of Authorship, Reading and Publishing, and he currently coedits (with Ezra Greenspan) the journal *Book History*.

JOHN P. ROSSI is a Professor of History at La Salle University in Philadelphia. He has written widely about Orwell's career.

MARGERY SABIN is Lorraine Chiu Wang Professor of English at Wellesley College. She is the author of *English Romanticism and the French Tradition* (1976), *The Dialect of the Tribe: Speech and Community in Modern Fiction* (1987), and *Dissenters and Mavericks: Writings about India in English: 1765–2000* (2002), as well as essays and reviews in journals, including *Raritan*, *Essays in Criticism*, *Prose Studies*, and *College English*. An earlier and partial version of her essay here was presented at the George Orwell Centenary Conference at Wellesley College (May, 2003), and published as 'Outside/Inside: Searching for Wigan Pier', in *George Orwell Into the Twenty-First Century*, edited by Thomas Cushman and John Rodden (2004).

IAN WILLIAMS'S book *Rum: A Social and Sociable History of the Real Spirit of 1776* was published in August 2004 which Kirkus Reviews calls 'rambunctious, rollicking history, sodden with tasty lore'. His previous was *The Deserter: Bush's War on Military Families, Veterans and His Own Past*. His first, *The Alms Trade*, was published in 1989, and his second, *The UN For Beginners*, was published in 1995. He has chapters in *George Orwell Into the Twenty-First Century*, edited by Thomas Cushman and John Rodden (2004), *Why Kosovo Matters: The Debate on the Left Revisited*, edited by Danny Postel (forthcoming), *Irving Howe and the Critics: Celebrations and Attacks*, edited by John Rodden (2005), and *The Iraq War*, edited by Rick Fawn and Raymond Hinnebusch (2006).

PREFACE

JOHN RODDEN

George Orwell's public reputation far exceeds that of any other writer of his generation, and indeed of any other political writer of the twentieth century. Six decades of commentary about his work and life – which has included five biographies, at least four dozen book-length scholarly studies, and hundreds of literary essays and scholarly articles – has all become part of an Orwell cottage industry that continues to churn at a phenomenal rate. His centennial year in 2003 alone witnessed the publication of three new biographies as well as at least a half-dozen critical books and dozens of essays and articles. This enormous secondary literature has taken on a life of its own and gone beyond the work of Orwell to cover also the phenomenon of 'Orwell' – the cultural icon and mythic figure who is probably more quoted and referenced than any other modern writer.

Given the plethora of Orwell criticism, one could argue that another critical study of Orwell is superfluous and unnecessary. But the fact is that this massive critical literature has not only become extremely specialised, and therefore somewhat inaccessible to the nonscholar, but it has also contributed to and even created misconceptions about the man and writer and his literary legacy.

These realities make clear that an overview covering the broad range of Orwell's writing and influence can be an indispensable resource. Accordingly, this Cambridge Companion serves as both an introduction to Orwell's work and furnishes numerous innovative interpretations and fresh critical perspectives on it. It is designed to address both the needs of a general reader newly acquainted with Orwell and to challenge the student or scholar of Orwell thoroughly familiar with his work and the controversies swirling about it. The diversity of critical perspectives – literary, cultural, political and historical – reflects the extraordinary range and scope of commentary devoted to Orwell. Most importantly, they do what excellent critical essays ought to do, which is indeed to function as a 'companion' to the original literary work, whereby they stimulate the reader to discover (or rediscover) the author's achievement for themselves.

Orwell presents special challenges for an editor who seeks to be comprehensive. He is regarded as the greatest political writer in English during the twentieth century. The world fame of George Orwell is due to a combination of high esteem from intellectuals and immense popularity with the general reading public. Although he died at the early age of forty-six, his last two works – *Animal Farm* (1945) and *Nineteen Eighty-Four* (1949) – have sold more than forty million copies and stand as the most influential works of political fiction of the twentieth century.

Yet Orwell was far more than a novelist; he wrote essays, reportage, opinion columns, book reviews and even film reviews and poetry. *The Complete Works of George Orwell* comprise twenty thick volumes in Peter Davison's monumental edition published by Secker and Warburg. In addition, there is 'Orwell', the cultural icon, the mythic literary and public personality, the canonised author in the schoolbooks, and the literary Cold Warrior who towers over political events of the past six decades and has become a culture hero for intellectuals across the ideological spectrum. No critical survey of his writings and heritage can ignore this remarkable development.

Rather than survey in cursory fashion the full range of Orwell's life, work and reputation – that is, the achievement of Orwell and the phenomenon of 'Orwell' – the chapters in this Cambridge Companion address what is central to his work and legacy, with an occasional foray into an unfamiliar area of interest. They concentrate on the fiction and documentary writings, but they also cover Orwell's prose style and such topics and issues of keen interest to readers as his literary style, his patriotism, his positions on war and pacifism, and his anti-Communism. Throughout this Companion, Orwell's work is also placed within the context of the political and social climate of the time. His response to the Depression, British imperialism, Stalinism, the Second World War, and the politics of the British Left are all examined. The contributors also discuss Orwell's status among intellectuals and in the literary academy.

The volume closes with a bibliographic essay that highlights the key issues and critical studies of Orwell, and it opens with a detailed chronology of Orwell's life and work.

CHRONOLOGY

1903	25 June. Eric Arthur Blair born in Motihari, Bengal.
1904	Ida Blair returns with children Marjorie and Eric to England and settles at Henley-on-Thames, Oxfordshire.
1908–11	Attends day-school at Henley run by Ursuline nuns (as did his two sisters, Marjorie and Avril).
1911–16	Boards at St Cyprian's, private preparatory school at Eastbourne, Sussex.
1912	Richard Blair retires from the Indian Civil Service and returns to England. Family moves to Shiplake, a village two miles south of Henley in Oxfordshire (probably late autumn).
1914	2 October. First appearance in print with poem, 'Awake! Young Men of England', *Henley and South Oxfordshire Standard*.
1917–21	King's Scholar at Eton. Contributes to *The Election Times* and *College Days*.
1917	13 September. Father commissioned as 2nd Lieut; posted to France, he spends eight months 'in the field', and the last four months of the war with the Royal Artillery in Marseilles.
1922–27	Serves in Indian Imperial Police in Burma; resigns while on leave in England in November 1927, effective in January.
1927	October. First tramping expeditions to East End of London.
1928	Winter. Tramping in vicinity of London.

1928–29	Lives in working-class district of Paris; writes (and destroys) one or two novels. Begins early drafts of *Down and Out in Paris and London* and *Burmese Days*.
1929	7–22 March. Admitted to Hôpital Cochin, Paris, after coughing up blood.
1930–31	Uses parents' home in Southwold as base, writing there but going off to tramp and live with down-and-outs in London.
1932–33	Teaches full-time at The Hawthorns, a small private school for boys, in Hayes, Middlesex.
1933	9 January. *Down and Out in Paris and London,* by 'George Orwell', published by Victor Gollancz.
1933	Autumn. Teaches French at Frays College, Uxbridge in Middlesex.
1934	January–October. Lives with parents in Southwold. Writes *A Clergyman's Daughter*.
1934	25 October. *Burmese Days* published by Harper & Brothers, New York.
1934–36	October–January 1936. Part-time assistant (with Jon Kimche), at Booklovers' Corner, 1 South End Road, Hampstead.
1935	11 March. *A Clergyman's Daughter* published by Gollancz.
1936	31 January–30 March. In North of England to collect material for a book commissioned by Gollancz on unemployment conditions.
1936	20 April. Publication of *Keep the Aspidistra Flying* by Gollancz.
1936	9 June. Marries Eileen O'Shaughnessy at parish church in Wallington, Hertfordshire.
1936	September. 'Shooting an Elephant', *New Writing*.
1936	November. 'Bookshop Memories', *Fortnightly*.
1936	Christmas. Leaves to fight for Republicans in Spanish Civil War.

1937   January–June. Serves in Independent Labour Party contingent with militia of the POUM (Workers' Party of Marxist Unification).

1937   8 March. *The Road to Wigan Pier* published by Gollancz in trade and Left Book Club editions.

1937   28 April–10 May. On leave in Barcelona during Communist attempt to suppress revolutionary parties (including POUM). Spied on by Communist agents.

1937   20 May. Shot in throat by Fascist sniper at Huesca and taken successively to hospitals in Monflorite, Sietamo and Lerida, then to sanatorium outside Barcelona.

1937   23 June. Escapes with Eileen from Spain into France by train.

1937   Early July. Arrives back at Wallington; begins writing *Homage to Catalonia*.

1938   25 April. *Homage to Catalonia*, having been refused by Gollancz, is published by Secker & Warburg.

1938   June. Joins the Independent Labour Party.

1938   24 June. 'Why I Joined the I.L.P.', *New Leader*.

1938–39   12 September–26 March. In French Morocco (mainly at Marrakech); writes *Coming Up for Air*.

1939   12 June. *Coming Up for Air* published by Gollancz.

1939   3 September. War breaks out. Shortly thereafter, Orwell leaves Independent Labour Party because of its opposition to the war.

1940   11 March. *Inside the Whale and Other Essays*.

1941   19 February. *The Lion and the Unicorn* published by Secker & Warburg (first of 'Searchlight Books' edited by Orwell and T. R. Fyvel).

1941–43   August 1941–November 1943. Talks Assistant, later Talks Producer, in Indian section of BBC's Eastern Service.

1941   September. Writes 'The Art of Donald McGill', *Horizon*.

1943   24 November. Resigns from BBC and joins *Tribune* as Literary Editor (until 16 February 1945).

1944	14 May. Birth of Orwell's son; adopted June 1944 and christened Richard Horatio Blair.
1945	15 February–end March. War correspondent for *The Observer* and *The Manchester Evening News* in France and Germany.
1945	29 March. Eileen Blair dies while under an anesthetic to undergo a hysterectomy. After the funeral, Orwell returns to Europe to report the aftermath of the war.
1945	17 August. After many rejections, publication of *Animal Farm* by Secker & Warburg in an edition of 4,500 copies.
1946	14 February. *Critical Essays* published by Secker & Warburg.
1946	April. 'Politics and the English Language', *Horizon*.
1946	Summer. 'Why I Write', *Gangrel*. 26 August. *Animal Farm* published in USA.
1947	31 May. Sends Fredric Warburg a version of 'Such, Such Were the Joys'; final version probably completed about May 1948. First draft composed as early as 1946.
1947	20 December. Patient in Hairmyres Hospital, East Kilbride (near Glasgow), suffering from tuberculosis; stays seven months.
1948	13 May. Publication of *Coming Up for Air*, first volume in Secker's Uniform Edition.
1948	28 July. At Barnhill, Jura for five months.
1948	15 November. Publication of first volume of *British Pamphleteers,* by Allan Wingate, introduced by Orwell.
1949	6 January–3 September. Patient in Cotswold Sanatorium, Cranham, Gloucestershire, with serious case of tuberculosis.
1949	8 June. Publication of *Nineteen Eighty-Four* by Secker & Warburg. July. *Nineteen Eighty-Four* appears as Book of the Month Club selection.
1949	3 September. Transferred to University College Hospital, Gower Street, London.

| 1949 | 13 October. Marries Sonia Brownell and names Sonia and Richard Rees as his literary executors. Plans extended trip to Swiss sanatorium. |

1949 13 October. Marries Sonia Brownell and names Sonia and Richard Rees as his literary executors. Plans extended trip to Swiss sanatorium.

1950 21 January. Dies of pulmonary tuberculosis, age 46.

1950 26 January. Funeral at Christ Church, Albany Street, London. Buried, as Eric Arthur Blair, All Saints Cemetery, Sutton Courtenay, Berkshire.

I

JOHN ROSSI AND JOHN RODDEN

A political writer

George Orwell was primarily a political writer. In his essay 'Why I Write' (1946), Orwell stated he wanted 'to make political writing into an art'. While he produced four novels between the years 1933 and 1939, it was clear that his real talent did not lie in traditional fiction. He seems instinctively to have understood that the documentary style he developed in his essays and his semi-autobiographical monograph, *Down and Out in Paris and London* (1932), was unsuitable to the novel format. Ultimately, the reason for this is simple – what profoundly interested Orwell were political questions. His approach to politics evolved during the decade of the 1930s along with his own idiosyncratic journey from English radical to his unique, eccentric form of socialism.

Orwell claimed he had an unhappy youth. If one believes the memories of those like his neighbour Jacintha Buddicom, who knew him as a carefree, fun loving young boy, Orwell's claim of unhappiness seems exaggerated. In his essay 'Such, Such Were the Joys', he portrays his school, St Cyprian's, as an unpleasant amalgam of snobbery, bullying and petty acts of tyranny. The truth lies somewhere between these two extremes, something Orwell himself understood. 'Whoever writes about his childhood must beware exaggeration and self-pity', he wrote of his years at St Cyprian's.

Orwell's experiences at Eton were more positive. Although he failed to distinguish himself academically, he received a solid education, one that he drew on for the rest of his life. But what is true is that in these years Orwell first began to carve out for himself the persona of the outsider, a role he would play the rest of his life.

Too young for the First World War, Orwell at Eton experienced the reaction against the twisted nationalism and extreme propaganda of the war that became commonplace in the early 1920s. The young generation of the 1920s despised the 'old men' who had sent England to war and rejected all the values the pre-war generation believed in. Orwell says at this time he was, in reality, both a snob and a revolutionary. 'I seem to have spent half the time in denouncing the capitalist system and the other half in raging over the insolence of bus-conductors'. At this stage of his life Orwell's political ideas were largely unformed, although he says he flirted with socialism like most young men. During his school years he rebelled against all forms of authority, or as he puts it in *The Road to Wigan Pier*, 'a revolt of youth against age'. His rebellion was rooted in a belief that he didn't fit in. One form this anti-authoritarian stance took was a simple dislike of his better-off, nouveau riche fellow students. His initial political opinions – if they deserve to be called that – were little more than a facile form of egalitarianism.

The maturing of Orwell's political beliefs really can be dated from the five years (1922–27) he served as a policeman in Burma. Instead of following the traditional route of bright young men of going up to Oxford or Cambridge after graduating from Eton in 1921, Orwell joined the Indian Civil Service. He was young and a keen admirer of Kipling, and India promised adventure as well as a comfortable income. Perhaps it was also a way of appeasing his father for his mediocre performance at Eton.

Burma saw Orwell's naïve rebellion against authority take on a bitterly anti-imperial atmosphere. His egalitarianism now gave way to a hatred of the British Empire and all it represented. Culled from his essays about his job as a policeman and from references sprinkled throughout his other writings, it appears that Orwell grew disgusted ruling over people who despised him. He says in the autobiographical second part of *The Road to Wigan Pier* that 'in order to hate imperialism you have to be part of it'.

Orwell was highly regarded by his superiors. His anti-imperialism took on a peculiar form. Orwell came less to identify with the Burmese and other oppressed races of the Empire than to see the whole process as debasing the ruler even more than the ruled. The imperialist deceives himself, he argued, when he believes he is doing civilising work. The imperialist, he says, 'wears a mask and his face grows to fit it'. His Eton contemporary, Christopher Hollis, wrote that when he visited Orwell before he left the police, he already was a critic of what he called the racket of imperialism.

In his best writing about Burma, the novel *Burmese Days* (1934) and the essays 'Shooting an Elephant' (1936) and 'A Hanging' (1933), one can follow the development not only of Orwell's disenchantment with Empire, but also his growing radicalism. He came to hate not only what he was doing but also what he was becoming. As he writes in 'Shooting An Elephant': 'with one part of my mind I thought of the British Raj as an unbreakable tyranny . . . with another part I thought of that the greatest joy in the world would be to drive a bayonet into a Buddhist priest's guts'.

When Orwell resigned his position in the Indian Civil Service, his political development had not progressed much beyond the frustrated anger he felt as a young man fresh from Eton. He hated the Empire, had difficulties dealing with authority, and was radical in a superficial way. His political ideas remained unformed. The only thing he was sure of when he returned to England was an 'immense sense of guilt that I had to expiate' for his part in enforcing the rules of an Empire he despised. All he wanted to do he says in *The Road to Wigan Pier* was 'to submerge himself, to get right down among the oppressed, to be one of them on their side against the tyrants'.

If Burma confirmed Orwell's radicalism, unfocused as it was, the next four or five years gradually moved him further to the left, to an identification with the poor and the downtrodden.

Between 1930 and 1935 Orwell worked at becoming a writer. In those years he published three novels, numerous essays, book reviews, as well as a semi-autobiographical documentary of life on the edge of society, *Down and Out In Paris and London* (1933). The novels were traditional works of fiction without a strong political bent, although they all reflected a kind of vague radicalism and discontent with the direction of society. From *Down and Out* it would be difficult to extract any political meaning other than a general bias in favour of the poor and downtrodden. Running through all his early writing was an unfocused anger at the injustices of the capitalist system. Orwell, however, had no programme or even clear suggestions of how to solve society's ills. The best that one can say of Orwell's political views before 1935–36 is that they were a cross between Tory Anarchism and leftist outrage. Later he would say that he was something of a socialist even then but the evidence is lacking. Orwell was angry and in rebellion against the English society of his time, but as the novelist Anthony Powell shrewdly noted: 'Like most people in rebellion, he was more than half in love with what he was rebelling against'.

It was not until his publisher, the left wing socialist Victor Gollancz, asked him to study the conditions of the poor and unemployed in the North of England, that Orwell's views advanced beyond political pique. In January 1936 Orwell travelled north to investigate this area, among the hardest hit by the Depression. It was the turning point of his life. Bernard Crick, his biographer, calls this period of Orwell's life, 'The Crucial Journey'.

The book that emerged from Orwell's investigation, *The Road to Wigan Pier*, achieved two things. It made his reputation as a sharp critic of capitalism and it launched him on the road to his own eccentric brand of socialism. Orwell only spent a couple of months in the North of England gathering material for his book. Gollancz adopted *The Road to Wigan Pier* as part of his highly successful Left Book Club which he controlled. Gollancz got more than he bargained for.

The Road to Wigan Pier divides into two distinct parts. The first section is a brilliant piece of reportage on what unemployment did to the working people of the north of England. There are unforgettable portraits of poverty: the tripe shop filled with black beetles in the house where he boarded, his trip down a coal mine, a woman glimpsed from a moving train trying to clear a blocked drain. Orwell's vivid, colloquial, almost matter-of-fact prose, first evidenced in 'A Hanging', reached maturity in part one of *The Road to Wigan Pier*. While completing the book, Orwell would write the essay, 'Shooting An Elephant', which clearly showed that he had found his voice. By 1936 Orwell had mastered the distinctive sense of someone talking directly to the reader that made his writing unique. He had come a long way as a writer in six years.

The second half of *The Road to Wigan Pier* embarrassed Gollancz. Orwell argued that in order to convince the public that socialism was the answer to England's problems, you first had to analyze why the movement failed to attract a mass following. The answer, he wrote, lies in the flaws of the socialists themselves. They were isolated from the working classes, and what is worse, looked down their noses at them. Unlike the working classes who Orwell argued possessed a real culture, socialism attracted a strange type of intellectual cut off from the people – in a celebrated passage he labelled them an unhealthy amalgam of fruit juice drinkers, nature cure quacks and nudists.

Until the socialists overcame this sense of distance from the working classes, Orwell believed there was little chance of their movement succeeding. The Marxist class argumentation he rejected as worthless logic chopping. The bourgeois baiting of the typical Marxist, he said, was a sign of weakness antagonising the very people you needed to convert. Despite his left wing views Orwell had little time for class warfare. He was an old-fashioned English radical in the sense that he believed that the English people had more features of their lives and history that united than divided them.

By the time he finished writing *The Road to Wigan Pier* in December 1936, Orwell had taken a major step toward socialism. For the rest of his life he would describe himself as a socialist. His brand of socialism, however, remained idiosyncratic, as eccentric as the man himself, combining egalitarianism, idealization of working class culture, and an intense dislike of Marxist bickering. Orwell's emphasis on egalitarianism is what separated him from many of his fellow socialists. He thought they wanted power, and he feared they wouldn't use it in the best interests of the working class. One could describe Orwell as a twentieth-century utopian socialist but for the fact that he distrusted all intellectual formulae based on power worship.

If *The Road to Wigan Pier* demonstrated Orwell's embrace of socialism, his experiences in Spain during the Civil War completed the process while adding another dimension to his thought – a pervasive distrust of communism.

Early in 1937 Orwell went to Spain to fight on the Republican side. He spent six months there as a member of a Trotskyist-anarchist group, POUM, stationed on the Catalonia front. Spain changed him forever. When he first visited Barcelona he was thrilled to see a society in which the working classes were in control and where class distinctions seemed to have disappeared. He enjoyed the military atmosphere in Spain, spending about 100 days at the front. Toward the end of his stay, he was shot through the throat and invalided out of the war. Orwell had not understood the bitter divisions within the Republican camp when he went to Spain, and he underestimated the determination of the Communists to control all the Republican forces. He was shocked when his comrades in the POUM were labelled as objectively pro-fascist and then ruthlessly purged. Among the lasting impressions Orwell took from his time in Spain was that true socialism was possible, but the Communists would destroy any left wing forces they could not control.

Orwell was outraged when he returned to England and tried to tell how Stalin's agents were betraying the revolution in Spain. He discovered that his views were unacceptable. They contravened the Popular Front line of 'no enemies on the left'. Those parties not cooperating with the Communists were regarded as objectively fascist.

Orwell was disgusted by the way the war in Spain was distorted for political reasons and for the first time began to fear that the idea of objective truth was in danger of disappearing. 'I saw great battles reported', he wrote later, 'where there had been no fighting, and complete silence where hundreds of men had been killed . . . I saw newspapers in London retailing these lies and eager intellectuals building emotional superstructures over events that never happened'. ('Looking Back on the Spanish War', p. 197)

Orwell found that articles and reviews he wrote about Spain were rejected by leading left wing journals such as the *New Statesman*. The editor, Kingsley Martin, refused to run one of Orwell's Spanish articles on the grounds that it would 'cause trouble'. As a sop he offered Orwell a book on Spain to review but then rejected Orwell's review too. What pained Martin was Orwell's insistence that in Spain Fascism and Communism differed 'in degree, not in kind'. Orwell never forgave Martin whom he described as a 'decayed liberal'. Years later Orwell and Malcolm Muggeridge were having lunch and Orwell asked to change seats. When Muggeridge enquired why, Orwell said Martin was at an opposite table and he couldn't abide looking at his corrupt face.

Orwell began writing a memoir of his Spanish experiences almost as soon as he returned in June 1937. Despite owning a contract for Orwell's next two publications, Gollancz rejected the book because of its political opinions. Fredric Warburg's small firm, Secker and Warburg, took it on and *Homage to Catalonia* was published in April 1938. It is in many ways one of the most personal of Orwell's books and the most powerful. His anger at the betrayal of socialist forces in Spain is overpowering. He tells the story from his personal standpoint while weaving in examples of communist perfidy.

Homage to Catalonia received decent reviews including a comment in *The Observer* that 'Mr. Orwell is a great writer', the first time that had been said of him. It was savaged in the left wing press, the communist *Daily Worker* calling it Trotskyist propaganda. *Homage to Catalonia* sold poorly in the Popular Front atmosphere of the late 1930s but it cemented Orwell's reputation as an arch-foe of communism.

Spain embittered Orwell and made him pessimistic about the future. He argued that Europe was drifting toward an imperialist war which would see the eventual triumph of some form of Fascism. If a war broke out between England and Germany, he said it would just be 'one band of robbers against another'. With all its flaws, socialism was the 'only real enemy Fascism has to face'. His faith in socialism remained strong but he was disgusted by its adherents' blind hero worship of Stalin's Soviet Union. Looking for a political home, Orwell joined the radical Independent Labour Party in 1938. He found their combination of a fierce anti-communism and a slightly anarchist version of socialism appealing. His conviction that the next war would lead to a fascist triumph even made their pacifism palatable. By this time Orwell knew what he was against: Fascism in all its forms. But he had difficulty articulating what kind of socialist he was. He would spend the last decade of his life defining his own esoteric brand of socialism.

On the eve of the Second World War, Orwell was in conflict with himself. He had lost his faith in the left in England. Aside from his novel, *Coming Up For Air*, which was published in June 1939, he wrote little in those two years save for some reviews and one significant essay, 'Marrakech', a reflection on how long it would take before the non-white races overthrew the domination of white imperialism. Orwell was rethinking his role as a writer. He had published four novels, none of which sold well or showed much understanding of traditional fiction. On the other hand, his documentary, semi-autobiographical, non-fiction revealed unique qualities. His best essays showed a talent for sociological insight combined with a crisp, adjective-free prose style. While considering his future, the Second World War broke out in September 1939.

The war alleviated Orwell's pessimism. In fact he enjoyed its hardships and crises. He believed that a major conflict could create a revolutionary situation in England. His own bedrock patriotism had surfaced on the eve of the war and he was convinced that this concept could unite the otherwise class-ridden English nation.

During the first two years of the war, when England faced a serious threat of invasion and defeat, Orwell stressed the importance of revolutionary patriotism. He saw no contradiction between socialism and patriotism. In the face of the critical struggle against Nazi Germany, he wrote: 'a revolutionary has to be a patriot and a patriot has to be revolutionary'. It even was possible, he argued, to build 'socialism on the bones of a Blimp'.

The war also matured Orwell's socialism. He saw it as necessary if England was to survive and win the war. Over the next two years Orwell argued in a series of essays – most importantly, 'My Country, Right or Left', and the book, *The Lion and the Unicorn* – that the left wing intelligentsia failed to grasp that patriotism was the glue that bound the middle and working classes together and that it could serve as a lever for a people's revolution. By stressing the revolutionary nature of patriotism, Orwell was reacting against the way his enemies had portrayed him as a frightened bourgeois. He believed that 'the class racket', as he always referred to it, was a fraud. Unlike most Marxists, Orwell was convinced that nationalism trumped class identity. His fellow socialists, he said, had lost their fatherland but still needed something to believe in. For most socialists that belief was a romanticised version of the working class or, what was worse, Stalin's Russia. He noted that English leftists were 'ashamed of their own nationality'.

Orwell's linking of socialism and patriotism was too much for many on the left. They especially disliked *The Lion and the Unicorn*, dismissing it as little more than an argument in favour of social fascism. As in Spain, Orwell found himself politically isolated on the left. At the same time he was gaining recognition as an unorthodox, often original, political thinker.

Unable to secure a military commission because of his poor health, Orwell joined the BBC in June 1941, specialising in cultural programming aimed at India. By this time he believed that the quasi-revolutionary conditions that had prevailed in 1940 were disappearing. The focus in England, especially once Hitler attacked the Soviet Union, was on defeating the Axis. The English left, many of whom had been neutral up to this point, rallied to the Soviet cause. The left's amnesia about Stalin's purges and the Nazi-Soviet Pact reaffirmed Orwell's distrust of communism and its fellow travellers in England. For the left, Orwell wrote in 'Inside the Whale', communism was nothing more than 'the patriotism of the deracinated'.

Orwell spent a little over two years at the BBC, years he regarded as wasted. He wrote numerous scripts for the Indian audience plus an occasional essay for Cyril Connolly's monthly, *Horizon*. The best of these, a study of comic postcards, 'The Art of Donald McGill', is a classic example of how Orwell could take a popular topic and mine it for profound insights about the nature of English society. From his time at the BBC Orwell absorbed many of the ideas that would later surface in *Nineteen Eighty-Four*. The Ministry of Truth, some elements of Newspeak, and the ghastly cafeteria in *Nineteen Eighty-Four* were inspired by Orwell's time at the BBC.

In September 1943 Orwell resigned from the BBC. Two months later he was named the literary editor of the left wing weekly, *Tribune*. He was happy to return to serious writing and had already begun work on the book that would make him famous, *Animal Farm*.

Animal Farm had been incubating for years, at least as far back as Orwell's experiences with communist perfidy in Spain. He wanted to write a satire – he called it a fairy tale – about the way a revolution can be corrupted. *Animal Farm* perfectly correlates with the events in the Soviet Union in the years after the revolution, but does so through the guise of a beast fable. The allegory was both ingenious and ingenuous: a child and a sophisticated adult could understand *Animal Farm* at different levels.

It took less than a year to complete *Animal Farm*. Orwell then confronted the problem of finding a publisher because of the implied criticism of the Soviet Union. Gollancz wouldn't touch *Animal Farm* and the rest of the English publishing community rejected it out of hand. The Ministry of Information let it be known that they regarded the book as not in the national interest. It was the same argument over *Homage to Catalonia* again – Orwell was causing trouble for the left.

Fredric Warburg again came to the rescue. He took a chance and brought *Animal Farm* out in August 1945, just as the war ended. The first edition sold out in a matter of days and a second printing of 10,000, a large print run in those days of paper shortages, also sold out quickly. A year later *Animal Farm* appeared in the United States where it achieved greater success. Almost a half million copies sold, largely because the book was adopted as a Book of the Month Club selection. After fifteen years of struggling as a writer, Orwell had become famous and financially comfortable.

Animal Farm's timing was perfect. It came out just as the Cold War was intensifying. It also captured the growing doubts and fears about the future of Stalin's Russia that would crystallise in the West six months later with Winston Churchill's 'Iron Curtain' speech.

The popularity of *Animal Farm*, followed shortly by the successful publication of his *Critical Essays* in February 1946, enabled Orwell to leave

London, a city he never liked. The death of his wife on the eve of his triumph with *Animal Farm* left him alone to raise their adopted son, Richard. Her death also reaffirmed an idea Orwell had to move to the island of Jura off the west coast of Scotland. In May 1946 he took up residence there, entering what would be the last phase of his life.

By the war's end Orwell's health had deteriorated badly. His tuberculosis was serious – both lungs were infected. He would be in and out of hospitals for the rest of his life. None of this deterred him from starting a new life on Jura and beginning work on his last great work, *Nineteen Eighty-Four*.

Orwell started the novel in August 1946. Like *Animal Farm*, *Nineteen Eighty-Four* had been forming in his mind for years. His Spanish experiences, his frustrations with the BBC's bureaucracy and his growing conviction that the idea of objective truth was being undermined by totalitarianism all played a part in giving birth to Orwell's dystopia.

Nineteen Eighty-Four was written in a series of drafts between 1946 and the end of 1948. The title was a play on reversing the last two digits of the year he finished the novel. None of Orwell's work has generated such controversy. Some critics see it as an example of profound pessimism, Orwell's dark vision of what the future would be like. Others have argued that it was a reflection of the last stages of the tuberculosis that would eventually kill him. Christopher Hitchens believes that *Nineteen Eighty-Four* is Orwell's only work of fiction that rises to the literary level of his essays.

The evidence that Orwell was depressed about the future is weak. He was doing what he had done so well since 1936 – writing a book which he hoped would point out the dangers of what happens when a revolution is betrayed. He had been gathering material on images of dystopia for years. *Nineteen Eighty-Four* was designed to show how one man, Winston Smith, representing everyman, was controlled by the all-powerful forces of the state. The book posed the question: Can the individual survive in the face of the collective power of the modern state? Some of Orwell's insights were prophetic: the omnipresent telescreens, the manipulation of language by Newspeak, etc. But Orwell was not saying this had to happen. He was arguing that it *might* if the people were not alert to the way government can be corrupted by those who abused power. The book had clear connections to events in the Soviet Union under Stalin, but Orwell meant to generalise about what will happen to the free individual if the trend of concentrating power in the hands of the state wasn't reversed.

Many critics seized on *Nineteen Eighty-Four* as an indictment of socialism, which Orwell forcefully denied. He told an American labour leader, Francis A. Henson, that his book was not an attack on socialism or the British Labour Party but was designed to show 'the perversions to which a centralized economy is liable and which have already been partly realized in Communism and Fascism'.

When *Nineteen Eighty-Four* was published in 1949, Orwell was hospitalised in London. While there he married a second time. His wife Sonia Brownell had been Cyril Connolly's assistant at *Horizon* and was a well-known figure in London literary circles. For Orwell marriage was a defiant gesture – a way of saying he wanted to live. He kept a notebook during the last months of his life, which contained material for essays and articles he planned to write – hardly the sign of a man expecting to die. But die he did on 21 January 1950 of a massive hemorrhage of the lungs. He was six months shy of his 47th birthday.

The Politics of Posthumous Reputation

George Orwell died, but 'Orwell', the brilliant Cold Warrior and the man within the writings with the ever-living voice and compelling literary personality, did not die. Indeed, more than six decades after his death, he has still not died.

To the contrary, 'Orwell' is in some respects more alive today – as an intellectual and moral presence in Anglo-American culture – than he was during his own lifetime. Certainly the catchwords of *Animal Farm* and *Nineteen Eighty-Four* – 'Some animals are more equal than others', 'Big Brother', 'Newspeak', 'doublethink', 'thoughtcrime', and so on – are in far wider circulation today than they were at the time of his death. Orwell's afterlife brings to mind a famous line of Horace in his *Odes*: '*non omnis moriar*'. 'Not all of me will die'.

Without doubt, not all of 'Orwell' has died. His last two books, *Animal Farm* and *Nineteen Eighty-Four*, have sold almost fifty million copies in sixty-two languages, more than any other pair of books by a twentieth-century author. No other English writer of his generation – for example, not even Graham Greene or Evelyn Waugh – has matched his influence. His works remain in print and are still widely read.

But the outsized scale of Orwell's literary reputation is rivaled by the intense degree of political controversy surrounding it. As we have seen, he was chiefly a political writer during his lifetime, and the main interest in his work since his death has been shown by politically minded critics and readers.

Unfortunately, his politicised reception has resulted in his work undergoing distortion by admirers as well as adversaries. His last two works are variously taken as direct political statements or prophesies or satires, his fictional characters are read as autobiographical mouthpieces, his non-fiction is invoked where expedient to buttress both these practices, and his alleged 'failure' to provide any comprehensive summa of his politics is exploited as a rationale for 'extending' his ideas in various partisan directions. Moreover, the debates about Orwell's legacy have occurred not just among scholars and critics, but have witnessed the participation of a broad reading public. Argument about Orwell's writings has frequently entered the conversation in the public sphere, as the letter columns of Anglo-American newspapers from the mid-1950s through his centennial year of 2003 attest.

In fact, Orwell's controversial political legacy has so intertwined with the complexities of postwar Anglo-American ideological politics that a culture war has periodically raged over which groups stake a claim to him as a forerunner. The competing claims to his mantle range from neo- and cultural conservatives on the Right to democratic socialists and independent or libertarian radicals on the Left. Indeed, what is most strikingly distinctive about Orwell's posthumous history is that the claims and counter-claims to him occur at all points on the ideological spectrum – Right, Centre and Left. As the twenty-first century unfolds, Orwell continues to 'be a writer well worth stealing', in his famous phrase on Dickens – and not for reasons entirely separable from the character of his work and life, including his aspiration to become a political writer.

2

GORDON BOWKER

Orwell and the biographers

Days before dying, on 21 January 1950, George Orwell inserted a clause in his will asking for no biography. Biographers of Orwell have therefore often been accused of disregarding a dying man's wishes. However, viewing this final request in the context of Orwell's life raises the question of its authenticity. Was it made freely or under the pressure of circumstances?

There is no evidence that Orwell was 'anti-biography'. On the contrary, it is perfectly clear from what he wrote, that he valued literary biographies as means to understanding authors' works. His first published review, of Lewis Mumford's life of Herman Melville, shows him identifying strongly with a writer whose career was as troubled and penurious as his own. Throughout his life he read biographies avidly, in 1934 himself offering to write a centenary biography of Mark Twain. In 1942, he called for a much-needed life of Joseph Conrad, in 1945 for 'a definitive one' of Conan Doyle and in 1948 for one of George Gissing. In 1946, shortly after *Animal Farm* appeared, he urged his publisher, Fredric Warburg, to bring out Trotsky's biography of Stalin. He readily supplied autobiographical details to publishers, critics and writers' directories, cooperated happily with biographers of others, and approved his friend George Woodcock's plan to make him the subject of a biographical essay.

'The qualities needed for a biographer', he wrote, 'are piety and wit'. He favoured 'the analytical, interpretative method'[1] over one too fixated on chronology and the external life which 'enumerates the various activities' of the subject, with 'a morbid interest in everything'.[2] Nor did he care for studies 'merely . . . of . . . character', which ignored the literary work, even while acknowledging that the interweaving of biography and criticism required both skill and conscientious effort. However, 'character', he thought, should not be ignored, and authors' works should be mined to reveal the inner lives of subjects. Thus, of Stendhal he wrote, '[His] life was of the kind that is absorbingly interesting when one sees it from the inside, as one does in certain passages in his novels'.[3] And of a life of Tolstoy, 'The most valuable part of [the author's] biography is the careful exposition that he gives to each of Tolstoy's books in turn, showing just how it related to Tolstoy's spiritual development'.[4] And while cautiously acknowledging that with many writers their private character differs from that which emerges from their work, he could also claim to 'see' that Pip's attitude towards Magwitch in *Great Expectations* was 'obviously the attitude of Dickens himself'.[5]

More controversially, he argued that some 'inherently probable' historical claims, like Trotsky's assertion that Stalin had Lenin murdered, ought to be allowed even when not strictly demonstrable.[6]

Against Orwell's obvious partiality for the genre, Susan Watson, nurse to Orwell's adopted son, reported him opposing one of himself. 'He said that if anything was to be written, he was the person to do it, but he did not intend to, because in an autobiography you had to tell absolutely the whole truth'.[7] However, while Watson was still working for him he told his literary executor, Sir Richard Rees,

> I don't know if I would, as it were, get up to the point of having anything biographical written about me, but I suppose it could happen and it's ghastly to think of some people doing it. All I can say is, use your discretion and if someone seems a B.F., don't let him see any papers. I am going to include among my personal papers, in case of this happening, some short notes about the main events in my life, chiefly dates and places, because I notice that when people write about you, even people who know you well, they always get that kind of thing wrong.[8]

And, as if to aid prospective biographers further, at about the same time he published the revealing autobiographical essay, 'Why I Write', and completed his controversial memoir of St Cyprian's preparatory school, 'Such, Such Were the Joys'.

Until the very end of his life, then, Orwell showed no real aversion to a biography. However, his second wife, Sonia, was, it appears, intensely antipathetic to the genre. Even before Orwell's death, her impatience with biographical enquiries is evident in her abrupt response to his French friend, Yvonne Davet, requesting some personal details for an article on him. 'As for your article', she wrote, 'he has absolutely nothing interesting to say about his life'. The irony here, which clearly eluded her, was that the whole of Orwell's writing career consisted of him trying to say interesting things about his life. It is 'inherently probable', therefore, that the request for 'no biography' in his will (discussed with Sonia), was her doing.

Sonia is often credited with having fended off biographers in deference to her late husband's dying wish. However, Orwell also requested 'no memorial service', yet his very public funeral held at Christ Church, Marylebone, with most of London's literati present, was effectively that. Ironically, only months previously he had written of Dickens, 'His body, against his clearly expressed wish, was buried in Westminster Abbey', suggesting that he was well aware that certain such final requests were likely to be disregarded.

The early posthumous history of Orwell's biography is dramatic, complex and fascinating. A major factor in the unfolding story was Sonia's capriciousness. At first, she readily deferred to Orwell's close friends – David Astor, Arthur Koestler, Tosco Fyvel, Malcolm Muggeridge and Warburg. Later she went her own inconsistent way, wanting a biography one moment, opposing it the next, first encouraging a writer then spurning him. Before long, she acquired a reputation for being awkward and unpredictable.

One early tussle involved Sonia, Warburg and Rees, Orwell's joint literary editor. Following Orwell's death (perhaps encouraged by Warburg and the accountant Jack Harrison, who later got control of Orwell's copyrights) Sonia moved to marginalise Rees, and take sole charge of the estate. Rees proved reluctant. He *was* prepared, he said, to renounce his right to oversee Orwell's will, determine contracts and film rights etc., but George, he thought, would have wanted him to continue having a voice in what was published. Yet, despite his readiness to accommodate the newly-bereaved widow, he found himself further at odds with her and Warburg who, disregarding Orwell's will, was eager to publish an early biography of his famous author.

A collection of autobiographical writings under Sonia's preferred title, *The Crystal Spirit*, was first proposed. Rees quickly expressed reservations. 'It is', he argued, 'rather a delicate matter to make up such a book without the help of the author himself . . . [and] . . . unsatisfactory for an author to be presented to the public in a book compiled solely or mainly by people much younger than himself'.[9] The contrary argument would later be used against appointing a biographer from among Orwell's contemporaries.

Another problem arose when both Sonia and Warburg wanted to publish 'Such, Such Were the Joys', which Rees thought grossly exaggerated, badly written, and likely to harm Orwell's reputation. When Sonia insisted, Rees told her, 'You're completely nutty about St Cyprians'.[10] Thereafter, Rees faded from the scene, and all subsequent permission-to-publish decisions devolved to Sonia. Sadly reflecting on their quarrel four years later, after the essay had appeared in America, Rees wrote to her, 'I seem to have rather forgiven you about St Cyp. Personally, I would either have cut it or held it back a bit longer, but it really doesn't seem to matter a damn'.[11] But by then, it seems, he was long out of the picture.

Something like an autobiographical anthology would eventually emerge, but meanwhile the biography question surfaced and interested parties soon took sides. Within four months of Orwell's death, Fyvel asked Sonia whether he might expand a 'sketch' about Orwell into a book. Evidently she demurred because Fyvel's memoir of Orwell did not appear until after Sonia's death. Next came Laurence Brander, one-time BBC colleague of Orwell. He completed *his* book *before* informing Sonia. He knew about George's wish for no biography, he said, and had used his life only as a general frame in which to discuss his work. Sonia's reaction is unknown, but Brander's study *did* appear, in 1954, as did one by John Atkins, Orwell's predecessor as literary editor of *Tribune*.

That same year, another Orwell friend, Julian Symons, proposed a full-scale biography. Meeting Sonia, Symons felt encouraged, believing that she might agree. But, perhaps aware of her reputation as 'a difficult woman', his formal approach was decidedly circumspect.

> If . . . you feel that you might permit me to write about George (which I should think a great honour) why not let me see the material you have? We could then talk about it – and you would remain uncommitted . . . I don't think I sufficiently stressed that in anything I wrote I would be anxious not to say anything unjustifiably painful to anybody – and particularly to you . . . About such things [as which documents seem relevant] I should value your advice and knowledge.[12]

Sonia consulted the inner circle of Orwell's friends before replying. Astor was opposed to any acquaintance of George's undertaking the task; Koestler proposed an archive rather than a biography. Sonia, about to leave for the New York film premiere of *Animal Farm*, rejected Symons. He replied, 'saddened . . . but not surprised by your decision', hoping she would change her mind one day, adding that 'a good biography would help to soften the crust of anti-Socialist propaganda which is being stuck on to George now. Inevitable perhaps, but nasty'.[13] After seeing how *Animal Farm* had been doctored by the film-makers, she was probably ready to agree with Symons, but by then he had already been rebuffed.

Now, however, with Warburg pressing and biographers lining up, Sonia decided to appoint someone 'official', someone unlikely to deliver but whose appointment could be used to repel all comers. In 1955, therefore, Muggeridge was designated Orwell's biographer. Some thought the choice bizarre. Reginald Reynolds called Muggeridge 'son of a failed Labour candidate, who has been going to the right at a huge rate of knots while Orwell moved erratically in exactly the other direction'.[14] According to Ian Angus, Sonia never expected the slothful Muggeridge to complete the job, despite attracting a great deal of publicity.

The publicity, however, did work, and the next contender, George Woodcock, was as cautious as Symons in approaching Sonia. 'I am writing about a subject which has doubtless caused you already a great deal of vexation', he wrote, 'and I hope I shall not add unduly to it'. How would she regard a book of an 'essentially critical character', using George's life 'partly as a frame to hold his books and partly as a source from which to elucidate them?' He would not, he said, be prying into intimate details and would use only what biographical detail was already published.[15] Sonia, clearly suspicious, asked him to wait until Muggeridge's book had appeared. It never did, but Woodcock's *The Crystal Spirit*, even though quoting Orwell with Sonia's permission, did not appear until 1967.

Following Woodcock came the Catholic writer Christopher Hollis who knew Orwell at Eton and then fleetingly in Burma. He was planning a book about George, he told Sonia, hoping that she would find it 'a friendly book', even if she disagreed with some of his judgements. He promised to show her the typescript and change anything she found unacceptable. 'My last wish', he said, 'would be to cause any pain in such a matter as this'.[16] Perhaps because Hollis was an MP and himself a publisher, Sonia did not object, merely asking him not to present George as 'a crypto-Catholic' or stray onto Muggeridge's territory.[17]

Despite his assurances to Sonia, however, Hollis could not resist presenting Orwell as some kind of right-wing convert. As for Muggeridge, his 'territory' quickly became a biographical wasteland, and, as Sonia expected, he soon became bored with it.

> I made various vague moves in the direction of doing it; such as going through whatever letters and other documents there are, meeting various people who had been connected with him, and trying to sort out my own thoughts on the subject. In the end the project defeated me, partly through my own indolence, and distaste for collecting and absorbing the masses of tape-recorded talk, much of it necessarily intensely boring, which would constitute the bulk of one's material. It seemed to me that Orwell, with a cunning he sometimes displayed in life, had posthumously laid down a great smoke-screen of boredom between himself and any explorer who tried to invade the privacy in which he had lived and died.

He also doubted the truthfulness of Orwell's autobiographical writings, especially his schooldays memoir, advancing the argument later adopted by Sonia. 'Orwell is an artist, and as such lived and wrote his own biography'.[18] Orwell's friend Inez Holden claimed that *she* persuaded Muggeridge to withdraw, suggesting that 'he'd only make himself look a bloody fool'. His questioning, she thought, was irrelevant and in any case he had never known Orwell at all well.[19]

The formal end to Muggeridge's reign as 'official' biographer in 1959 is said to have coincided with the cooling of an affair he was having with Sonia. Now she needed another excuse for brushing off would-be biographers. Warburg and Catherine Carver of Harcourt Brace, Orwell's American publisher, provided one. Both had long favoured a collection representing 'a kind of autobiographical report on Orwell'. E. M. Forster was even once invited to write an introduction.

A classic 'guardian of the flame', Sonia was sedulous in policing access to Orwell's papers. Following Koestler's suggestion, a committee under Astor had begun organising an Orwell Archive to be housed at University College, London. Koestler's proposal for a collection of tape-recorded memoirs of Orwell was vetoed by Sonia, who, according to Astor, feared that 'miscellaneous American literary students . . . will construct weird psychological theories on the scraps of evidence'.[20] Although this project floundered, reminiscences of Orwell recorded for various radio and television programmes *were* deposited with the archive, some appearing later in published form. The Archive Committee's rules gave Sonia power to deny access to would-be biographers, a power she never hesitated to exercise.

With Muggeridge's departure, Orwell's publishers pressed for a replacement. Warburg consulted Rees, who had once thought that such a person must be of Orwell's generation, but now said he preferred 'one of the younger writers'. 'Every friend . . . would find himself writing defensively and so be less convincing'.[21] The name of Richard Hoggart, author of *The Uses of Literacy*, was briefly floated, but by the end of the year, Warburg found himself confronting Astor, who thought it premature for an Orwell biography. His line echoed Rees's. No contemporary writer, he said, could be uninvolved in 'the various disputes of the thirties in which George played such a heroic part'. Consequently, 'they would be grinding the axe of their own opinion and feelings about these controversies, instead of making a detached and objective study of George'.[22] Warburg disagreed, saying, 'I believe that detached and objective studies of any man, including Orwell, are most undesirable'.[23]

Meanwhile, taking the initiative, Sonia approached Dwight Macdonald, the American journalist and editor in turn of *Partisan Review* and *Politics*, to both of which Orwell had contributed, suggesting he accept the job. Publishers, she told him, were in the mood to offer a generous advance. Macdonald took eight months deciding to accept, by which time enthusiasm had waned. Sonia was apologetic. The publishers were now 'off the mood of generosity with which they were suffused when I spoke to you'. She blamed this change of heart on Orwell's English friends. Over the past few months, she said, the feeling against a biography had grown. 'This is partly – I suspect – that with such a difficult decision going against George's specific request that no biography be done, people can seldom stick to one line for long'.[24]

The inconsistency she ascribed to others was almost certainly her own, and Macdonald, like Symons, would not be the last to be led on by her only to be dumped. However, he had his own suspicions about what had happened. 'The publishers think I'm too critical and sharp-penned and fear . . . my re-evaluation' which might disrupt 'the semi-established and tranquil phase of Orwell's reputation at the moment'. Sonia was quick to reassure him. Personally she thought him 'the right person to do an Orwell biography', and 'it is not you [the publishers and others] are against'. However, she added,

> I simply don't have the moral courage to stand out against the gang . . . Astor and Co fundamentally don't want anyone – not just you but anyone at all – disturbing their own precious personal pictures of George. They are all severe cases of over-prolonged-adolescent-hero-worshippers – in fact Englishmen.[25]

She was wrong about publishers' attitudes toward Macdonald. Only two months later, Warburg told William Jovanovich of Harcourt Brace, that he 'and a good few others in England' objected to Macdonald personally.[26] The American, it was thought, was no more likely to have completed a biography than Muggeridge, having recently been considered and then rejected as unreliable for the co-editorship of *Encounter*. However, neither opposed recruiting another Orwell biographer, and a notable literary event was already exciting them. In September 1959, Richard Ellmann's new biography of James Joyce had appeared to considerable critical acclaim. In the wake of this tidal wave of encomia and the subsequent large sales, Jovanovich thought they had found the perfect candidate, saying, 'There is no doubt that he is a meticulous workman, and he most particularly enjoys ferreting out materials at their source'.[27] Warburg agreed. 'I think very strongly that an Ellmann book on Orwell would make a mighty seller, perhaps even in excess of his book on Joyce'.[28] Even Koestler gave grudging approval. 'I still think it is too early for a biography, but if anyone is to do it, I think Ellmann would be a good choice'.[29]

Cautiously they delayed mentioning Ellmann's name to Sonia until mid-May. They knew they had to get her onboard but also knew that Ellmann was still uncommitted. Eventually Jovanovich pressed home the case to Sonia:

[Ellmann] is now the toast of the American academic world, for the James Joyce book has been a tremendous success here both in the prestige it had been afforded and in its sales (even at a $12.50 price!) apparently, [he] has had half a dozen publishers approach here with proposals (and a number of university posts that have been offered to him) and he was in the process of sorting things out when I first wrote him about the Orwell book . . . [He] is distinctly interested and I feel that he would like to write this book more than any other in the offering . . . [He] and I left the matter with his saying that he cannot make up his mind until he had a chance to talk with you . . . I hardly need say that Ellmann is a superb scholar and perceptive critic: he is thorough, careful, and exacting, but he doesn't lack imagination and grace of style. I am hoping that you like him and that you will want us to proceed.[30]

Ellmann, added Warburg, was most likely 'to produce a book worthy of its subject . . . to do justice to what is the essence of the Orwell genius'.[31] Sonia, however, once she had spoken with Ellmann by phone and noted that he was asking for a $25,000 advance, characteristically began to prevaricate. 'I just felt after talking to him that none of us had real proof of his desire to do the book apart from money or of his ability to understand the mental climate – for want of better expression – which prevailed when George was writing'.[32]

A few weeks later the matter was settled. On 8 August, Jovanovich informed Sonia that 'after much agonizing reappraisal' Ellmann had decided that he was not the man for the job.

What ability I have [he had written], I think [lies] partly in the attempt to reclaim the unwieldiness of the literary mind in experiences, a point where Orwell is of course interesting, but also in dealing with a specific literary problem of complexity, which he does not pose. I am well aware that to study Orwell intensely would be to study the cultural history of the last forty or fifty years, and I am very interested in that, but not as a biographer.[33]

On 26 October 1960, the establishment of The George Orwell Archive at University College was announced as follows: 'In accordance with George Orwell's own wish, his literary executors, Sonia Pitt-Rivers (she had remarried in 1958) and Sir Richard Rees, have never commissioned an official biography. They have, however, always wished to establish a collection of Orwell material in a scholarly library which would preserve it, add to it whenever possible and make it available to scholars . . .' There was no mention of Muggeridge, Macdonald or Ellmann, so the myth of the devoted widow remaining faithful to her husband's testamentary request was thereby maintained.

Despite failing to get a biography, however, his publishers were still pressing for an anthology representing 'a kind of autobiographical report' on
Orwell. By 1961, Sonia had appropriated this idea, arguing that Orwell's
biography was to be found in his own work and that therefore any biography by another party would somehow lack authenticity. She now invited Ian
Angus, then administering the Orwell Archive, to help her edit a collection
which could 'stand as a biography'.

But if Sonia believed that all thought of a conventional biography had
been quashed she would soon be disillusioned. In 1962, Rees produced his
own memoir of Orwell, and two Americans, Peter Stansky and William
Abrahams, arrived in London to research 'a number of your English writers
of the 1930s, among them George Orwell, who had fought on the side of
the Republic in the Spanish Civil War'. Sonia reported having met them and
having been charmed. However, she soon began to suspect that they were
contemplating an Orwell biography. As Jovanovich told Warburg, 'She saw
they were moving in the direction of writing about personalities rather than
"history" [so] she cut off correspondence'.[34] Learning that they had already
spoken to Avril, George's sister, and to Rees, heightened her suspicions, and
she refused them access to the archive. It was a decision she probably came
to regret.

More directly, in October 1964, Roger Klein, a young Harper and Row
editor, visited Europe eager to commission an Orwell biography. Coincidentally, Warburg had a prospective biographer in mind, the critic and broad-
caster Walter Allen. Sonia, now divorced and living in Paris, met Klein for
lunch and again found herself enchanted by a clever young American who
went away, like so many before him, feeling encouraged. In London he met
Allen, who impressed him, and shortly afterwards he broached the idea to
Sonia, saying that Allen was keen to meet her. 'As he said very convincingly,
someone will inevitably be doing a biography of George Orwell, and it's
certainly best to have it done by someone serious and competent. I do hope
you will see Walter Allen and at least let him put the case before you'.[35]

But Klein would suffer the usual disappointment. Not only did Sonia see
herself and Angus as already composing a biography of Orwell from his own
words, but Klein had inadvertently struck a raw nerve with her. She would,
she told him, ponder the matter, but, 'In the meantime *please*, please, please
realise that nothing irritates me more than the blackmail of "someone will
inevitably do a biography etc., so why not authorise one"!!' The situation,
she said, was very difficult for her. 'Anyhow . . . I will make a statement on
my feelings as soon as I can! And give you advance notice'.[36] When Warburg
saw her letter, he told Klein, 'She has had 15 years to know what her feelings

on the subject are and if she doesn't know now, when will she know?'[37] Klein hoped that Allen would win over Sonia, but should he fail, suggested John Gross, assistant editor of *Encounter*, as an alternative. However, although Warburg reported Allen 'mad keen' to proceed, that 'keenness' was soon blunted by Sonia's by now predictable rejection.

The four-volume *Collected Essays, Journalism and Letters of George Orwell*, edited by Sonia and Angus, was published in Autumn 1968 on both sides of the Atlantic. The material was arranged chronologically and its autobiographical significance emphasised, while the cover blurb declared 'Mrs Orwell's wish' that the collection 'stand in for a biography'. No doubt she hoped thereby to silence calls for a separate *Life* for some considerable time. She would be sorely disappointed.

By now, Stansky and Abrahams had returned to the fray. Curiously enough, while Sonia refused contact with them, Rees, Orwell's other official literary executor, was actively encouraging them. As they wrote in *The Unknown Orwell*, on visiting him in May 1967 he told them, 'If you want to understand Orwell, you have to understand Blair . . . and to understand Blair – well, there's your book'. Sonia had firmly denied them access to the archive, so they set out to gather what material was otherwise available – published works and reminiscences, public records, uncollected letters etc. And, when the *Collected Essays Journalism and Letters etc.* appeared, a good deal of Orwell material was suddenly made public. All that remained to Sonia was to refuse permission to quote his words. At this juncture, Angus, her co-editor, unaware of her distaste for the argument, told her that someone was bound eventually to produce an unauthorised biography, so why not again make an 'official' appointment?

Coincidentally, the appearance of their collection had re-ignited the interest of Julian Symons. Having once been rebuffed by Sonia, he asked David Farrer, one of Warburg's editors, to sound her out. Orwell's request, he argued, was 'a stipulation that a man of sufficient interest can't make successfully (cf. Carlyle). If a good book is not written there will be a bad one, if a serious interpretation is not made half a dozen trashy ones will replace it'. He knew that Sonia thought her published collection was 'as complete as it can be', but there were undoubtedly gaps. 'A biography would present a picture partly complementary to the letters and autobiographical material but of course greatly enlarging it, and including much information about his life which of necessity found no place in such a collection'. He promised that his picture would be sympathetic, adding that Muggeridge had offered to hand over what material he had gathered a decade earlier.[38] Sonia's reply to Farrer is both interesting and revealing.

I really hate the whole of this biography situation and just know I really can't authorise one. Even if I did, I would never, myself, talk to any biographer about George and there really is fairly scant written material available. Judging by the things most of his friends have said on the BBC or written about him, I don't think their information is wildly accurate – as far as I can judge it – or very understanding. But I suppose that's not for me to judge! I do see it's maddening because I suppose one will be written as soon as I'm dead *or* the copyright expires, but quite honestly I cannot find it in myself to authorise one, even though I do see it might be sensible! I'm sorry to feel so fearfully vague and grumpy about the whole question. I really don't know what to do for the best and so, in a cowardly way I tend to refuse to face the situation![39]

Farrer suggested Symons take Sonia to lunch, hoping she might change her mind, but Symons, knowing Sonia of old, thought it pointless. 'Even if I were persuasive enough to make her change her mind (doubtful) I think it's likely that she would change it again in a week'.[40]

Three years later, however, the situation changed dramatically. In November 1972, Stansky and Abrahams's *The Unknown Orwell*, covering his early years, appeared. Sonia wrote angrily to the *TLS* attempting to discredit it.

I wish to point out that this book has been written without my cooperation and without my permission to quote from the work in copyright. In my opinion this book contains mistakes and misconceptions. Rather than let it stand as the only existing biography of George Orwell I have regretfully decided to go against Orwell's own wishes in the matter and to authorize a full biography which makes use of all the available material.

She then announced Muggeridge's successor.

I have asked Professor Bernard Crick, who for some time has been preparing a study of Orwell's political thought, to expand his work to include a biography. I shall of course give him all the help I can and I would ask all George Orwell's friends to do the same.[41]

The mantle had fallen on Crick after Sonia had read his *New Statesman* review of Miriam Gross's *The World of George Orwell*. He admitted being surprised by the invitation, but agreed on two conditions. One, he must first read Stansky and Abrahams's book. If he thought this was good enough, he wouldn't want to spend years covering the same ground and would urge Sonia to let the two Americans see everything. Two, he wanted unrestricted access to all papers, and prior waiver of copyright whatever reservations she might have on reading the final product.

Some thought her decision strange. Crick, a London University Professor of Politics, had never written a biography. Sonia was interested neither in politics, nor in Orwell's political writing. Her *Collected Essays Journalism and Letters* had focused more on the 'literary' Orwell than the 'political' one. Furthermore, Crick was a profound sceptic, bound to approach Orwell's autobiographical writings with suspicion, something likely to provoke serious conflict between widow and biographer. Seeing a final typescript, she tried unsuccessfully to get the book suppressed, and refused it the title 'authorised'. Harcourt Brace's 'Cold War Warrior' director, Jovanovich, rejected Crick's 'socialist' Orwell, and the US edition came instead from Little Brown. The UK edition appeared in November 1980; Sonia died a month later.

Since her demise, the number of major Orwell biographies has grown to six. Approaches differ, but one chose to be prescriptive. Crick adopts the strictly empirical line that attempts to reconstruct a subject's mental state are no business of the biographer. He is particularly critical of what he styles 'the English cult of biography' focusing on 'character' and admitting speculation. However, it is clear that Orwell himself favoured the English camp over Crick, whose prescription excludes the 'inherently probable'. The issue is whether Biography is a mere sub-division of History or whether it is a genre in its own right. The 'English' biography presupposes that the biographical subject is not merely a physical presence to be observed, measured and charted, or reflected through the memories of contemporaries, but also a conscious being; consequently any theory of biography requires also a theory of the self, however implicit.

Biographies are readings of relics, word-portraits reflecting the cultural preconceptions and preferred methods of their creators, which invariably contribute to debates about their subject's reputation.[42] Stansky and Abrahams, unable to quote Orwell, rely heavily (as their end-notes demonstrate) on a range of voices evoking Orwell – a multiple mirror-image glimpse of the man, incomplete though intriguing. Crick, politics professor, eschewing 'character' and doubting Orwell's autobiographical writing, offers the *political* Orwell perceived externally, eschewing speculation about his psychological state. Michael Shelden, English Literature professor, portrays the *literary* man but also the conscious being, while Jeffrey Meyers, long-time Orwell scholar and prolific biographer, ventures for the first time a systematic probing of Orwell's mental world. D. J. Taylor, critic and novelist, lends his critical imagination to the task, while, from a literary-sociological background, I endeavour to map Orwell's evolving consciousness within a changing socio-political context. The last three, published since 2000, benefit from Peter Davison's *Complete Works of George Orwell*, which places most of Orwell's archive into the public domain.

These various Orwell biographies illustrate the nature of the genre and the issues it raises. Is a human life a reality available to us only by means of a 'correct' method? Can the empirical approach, lacking a theory of self – and society, ever deliver a fully-realised life-story? How far can speculation go before biography becomes fiction? While this is no place to address such questions, it is nevertheless instructive to raise them.

Denied access to the Orwell Archive, Stansky and Abrahams were forced into a principally investigative mode – tracking witnesses, ferreting out documents, piecing together clues – and the paraphrasing of texts to avoid copyright infringement. They acknowledge five institutional sources, and assistance from more than thirty of Orwell's friends and acquaintances, some lost to subsequent biographers through death, including Mrs Vaughan Wilkes, Orwell's headmistress-villain of 'Such, Such Were the Joys'.

Crick acknowledges fourteen libraries and over a hundred witnesses. With full access to the archive, he had nevertheless to fill many gaps for himself. Consequently, here too is an emphasis on primary research, the evidential underpinning of the story. But here memoirs of others are presented without interpretation. This enables him to claim a certain status for his narrative, an evidential account tempered by scepticism. Following his own bent and reflecting his own set of intellectual priorities, Crick presents the very Orwell Sonia found uninteresting, and barely recognised in her *Collected Essays etc* – the *political* animal.

Shelden, acknowledging fifty Orwell contacts and seven libraries, provocatively styles his book 'The Authorized Biography'. He lacks Crick's aversion to interpretation and speculation and feels no compulsion to doubt the autobiographical Orwell. Unlike Crick, and following essentially literary priorities, he recreates the *literary* Orwell. His field researches also produced important discoveries, such as Orwell's 1937 medical record and his annotated copy of *Down and Out in Paris and London*.

Meyers (forty-seven Orwell contacts, and eighteen research institutions acknowledged), is also unconstrained by Crick's restrictive theory of biography. Furthermore, he is rather more willing than his predecessors to explore his subjects' mental life, to investigate the 'darker' side of Orwell and question his often 'saintly' image. He traced Orwell's model for Rosemary in *Keep the Aspidistra Flying* and was the first biographer to mention an NKVD report on Orwell in Spain. He was also first to draw on Davison's *Complete Works*, the archive made public.

Orwell: The Life is primarily text-based – drawing more on published memoirs and Davison's twenty volumes than first-hand research. Three archives, twenty-six witnesses and twenty-three literary editors are acknowledged. Written rather than enumerated end-notes read like extensions of the text itself, and a form of experimentation pioneered by Andrew Field and Peter Ackroyd (on Nabokov and on Dickens) is attempted – the narrator disrupting the story-line, here with discrete authorial reflections on aspects of Orwell's character. Although more literary than political, its posture, like Crick's, is sceptical of the autobiographical Orwell – perceived as contrived to promote the 'myth of Orwell'. The second half of *The Road to Wigan Pier*, for example, is regarded as his amateur, ill-informed view of socialism rather than evidence of a growing suspicion of people attracted to socialism, culminating in the savage satire of his last two novels. Discoveries include a youthful rival in love to Orwell, some remarkable new photographs, and some 'lost' Orwell-Muggeridge letters.

George Orwell (US title: *Inside George Orwell*) acknowledges eighty-two witnesses and forty-one libraries, reflecting a more research-oriented literary-sociological background. Following Orwell's prescription to explore the writer's inner world through his work, clues and allusions are followed to both highlight motives and unearth new discoveries – about Orwell's ancestry, his early education, dramas at Eton, some 'lost' love-letters, spy-induced paranoia in Spain leading him to go armed back in Britain. Unadventurously, no formal experiments are attempted, and reflections on Orwell's character are subsumed within what is offered (hopefully) as a seamless narrative. While sceptical of some autobiographical material, it is treated here more as evidence of a self-consciousness at work.

Debates about biography are bedevilled by a fundamental misconception. As Ira Nadel writes, 'The problem for biography is that readers accept facts literally, although their presentation is always figurative – that is readers misinterpret the artistic ideal of coherence for the historical ideal of objectivity'.[43] The figures which characterise any given biography will embody the vision, prejudices, literary and research skills, stock of knowledge and critical disposition of the biographer, often revealing as much about him/her as about the subject. On this view, no biography can be 'definitive', implying 'final' ('authoritative' is another matter, of course). As a figurative form, biography stands closer to portraiture than history revealed empirically. Biography so considered is more art than science. Biographies of Orwell, therefore, are better regarded as works of informed imagination than photographic realism.

Letters not otherwise indicated are lodged in the Department of Archives and Manuscripts at the University of Reading.

NOTES

1. Review of *Herman Melville* by Lewis Mumford, *New Adelphi*, March–May, 1930, in Davidson, Peter (ed.), *Complete Works of George Orwell* (London: Secker and Warburg, 2000), Vol. 10, p. 183.

2. Review of *The Life and Times of Henry Crabb Robinson* by Edith J. Morley, *Adelphi*, October, 1935; *Complete Works*, Vol. 10, p. 398.
3. Review of *Stendhal* by F. C. Green, *New English Weekly*, 27 July 1939; *Complete Works*, Vol. 10, p. 378.
4. Review of *Tolstoy: His Life and Work* by Derrick Leon, *Observer*, 26 March 1944; *Complete Works*, Vol. 6, p. 36.
5. 'Charles Dickens', 11 March 1940, *Inside the Whale* (London: Victor Gollancz, 1940) p. 43; *Complete Works*, Vol. 12, p. 36.
6. George Orwell-Fredric Warburg, 4 May 1946; *Complete Works*, Vol. 18, p. 305.
7. Bernard Crick and Audrey Coppard (eds.), *George Orwell Remembered* (London: Ariel Books, 1984), p. 221.
8. George Orwell-Sir Richard Rees, 5 July 1946, *Complete Works*, Vol. 18, pp. 340–1.
9. Rees-Sonia Orwell, 5 February 1951, Orwell Archive, University College, London.
10. Rees-Sonia Orwell, 1 August 1951.
11. Rees-Sonia Orwell, 17 January 1955.
12. Julian Symons-Sonia Orwell, 10 December 1954, Orwell Archive University College, London.
13. Symons-Sonia Orwell, 30 December 1954.
14. Reginald Reynolds, *My Life and Crimes*, London, Jarrolds, 1956, p. 215.
15. George Woodcock-Sonia Orwell, 20 February 1955, Orwell Archive, University College, London.
16. Christopher Hollis-Sonia Orwell, 21 August 1955.
17. Hollis-Sonia Orwell, 9 November 1955[?].
18. Malcolm Muggeridge, 'A Knight of the Woeful Countenance', in Miriam Gross (ed.), *The World of George Orwell* (London: Weidenfeld and Nicolson, 1971), p. 175.
19. Inez Holden-Ian Angus, 2 January 1967.
20. David Astor-Warburg, 25 September 1959.
21. T. R. Fyvell-Warburg, 5 February 1959.
22. Astor-Warburg, 25 September 1959.
23. Warburg-Astor, 28 September 1959.
24. Sonia Orwell-Dwight Macdonald, 15 January 1960.
25. Sonia Orwell-Macdonald, 15 March 1960.
26. Warburg-William Jovanovich, 4 April 1960.
27. Jovanovich-Warburg, 13 April 1960.
28. Warburg-Jovanovich, 28 March 1960.
29. Arthur Koestler-Warburg, 20 April 1960.
30. Jovanovich-Sonia Orwell, 10 May 1960.
31. Warburg-Sonia Orwell, 13 June 1960.
32. Sonia Orwell-Warburg, 15 June 1960.
33. Jovanovich-Sonia Orwell, 8 August 1960. A letter from Sonia to Jovanovich dated 20 July 1960 doubted whether Ellmann, as an American, was a suitable biographer for Orwell. It must have been this letter, forwarded to Ellmann, that prompted him to withdraw from the project.
34. Jovanovich-Warburg, 11 October 1966.
35. Roger Klein-Sonia Orwell, 9 November 1964.

36. Sonia Orwell-Klein, 4 January 1964.
37. Warburg-Klein, 11 January 1965.
38. Symons-David Farrer, 6 December 1968.
39. Sonia Orwell-Farrer, 14 April 1969.
40. Symons-Farrer, 18 April 1969.
41. *Times Literary Supplement*, 13 October 1972, p. 1226.
42. For the history of Orwell's biographies up to 1989 and their part in the construction of his reputation, see John Rodden's *The Politics of Literary Reputation: The Making and Claiming of 'St George' Orwell* (New York/Oxford: Oxford University Press, 1989).
43. Nadel, Ira Bruce, *Biography: Fiction, Fact and Form* (London: Macmillan, 1984), pp. 156–7.

3

JONATHAN ROSE

Englands His Englands

To say that England made George Orwell is both true and far more complicated than it seems. After all, there is, and always has been, more than one
England. In the first half of the twentieth century there were Englands of the
left and of the right; a hopeful and idealistic England and a depressingly pessimistic England. There was an England of law and liberty, and (especially
in wartime) an England infected by strains of totalitarianism. Of course the
nation was riven by class, but Disraeli's 'Two Nations' had by now divided
into several new subgroups: the old working class (for instance) had split
between those who enjoyed some of the trappings of mass affluence and
those mired in permanent unemployment.

Orwell knew all of these Englands, perhaps better than any other author
of his generation. His contemporaries tended to focus on particular social
niches, with middlebrow writers writing about Middle England, proletarian writers concentrating on proles, and Bloomsbury intellectuals telling
all you need to know about Bloomsbury. But Orwell had a genius for
ranging across the boundaries of class, culture, ideology and literary fiefdoms. He was a sociologist of remarkable breadth, and his writings, taken
together, may offer the most comprehensive profile of modern English society ever produced by one individual. He was able to explore and explain
all of the many coexisting Englands, because he half-belonged to each
of them.

First, there was Tory England. Aristocratic, Anglican, imperial, insular,
unintellectual, it was the realm of the armed forces and the public schools:
in short, his father's England. On that side of his family, Eric Blair was
descended from an earl and an Established Church deacon with a remunera-
tive living. George Orwell may have repudiated that England but, like most
rebels, he never broke completely free of what he rejected. He admitted that,
in a less political age, he probably would have followed a path of contented
conventionality:

A happy vicar I might have been
Two hundred years ago,
To preach upon eternal doom
And watch my walnuts grow . . .[1]

But he was also a citizen of Bohemian England, which was cosmopoli-
tan, literary, epicurean, more or less artistic, and more or less socialistic.
That legacy Orwell inherited from the family of his half-French mother, Ida
Limousin, who studied painting with a French artist and wore agate drop
earrings. When he complained that 'the English intelligentsia . . . take their
cookery from Paris and their opinions from Moscow' (CELJ 2:74), he might
have had his mother's casseroles in mind. Her sisters hosted Fabian Society
tea parties; one of them settled in Paris with an Esperantist. Even as a boy,
Eric Blair absorbed much of that milieu. He was a dedicated fan of Bernard
Shaw and H. G. Wells, and in 1922 he participated in a socialist conference at Dunsford, also attended by Sidney and Beatrice Webb. According to
Jacintha Buddicom, a childhood friend, Eric was already a socialist of sorts:
like many Fabians, he believed sincerely but vaguely in social equality, and
he cultivated a mildly subversive turn of mind.

From the beginning, then, George Orwell had his feet planted firmly in
two different and antagonistic worlds. That helps to explain why, for all
his professed clarity and straightforwardness, he was in fact a marvellously
paradoxical observer of the English scene, contradictory in the finest sense
of the term. Whether he was discussing the Left or the Right, imperialism
or pacifism, public schools or socialism, intellectuals or proletarians, he was
always capable of turning on himself, shifting his weight from one perspective
to another. An eternal contrarian, he usually differed with whomever he was
speaking with and sometimes disagreed with himself, because he understood
these Englands too well to entirely embrace or reject any of them.

Eric Blair attended school with boys from much wealthier families, and
thus became aware of the gross economic gulfs that separated the various
strata of British society. In 1911–13 the richest 10 per cent of the population owned 92 per cent of the national wealth, a proportion which had
scarcely changed (88 per cent) by 1936–38. Orwell memorably placed his origins in the 'lower-upper-middle class' earning £400 to £500 a year. That class
included mid-level imperial officials, like Orwell's father, as well as bohemian
intellectuals such as E. M. Forster and Virginia Woolf. The latter lived off
inherited money, which was often invested in colonies that were managed,
in turn, by men like Richard Blair. In 1912 the British had a net investment
abroad of more than £3.5 billion, earning a comfortable 5.2 per cent average

interest, which worked out to about £185 million annually and effortlessly flowing into the pockets of the shareholding class. When socialists denounced the 'bourgeoisie' they particularly had in mind the coupon-clipping rentier: this product of mature capitalism was portrayed as an economic parasite who did no useful work and deserved to be expropriated. Whether they worked for the government, in business, or not at all, the lower-upper-middle class family could typically afford a couple of servants, given that housemaids and cooks usually commanded £12 to £24 a year. Above the Blairs, a High Court judge was paid £5000, a successful barrister could earn £20,000, and the Earl of Derby took in more than £300,000 from coal mines, urban real estate, and 70,000 acres of agricultural land. Below them, a public school master could earn up to £300, the majority of clerks and elementary school teachers less than £100. The wages of a skilled artisan might be about 40s. a week, an unskilled male labourer 22s. to 29s., and the average for women workers was just 11s. 7d. – that is, when they were fully employed. Given the mild inflation of 1896–1914, real wages were actually declining, a fact that may have contributed to a massive wave of strike activity between 1910 and 1914. Edwardian social surveys found that 25 to 30 per cent of the urban population was in dire poverty. In 1911 only 8.6 per cent of the population of England and Wales was living in overcrowded housing, but the proportion was much greater in city slums and as high as 45 per cent for all of Scotland.

Alongside the economic contrasts of Orwell's England were equally glaring contradictions in the realm of personal liberties. It is telling that the author of *Nineteen Eighty-Four* enjoyed a childhood in an exceptionally liberal and law-abiding society. The central government interfered little with the daily lives of its citizens, and even a ten-year-old could freely purchase a rifle and gunpowder. (Until the Firearms Act of 1920 there were no serious parliamentary efforts to restrict gun ownership, mainly because homicides using guns were quite rare – only about 10 per year in the early 1890s.) *Coming Up for Air* is saturated with nostalgia for that lost Edwardian Eden, which for Orwell represented the benchmark of a truly free (though unequal) society.

The First World War called into existence a profoundly new and disturbing England. Although *Nineteen Eighty-Four* is often described as a portrait of Britain in 1944, in many ways Orwell found his model for totalitarianism in the previous conflict. On 8 August 1914 the government was empowered to resort to virtually any measures necessary to the prosecution of the war – including imposing martial law on civilians – by the Defence of the Realm Act, popularly and sardonically known as 'D.O.R.A.' As Arthur Marwick observed, it 'conjured up in the public mind the image of a cruel and capricious maiden who at the snap of her fingers could close down a news-paper, requisition a ship, or prohibit whistling for cabs' (Marwick, *Deluge*, p. 36). This is not hyperbole: in fact D.O.R.A. was used to commandeer property, impose rationing and price ceilings, control war industries, prose-cute the venerable *Times* as well as antiwar publications, limit pub hours, and (in August 1916) ban whistling for taxis. D.O.R.A. was the Big Sister domi-nating the anonymous antiwar satire *1920: Dips into the Near Future*, which Eric Blair may have read: the similarities between this squib and *Nineteen Eighty-Four* extend well beyond their titles. In *1920* D.O.R.A. taps tele-phones, cuts rations, arbitrarily imprisons people without trial, and treats truth as something 'infinitely malleable and adaptable to the purposes of the State'. (*1920*, pp. 26–27). She also commissions historians to rewrite history in a true anti-German spirit, describing Blucher's treachery at Waterloo and proving the nonexistence of Immanuel Kant. In fact British historians were whitewashing the despotism of their Czarist Russian allies, just as the next generation of intellectuals would whitewash the despotism of their Soviet Russian allies. To an unprecedented degree, the government mobilised writ-ers and academics to churn out deceptive propaganda, climaxing in the cre-ation of a Ministry of Information under Lord Beaverbrook. And that was just one of several vast dictatorial bureaucracies that were created during the war: there were also Ministries of Munitions, National Service, Food and Shipping, and Labour, though many of them would be dismantled after the armistice.

Britain in the First World War anticipated Airstrip One in many other ways, with paranoid spy scares, bombs falling out of the sky (albeit delivered by zeppelins rather than guided missiles), and shortages of everything. By December 1917 there were inadequate supplies of milk, sugar, tea, butter, bacon and rice in London; the following May the weekly meat ration was cut to 12 ounces. Orwell once confessed that margarine was what he remembered most clearly about the great conflict: 'By 1917 the war had almost ceased to affect us, except through our stomachs' (*CEJL* 1:537). That became an obsession with him: all of Orwell's protagonists (not just Winston Smith) are ill-fed. In *Coming Up for Air*, George Bowling is reduced to eating processed pseudofoods, notably artificial marmalade and fish frankfurters: 'Everything comes out of a carton or a tin, or it's hauled out of a refrigerator or squirted out of a tap or squeezed out of a tube' (*CUFA* 26). But Bowling remembers another England, before the war, an England of 'boiled beef and dumplings, roast beef and Yorkshire, boiled mutton and capers, pig's head, apple pie, spotted dog and jam roly-poly' (*CUFA* 57). It was a highly romanticised memory, as Bowling half-admits. But given his comfortable childhood, gaunt George Orwell had some reason to be nostalgic about the time 'When good

King Edward ruled the land / And I was a chubby boy' (Crick, *Orwell*, pp. 4–5).

St Cyprian's was a typical nursery of Tory England, where young Eric Blair was steeped in ethos of games, cramming, patriotism and snobbery. But Eton offered a more varied environment. Of course it educated the sons of the English establishment in conventional ruling-class values. In the First World War a total of 4852 Etonians performed overseas military service, of which more than 20 per cent were killed, figures typical of the public schools and of Oxford and Cambridge universities. But the school also had a more offbeat, artistic niche: Blair was taught by Aldous Huxley, and his schoolmates included Cyril Connolly, Anthony Powell, Harold Acton and Brian Howard. As D. J. Taylor observes, Eton had never been forced into the public-school mould devised by Dr Thomas Arnold: it remained 'a magisterial collective entity full of obscure secret fiefdoms; unfailingly orthodox in its make-up but quietly sympathetic to more maverick elements; aristocratic but not exclusively so; self-governing and *sui generis*' (Taylor, *Orwell*, p. 42). And as a King's Scholar, exempt from tuition fees, Blair belonged to an elite within an elite, with a justifiable sense of intellectual superiority vis-à-vis other Etonians. The cohort of scholarship students admitted with Blair in 1916 constituted 'an oasis of enlightenment', recalled Connolly. They were 'scholar athletes, animated, unlike the rules of the college, by postwar opinions. They hated bullying, beating, fagging, the election system, militarism, and infringements of liberty, and believed in the ultimate victory of human reason' (Connolly, *Enemies of Promise*, pp. 244–45).

Because he spent the years 1922–27 in Burma, Orwell missed the heyday of English modernism, yet he was not completely cut off from literary crosscurrents back home. He was moved 'almost to tears' by Margaret Kennedy's middlebrow *The Constant Nymph*, but also impressed by D. H. Lawrence's 'The Prussian Officer' and 'The Thorn in the Flesh'. Once again he had a foot in each camp, the mainstream and the highbrow. Revealingly, he subscribed to the *Adelphi* – John Middleton Murry's leftish, arty little magazine – but also used it for target practice. Outwardly a conventional policeman, inwardly he was increasingly convinced that imperialism was a 'racket', yet he found intellectual critiques of colonialism infuriatingly naïve about the actual situation on the ground. That Tory/Bohemian ambivalence is manifest in his shifting attitudes toward a writer when he repeatedly came back to: 'I worshipped Kipling at thirteen [at St Cyprian's], loathed him at seventeen [at Eton], enjoyed him at twenty [in Burma], despised him at twenty-five [having quit the Burma police], and now [in 1936] again rather admire him' (*CELJ* 1:159).

In 'Inside the Whale' Orwell was able to sort most of the writers of the period 1910–40 into a few well-defined groups: first the Georgian poets, then the Modernists, followed by the Auden-Spender circle, while the middlebrows clustered around Sir John Squire and Hugh Walpole. Like Gordon Comstock, Orwell disdained these groups as mutual admiration societies that would not give an outsider a chance, and in fact English literary life between the wars was dominated by a few old boys' cliques. Though Orwell profited from his connections with his Etonian schoolchum, Cyril Connolly, he did not really belong to any of these circles: therefore, he could independently read and criticise them all, without confining himself to any one movement or school. At a time when English literary culture had fractured along high/middle/lowbrow lines, with most authors limiting themselves to just one of these audiences, Orwell exceptionally worked in all three literary strata, writing with equal facility and insight about D. H. Lawrence, J. B. Priestley and comic papers. These three levels of modern English literature are all embodied in *Nineteen Eighty-Four*, which is at once pulp science fiction, a popular political thriller, and (as Alex Zwerdling has noted) high modernism. Its opening line ('It was a bright cold day in April, and the clocks were striking thirteen') echoes that of *The Waste Land* ('April is the cruellest month . . .') and both employ the same modernist devices: they immediately put the world out of joint, disorient the reader, upset audience expectations with a discordant note, and introduce a mood of indefinable menace. But unlike other modernists, Orwell was able to work modernism into a best seller. In his uninhibited crossing of cultural boundaries, he anticipated the 'nobrows' of the postmodern era, though he more felicitously called them 'elastic-brows' (*CEJL* 1:254).

Orwell's oft-quoted sneer – 'that the mere words "Socialism" and "Communist" draw towards them with magnetic force every fruit-juice drinker, nudist, sandal-wearer, sex-maniac, Quaker, "Nature Cure" quack, pacifist and feminist in England' (*RWP* p. 174) – sounds like something his father might have said, if he had been that articulate. But it obscures the fact that, when Orwell resigned from the Burma police, he decisively quit Tory England and joined Bohemian England. His father was so appalled that he apparently hurled his foulest epithet (*'dilettante!'*), and the two were estranged for years (Taylor, *Orwell*, p. 88). Yet Orwell persevered in following the conventional route for unconventional creative people. Like Cyril Connolly, Hemingway, Fitzgerald and Gertrude Stein, he gravitated to Paris. He was assisted by arty people he knew, notably his Aunt Nellie and poet Ruth Pitter. Later, he landed the ideal bohemian job, which allowed him time for writing: as a part-time assistant in a second-hand Hampstead bookshop run by Independent Labour Party activists. Still later he damned the precious upmarket bohemians portrayed in Cyril Connolly's novel *The Rock Pool*, but meanwhile he was enjoying a downmarket bohemian life in a sixteenth-century country cottage, running a tiny general store and tending goats and hens in the garden. The cottage wasn't far from Letchworth Garden City, where Orwell mixed with the same avant-garde types he had caricatured in the above quotation. He didn't entirely like them, and often the Tory in him would snort at them, but (nudism aside) he shared many of their values.

Take, for example, their sexual attitudes. We tend to assume that the great revolution in mores happened in the 1960s, but in Orwell's time Victorian England was already beginning to give way to a more permissive society. Two-thirds of women marrying between 1935–39 used birth control, though it was often only withdrawal. When Orwell was 30, the birth rate was just over half what it had been when he was born. *Keep the Aspidistra Flying* reflects his ambivalence on that subject. Gordon Comstock obsesses about sex as an angry young man (angry mainly because he isn't getting much of it), but on another plane he looks back nostalgically to those enormous Victorian families. Ultimately he recognises and accepts what he really wants: suburban monogamy and domestic tranquillity. In reality, some English-women were beginning to enjoy sexual adventures of their own, without necessarily closing their eyes and thinking of England. A 1943–46 survey of 100 younger working-class wives reported that 49 of them had orgasms invariably or often, and another 36 infrequently. Just 19 per cent of married women born before 1904 had sex before marriage (often with their future husbands), rising to 36 per cent of those born between 1904–14. No doubt the proportion was much higher in bohemian circles, where Orwell met women like Sonia Brownell, who became his second wife and the model for Julia, the sexual outlaw of *Nineteen Eighty-Four*.

With the fruit-juice drinkers and sandal-wearers and so on, Orwell also shared an abiding concern with yet another England – down-and-out England, the England of 'The Spike' and 'Common Lodging Houses'. In 1934 the *New Survey of London Life and Labour* reported a poverty rate of 10 per cent, *The Social Survey of Merseyside* 16 per cent. In 1901 Seebohm Rowntree had found 28 per cent of the population of York living in poverty; in 1936 it was still 18 per cent, compared with just 1.5 per cent in 1951. Orwell has been criticised for his comments on the body odours of the proletariat, but the hard fact is that in 1939 nine out of ten Stepney families had no baths, as did half of all Glaswegians and two of five dwellings in Hull. And if Orwell was fixated on food shortages, it was because much of Britain was undernourished. John Boyd Orr's study *Food, Health, and Income* reported that in 1934 there were still glaring differences in eating habits across class lines. Fully half the population could not afford a completely adequate diet, and the diet of the poorest 10 per cent was 'deficient in every constituent examined'. All classes enjoyed a more or less equal share of bread, potatoes and sugar, but consumption of nearly every other important food group – meat, milk, eggs, butter, cheese, fish, fruit, vegetables – declined steadily with income.

In 1931 the National Government had allowed unemployment benefits of 15s. 3d. for an adult man, 8s. for his wife, and 2s. for each child, for a maximum of 26 weeks. Thereafter, the long-term unemployed could apply for 'transitional payments', sourly known as 'the dole'. Two hundred local Public Assistance Committees set the rates for the dole, which in a few cases could be as low as 16s. for a husband and wife. And even that was subject to a means test: military and widows' pensions, personal savings and the earnings of any family members (including children) were grounds for reducing or eliminating the allowance. In Lancashire a third of the unemployed were completely disqualified, though elsewhere some Public Assistance Committees defied or evaded the means test and awarded maximum payments to nearly all claimants. The Communist-led National Unemployed Workers' Movement organised 'hunger marches' and agitated for increased public assistance. The administration and guidelines governing unemployment benefits would be a subject of constant controversy throughout the decade, but the means test was not ended until 1941.

And yet Orwell recognised that, even in the Great Depression, a more affluent England was also beginning to emerge. When he wrote *The Road to Wigan Pier*, national industrial production was 75 per cent higher than when he had entered St Cyprian's. Poverty and long-term unemployment were strangling the mill towns and mining communities of northern England, Wales and Scotland. But in southern England modern light industries were creating a new working class that was 'more middle-class in outlook'. By 1934 half the insured workers in Abertilly were idle, two-thirds in Jarrow, but just 5.1 per cent in Coventry and Oxford, and only 3.3 per cent in High Wycombe. The great business success story of the 1930s was Marks and Spencer, which mass-marketed fashionable clothes for an upper-working-class/lower-middle-class clientele. The great publishing success story was the Penguin paperback, available at any Woolworth's for sixpence. The cinema offered entertainment that was cheap and classless, yet (in the grander picture palaces) suffused with an atmosphere of luxury: perhaps 80 per cent of young unemployed people went more than once a week. Many shipyards and steel mills were idle, but the number of distributive workers increased steadily every year of the Depression, from 1.5 million in 1929 to 1.88

million in 1937. By 1930 the electrical, automotive, aircraft, rayon, hosiery, chemical and scientific instrument industries accounted for 12.7 per cent of the industrial force, up from 5.2 per cent in 1907. Where only one in seventeen houses was electrified in 1920, two-thirds were in 1939, by which time radios were in 84.4 per cent of upper working-class homes (earning £2 10s. to £4 a week) and 57.7 per cent of lower working-class homes (earning less than £2 10s.). Spending on social services, only 4.1 per cent of the gross national product in 1913, had risen to 11.3 per cent in 1938, when the government was redistributing as much as £386 million to those earning less than £125 a year. Compared with the prewar period, per capita consumption of fruit was up 88 per cent, vegetables 64 per cent, eggs 46 per cent. Wigan was a terrible pocket of squalor, but nationwide consumption by persons earning less than £250 dipped only slightly during the first years of the slump and, by 1936, was above 1929 levels.

Thanks to low interest rates, government housing programmes, cheap labour, and cheaper construction materials imported from abroad, four million houses were built in England and Wales between the wars. Of these 1.1 million were council houses, but nearly 2.5 million were built by private contractors with no state subsidy. A suburban house could be had for £800, or as little as £450 for small cookie-cutter semi-detached homes, affordable to the lower-middle-class George Bowlings of England or even to better-paid workingmen. And Orwell noticed that, thanks to hire-purchase (accounting for 60 per cent of all furniture sold in 1938), 'the interior of a working-class house resembles that of a middle-class house very much more than it did a generation ago' (CEJL 3:22). All these developments were creating a new suburban England of

> labour-saving flats or council houses, along the concrete roads and in the naked democracy of the swimming-pools. It is a rather restless, cultureless life, centering around tinned food, *Picture Post*, the radio and the internal combustion engine. It is a civilization in which children grow up with an intimate knowledge of magnetoes and in complete ignorance of the Bible.

Orwell appreciated that 'the older class distinctions are beginning to break down' in the face of this suburbanisation (CEJL, 2:77–78). But at the same time he recognised that the old impoverished England and the new affluent England had produced a bastard offspring, a peculiarly modern poverty which, a generation later, would become characteristic of slums throughout the Western world. Permanent unemployment was now palliated by government handouts and bargain-basement consumerism:

... the youth who leaves school at fourteen and gets a blind-alley job is out of work at twenty, probably for life; but for two pounds ten on the hire-purchase system he can buy himself a suit which, for a little while and at a little distance, looks as though it had been tailored in Savile Row. The girl can look like a fashion plate at an even lower price. ... Whole sections of the working class who have been plundered of all they really need are being compensated, in part, by cheap luxuries which mitigate the surface of life. ... It is quite likely that fish and chips, art-silk stockings, tinned salmon, cut-price chocolate (five two-ounce bars for sixpence), the movies, the radio, strong tea and the Football Pools have between them averted revolution.   (RWP, 88–90)

There was much antiwar sentiment in the thirties, but here again England and Orwell were of two minds. In February 1933 the Oxford Union notoriously passed a motion 'that this house will under no circumstances fight for its king and country', but that produced a storm of protest, with the *Daily Express* vilifying the 'woozy-minded Communists, the practical jokers, the sexual indeterminates of Oxford'. The 'Peace Ballot' of 1934–35 polled more than 11 million citizens, who solidly supported the League of Nations, reduction of armaments, the abolition of air warfare, and a ban on arms sales; but they also backed, by a margin of nearly 3 to 1, the use of military force if necessary to stop an aggressor. Shortly before Chamberlain flew to Munich, a Mass Observation survey found that only 16 per cent of men supported his policy while 67 per cent denounced appeasement; women were more willing to abandon the Czechs, by 43 to 22 per cent.

In the months immediately leading up to the German attack on Poland, Orwell backed the antiwar agitation of the ILP. But once the fighting started he resolved to support 'My Country Right or Left', and vitriolicly denounced pacifists for expressing opinions that he himself had held just a short time before. One may venture a psychological explanation for that radical change of heart. An individual in the grip of a lifelong ambivalence may experience a burst of directed energy when he finds a way of resolving that conflict. Orwell had always been trying to work out the tension between the right and left sides of his political consciousness. His love of the flora and fauna of England may lie in the fact that reverence for nature and hostility to industrialism was one of the few points that Tory England and Bohemian England – the readers of *Country Life* and William Morris, respectively – could agree on. Likewise, he rallied to the flag during the Second World War because the conflict seemed to be forcing the birth of a new society that was neither his father's England nor his mother's, but something of both. As he put it, 'The divorce between patriotism and intelligence', where Blimps and Pinks did not speak to each other, 'cannot continue', because neither was capable of defeating Hitler alone. 'The Bloomsbury highbrow, with his mechanical snigger, is as out-of-date as the cavalry colonel. A modern nation cannot afford either of them. Patriotism and intelligence will have to come together again' (*CELJ*, 2:75).

They came together on 14 May 1940, when Anthony Eden broadcast an appeal for what later became known as the Home Guard. Volunteers began showing up at police stations even before he finished speaking, and within a few weeks almost 1.5 million had joined. In practice virtually anyone under age 65 could join, regardless of medical condition, and the result was an enthusiastic and often pathetically equipped force that seemed to unite all social classes, as if Burma police officers were commanding a Spanish workers' militia. Tom Wintringham, who had led the British contingent of the International Brigades, ran a guerilla warfare school for the Home Guard at Osterley Park, which Orwell attended. Orwell called it 'a People's Army officered by Blimps', and saw it as a potentially revolutionary force.

Meanwhile, the England of mass consumerism was suspended for the duration. Marks and Spencer had 234 stores at the beginning of the war; by the end half of its floor space had been requisitioned by the government or put out of commission by air raids. In August 1942 the weekly ration was only a pound of meat, four ounces of bacon and ham, eight ounces of sugar, two ounces of butter and four of margarine, eight ounces of cheese, four ounces of jam or marmalade, two ounces of candy, and the equivalent of one-and-a half dried eggs. One could always fill up on bread and potatoes, which were unrationed. It wasn't quite as bad as *Nineteen Eighty-Four*: note the fairly generous allowances for sweets, and young children received special rations of milk, orange juice and cod liver oil. It made for a diet that was as nutritious as it was boring. Of course, as in Oceania, there was a black market, and elites contrived to obtain luxuries not available to the masses. Razor blades and cosmetics always seemed to be in short supply, and most toys were banned. Paper was strictly rationed: publishers were eventually reduced to 37.5 per cent of prewar consumption, while per capita book sales rose 50 per cent. Meanwhile, no less than 20 million volumes were destroyed by the Luftwaffe, including a particularly devastating raid on Paternoster Row, the centre of the publishing industry. The ever-increasing gap between supply and demand made it attractive to publish short books and pamphlets, such as *Animal Farm*.

Britain may have done more than any other belligerent nation (even the USSR) to mobilise women, who could be conscripted for essential war work up to age 50. The proportion serving in the armed forces or war industries was about twice that in the First World War, more than a million and a half in the engineering and metal industries alone. Counterintuitively, putting women into men's jobs and work clothes made them appear more sexy, as one Sheffield tram conductress complained: 'Numbers of passengers believe that the last act of a conductress and her driver or motorman each night before going home is the exercise of sexual intercourse' (Calder, *People's War*, p. 386). Orwell seems to have shared that assumption: after a long week attending a large electric motor, Julia secretly rendezvouses with Winston and rips off her overalls. In some ways Orwell had very traditional ideas about gender roles, but he also recognised that a woman who runs heavy industrial machinery can carry a tremendous erotic charge.

On 22 June 1940, the day France signed an armistice with Germany, parliament passed an Emergency Powers Act, which one historian called 'one of the most drastic pieces of legislation in English history – placing all persons and all property at the disposal of the Government as thought "necessary or expedient for securing the public safety"' (Havighurst, *Britain in Transition*, p. 299). In the wrong hands it could have been a mandate for totalitarianism, but it was administered mainly by Minister of Labour Ernest Bevin, chairman of the Trades Union Congress. He was trusted by the working classes and used his near-dictatorial powers with notable restraint, fairness, and the cooperation of both labour and management. At the time it all seemed to be leading inevitably to a socialist England. Orwell was convinced that Britain would have to conscript wealth and arm the people in order to win the war: 'Well, if only we can hold out for a few months, in a year's time we shall see red militia billeted in the Ritz, and it would not particularly surprise me to see Churchill or Lloyd George at the head of them' (*CELJ*, 2:352). The following April the Ritz was still in bourgeois hands, but Orwell remained optimistic: rationing had brought about economic levelling and fewer advertisements cluttering up newspapers. Even the popular tabloids had 'grown politically serious'; even the *Times* 'mumbles about the need for centralized ownership and greater social equality' (*CELJ* 2:112–13). In fact taxation rose dramatically for all, particularly for the affluent, and it hit Orwell hard when the royalties for *Animal Farm* began rolling in. Taxes for a family of four earning £1000 rose from £190 to £400, and the greatest incomes were taxed at a marginal rate of 97.5 per cent.

The Beveridge Report of December 1942 promised a national system of social insurance offering coverage literally 'from the cradle to the grave'. It would begin with maternity grants and end with burial subsidies: in between there would be benefits for unemployment, illness, disability, and workmen's compensation, as well as old age, widows', and orphans' pensions. The report sold an astonishing 635,000 copies and dominated public debate over postwar planning. In one poll nine out of ten respondents favoured enacting its proposals. In 1944 government white papers proposed a national health service and Keynesian public spending policies to head off unemployment. All these became the blueprints of the welfare state constructed by the Labour government after 1945, but as Orwell recognised, they fell short of outright socialism. They represented a compromise between two Englands, a consensus around welfare capitalism. 'Thirty years ago any Conservative would have denounced this as State charity, while most Socialists would have rejected it as a capitalist bribe', Orwell wrote. 'In 1944 the only discussion that arises is about whether it will be adopted in whole or in part' (CELJ, 3:14–16). That consensus would not break up until the election of Margaret Thatcher.

Mass Observation surveys conducted during the war indeed found that Britons had become less selfish, more critical of the existing order, and more concerned with economic justice. Even in the Blitz, most believed that the postwar world would bring more equality and better social services after the war, but 21 per cent predicted 'more state control', and 13 per cent expected 'fascism'. It was this fear that Churchill spoke to in his notorious 1945 political party broadcast:

> No Socialist Government conducting the entire life and industry of the country could afford to allow free, sharp or violently-worded expression of public discontent. They would have to fall back on some sort of Gestapo, no doubt very humanely directed in the first instance. And this would nip opinion in the bud: it would stop criticism as it reared its head, and it would gather all the power to the supreme Party and the party leaders, rising like stately pinnacles above their vast bureaucracies of Civil Servants, no longer servants and no longer civil.   (Hennessy, *Never Again*, pp. 77–78, 82)

Could this have been the origin of the intimidating ministries of *Nineteen Eighty-Four*, each 'an enormous pyramidal structure of glittering white concrete'? (*NEF* 7) One's first impulse is to dismiss the idea out of hand. Churchill's accusation was a smear and a blunder, which deservedly cost him votes. Nothing could have been more ludicrous than to compare humane, soft-spoken Clement Attlee to the recently-crushed Nazis. Orwell always denied that *Nineteen Eighty-Four* was a criticism of the Labour government, which certainly preserved basic civil liberties. True, postwar austerity measures meant several more years of material shortages, but if you were young or working-class or simply eager to make a better world, it was a good time to be alive. The severe housing shortfall was partly alleviated by prefab units, which actually could be popular starter homes for new families. The proportion of national income paid out in wages went from 39 per cent in 1938 to 48 per cent a decade later – in effect transferring a hefty 9 per cent slice of the economic pie from the upper and middle classes to the working classes. On top of that, real public spending on social services had doubled, and there was virtually full employment. By some measures there was more economic equality in Attlee's Britain than Stalin's Russia, and it had all been accomplished without gulags, without secret police, without even abolishing the House of Lords. The New Jerusalem was not yet built, but construction was clearly moving forward.

So why didn't Orwell write more about that new, hopeful England? In part, it was because he knew all too well the vast bureaucracies Churchill had alluded to. During the war he had worked for the BBC, and his wife Eileen for the Censorship Department and later the Ministry of Food. Back then he had adamantly refused to eat black market food: significantly, Winston and Julia don't share those scruples. In the summer of 1946, to free up food for the recently defeated Germans, bread rationing was imposed in Britain, a measure of desperation that had been avoided in both world wars. The following winter was brutal, severely straining the coal industry, and forcing the government to restrict the supply of electrical power. Orwell needed streptomycin from America to treat his lung condition, but austerity blocked the expenditure of precious dollars, and import restrictions could only be overcome through vigorous wire-pulling, going right up to the Minister of Health, Aneurin Bevan.

In that climate, Orwell was not alone in giving way to gloom. 'Nothing dreadful is ever done with, no bad thing gets any better, you can't be too serious', as Cyril Connolly summed it up. 'This is the message of the Forties from which, alas, there seems no escape, for it is closing time in the gardens of the West and from now on an artist will be judged only by the resonance of his solitude or the quality of his despair' (Hennessy, *Never Again*, p. 319). In the fall of 1947, Chancellor of the Exchequer Hugh Dalton watched his dollar reserves drain away and was overtaken by panic: 'I am haunted by the thought of a people starving, unemployed and in revolt!' (Hennessy, *Never Again*, p. 338). Meanwhile the newsreels, like the telescreens, remained stupefyingly upbeat: Churchill was still giving speeches and receiving medals (though out of office) and gallant Tommies were still policing a crumbling Empire. But the spectre of the atomic bomb haunted everyone: even Bertrand Russell, whom Orwell much admired, recommended a preemptive nuclear strike against the USSR. When the Soviets blockaded Berlin in June 1948, many thought the holocaust was at hand.

Orwell's final portrait of England was painted in the face of that nightmare. Perhaps inevitably, he could only see the end of the country he had spent his life documenting. For this is the ultimate horror of *Nineteen Eighty-Four*: there won't always be an England. The physical island survives, as do the half-destroyed cities, but the nation has been essentially vaporised.

The history, the literature, the law, the religion, the institutions, the odd money and weights and measures, even the name of England have all been permanently erased. Nothing remains but the English language – and the boys at Minitrue are working on that one.

NOTE

1. *The Collected Essays, Journalism and Letters of George Orwell*, 4 vols., eds. Sonia Orwell and Ian Angus (1968, Harmondsworth: Penguin, 1970), Vol. 1, p. 4. [Hereafter, cited in text as *CEJL* by volume and page number.]

4

MARGERY SABIN

The truths of experience: Orwell's nonfiction of the 1930s

'It is not easy to get hold of any facts outside the circle of one's own experience, but with that limitation I have seen a great deal that is of immense interest to me. . . . I hope I shall get a chance to write the truth about what I have seen. The stuff appearing in the English papers is largely the most appalling lies.'

Letter to Victor Gollancz (Barcelona, 9 May 1937)

In the decade following his demoralised return in 1927 from service with the colonial police in Burma, George Orwell quite determinedly widened his circle of experience. Afflicted with a condition of 'bad conscience' in Burma, he explains, he was driven by the need to escape 'not merely from imperialism but from every form of man's dominion over man. I wanted to submerge myself, to get right down among the oppressed, to be one of them and on their side against their tyrants' (148).[1] This feeling dictated the kinds of experience he would pursue: living on the rough with tramps and beggars in England; menial work in the cellars of fancy Parisian restaurants; wandering the streets of poverty in England's depressed North; fighting with the Catalonian workers' militia during the Spanish Civil War. Although Orwell recalls embarking on this programme out of a commitment to 'failure' – 'Every suspicion of self-advancement . . . seemed to me spiritually ugly, a species of bullying' – these ventures paradoxically inaugurated his success as a nonfiction writer: the authority of direct experience strengthened the impression of truth in his reportage about circles of social and political life remote from most of his readers.

Although biographers, social scientists and historians have sometimes found reasons to impugn what Orwell offers as 'truth', his nonfiction books have more often been applauded as models of social and political reportage. The *New York Times Book Review* praised *Down and Out in Paris and London* (1933) as 'a model of the realistic approach'; 'the best sociological reporting I know', attests Dwight Macdonald about *The Road to Wigan Pier* (1937); 'perhaps the best book that exists on the Spanish Civil War', was *The New Yorker*'s judgement of *Homage to Catalonia* (1938), still cited among the blurbs for the book's current paperback edition. The enduring popularity of these books and their influence on later reportage about the conditions of poverty and war call for further reflection on Orwell's art of truth telling, as it sets itself against what he repeatedly invokes as official errors, if not actual 'lies'.

One kind of falsity that Orwell's writing teaches us to recognise appears in the very tribute to him represented by the Heritage museum now constructed on an $8\frac{1}{2}$ acre site in the town of Wigan, immortalised through Orwell's book. The museum features a hall named 'The Orwell', now fixed up as 'the perfect venue for your wedding or private party'.[2] Costumed actors in the museum 'bring history to life performing short scenarios', the Museum website explains: 'At Wigan Pier, whatever your age, sex, or nationality you are sure to find something which will remind you of a special time or a favourite thing'.

It is safe to guess that Orwell would have been of at least two minds about this refurbishing of Wigan Pier in his name. He would have had to give one cheer that the fame of his book had created a remarkable opportunity of post-industrial commerce for at least a portion of the community that he had seen in 1936 suffering the prospect of permanent unemployment. Any new prosperity could hardly be regretted by anyone genuinely moved, as Orwell was, by the earlier poverty and hopelessness he recorded. But the Heritage museum's promise of universal enjoyment – every visitor reminded of 'a special time or favourite thing' – nullifies Orwell's distinctive accomplishment in *The Road to Wigan Pier*. That book tries to draw, and succeeds in drawing, readers *away* from their own favourite thoughts and things so as to grapple with the social and historical reality of Depression suffering in the north of England, almost the opposite of the 'restored and refurbished' promise of confirmed enjoyment of the visitor's own favourite things. Orwell's writing aims to move readers outside their own preoccupations, at the same time as Orwell insists on the ways that full access into other worlds is inevitably limited by the experiences and prejudices you cannot help but bring to them. In all his nonfiction writing, Orwell acknowledges the limitations of his experience and access to truth; but he also insists that truthfulness begins by overcoming the comfort of the familiar, whether it be rooted in the limitations of personal experience and taste, or the habit of accepting the official stereotypes of newspapers and other forms of propaganda.

My purpose in this essay is to identify the qualities in Orwell's three nonfiction books of the 1930s – *Down and Out in Paris and London, The Road to Wigan Pier, Homage to Catalonia* – that distinguish his writing from what one website calls a 'Museum of Memories' in Wigan. This approach must, however, recognise that all three of his major books are full of cautionary acknowledgements of the limitations of his experience and therefore of his authority. These disclaimers, however, have the effect of increasing more than they detract from Orwell's air of truthfulness; since partiality is inevitable, candor about it exemplifies a necessary scepticism toward all claims of absolute and objective truth. 'Beware of my partisanship', he warns the reader on the final page of *Homage to Catalonia*, 'my mistakes of fact and the distortion inevitably caused by my having seen only one corner of events. And beware of exactly the same things when you read any other book on this period of the Spanish war'.

I

Acknowledgement of partiality takes more than one form in Orwell's first book, *Down and Out in Paris and London*. The last page disparages the book as 'trivial' because: 'At present I do not feel that I have seen more than the fringe of poverty' (213).[3] Yet Orwell does not withdraw the book's reproach to middle-class prejudice against 'the poor' as an alien race of monsters, savages, or sinners. Orwell judges his experience sufficient to argue for the essential humanity of the poor – not exemplars of virtue but 'ordinary human beings' whose faults and even depravities are 'the result and not the cause of their way of life' (202). Orwell does not wish merely to enumerate evils and injustices, but to break through what he regards as middle-class oblivion, a state of false consciousness that in his representation of it amounts to a kind of lying. Orwell's corrective to such falsity comes first by immersion of his own body – a supreme measure of truth for Orwell – directly into the experience of misery. He can attest, for example, that constant hunger leads to a mental state of dull indifference: 'Only food could rouse you. You discover that a man who has gone even a week on bread and margarine is not a man any longer, only a belly with a few accessory organs' (19).

   Another, almost contrary, kind of partiality comes from Orwell's explicit preference for the kind of freedom that he discovers in his own downward plunge into menial labour in Paris and tramping among the rural English poor. A semi-voluntary element differentiates his experiment from the mental as well as physical entrapment he diagnoses among 'the slaves of the modern world' (116), since he perceives himself pursuing escape from other, more respectable forms of social entrapment. A certain air of freedom that animates even his accounts of deprivation affiliates him with the most independent types among the poor: vagrants, tramps, stray foreigners, casual wage workers, street artists: 'Poverty frees them from ordinary standards of behaviour, just as money frees people from work' (7). The book owes its comedy to Orwell's gallery of these eccentrics – a kind of aristocracy of the poor. Casting off the superfluities of civilisation in their company, Orwell re-experiences basic truths of human existence with new acuteness – Orwell's language at points recalls Shakespeare's Lear meeting Poor Tom, but Orwell absorbed the arts of necessity with more delight than torment. 'Work in the hotel', he reports of his interlude as dishwasher, 'had taught me the true value of sleep. . . . Sleep had ceased to be a mere physical necessity; it was something voluptuous, a debauch more than relief. I had more trouble with the bugs. Mario had told me of a sure remedy for them, namely pepper, strewed thick over the bedclothes. It made me sneeze, but the bugs hated it, and emigrated to other rooms' (91–92).

Orwell's experiment in downward mobility has struck readers as simultaneously poignant, gallant, amusing and somewhat absurd. *Down and Out in Paris and London* does include memorable, scathing exposés of the mostly invisible social underworld of Paris and England in the late twenties and early thirties, but it is the high spirit of the reportage that makes it the most entertaining of Orwell's nonfiction books. By the time he wrote *The Road to Wigan Pier* in 1937, Orwell himself had come to ridicule his own earlier fantasy of getting right down *inside* the life of the lowest social strata through what he came to call 'masquerade' (150). Orwell looked back on his down and out days with irony, if also with some nostalgia: 'I was very happy', he recalls: 'Here I was, among "the lowest of the low", at the bedrock of the Western world! The class-bar was down, or seemed to be down. And down there in the squalid and, as a matter of fact, horribly boring sub-world of the tramp I had a feeling of release, of adventure, which seems absurd when I look back, but which was sufficiently vivid at the time' (152–53).

In *The Road to Wigan Pier*, Orwell denies himself the naïve satisfaction of belief that he could breach the class-bar in England of the Depression years so easily or, even if he could, that release from his own inner demons would be his reward. If by 1937 Orwell had come to discard the costume of the tramp (which he stored at his sister's house), he also was refusing to mask himself in a socialist party line, or even in the more neutral objectivity of the documentary reporter. Orwell's attitude toward language in the book is overtly personal, even before the book's long autobiographical interpolation, and with more sharp turnabouts of judgement than is customary in documents of social reportage. The book's colloquial directness, along with its seemingly improvisational structure, adds up to an effect of the artless and the natural, so that we feel in contact with someone who is refusing masquerade. It is thus easy to forget that the writing in *The Road to Wigan Pier* is itself a style, with definable advantages and limitations. The chief advantage of its freedom from visible uniform or costume is the mobility and flexibility it allows, like ordinary well-worn clothes.

The style is better suited to scepticism than to polemic, but to a scepticism that is dynamic rather than paralysing. It is true that he becomes *almost* paralysed, or at least severely incapacitated, by the literal effort of experiencing from the inside the work of a coal miner. Yet the voice reporting his day following miners down into a coal pit is itself full of lively movement:

> for a week afterwards your thighs are so stiff that coming downstairs is quite a difficult feat; you have to work your way down in a peculiar sidelong manner, without bending the knees. Your miner friends notice the stiffness of your walk and chaff you about it. ('How'd ta like to work down pit, eh?' etc.) Yet even a miner who has been long away from work – from illness for, instance – when he comes back to the pit, suffers badly for the first few days. (28)

Orwell's skilled agility as *a writer* allows him to keep shifting angles. He vividly conveys the unnatural physical contortions demanded by this arduous work while also distinguishing between his agonies as a novice and the skilled agility of the regulars. 'Certainly, it is not the same for them as it would be for you or me' (29). He admires the Wigan miners, but also sees their learned ability to skip crouching around the low pit props to make them move 'almost like dogs'. The work dehumanises the bodies of miners, but Orwell goes on to reinstate their humanity against the errors of stereotype by insisting that, as human beings, they are conscious of their condition: 'it is quite a mistake to think that they enjoy it' (29).

Although the employed miners are not strictly within Orwell's assignment from the Left Book Club to study the conditions of *un*employment, the famous chapter about their work has a rightful place near the beginning of the book, as Orwell's exemplum of what the reader (the 'you' addressed throughout Part I) as well as he himself can hardly imagine or, more to the point, ordinarily doesn't bother to imagine at all:

> More than anyone else, perhaps, the miner can stand as the type of the manual worker, not only because his work is so exaggeratedly awful, but also because it is so vitally necessary and yet so remote from our experience, so invisible, as it were, that we are capable of forgetting it as we forget the blood in our veins. In a way it is even humiliating to watch coal-miners working. It raises in you a momentary doubt about your own status as an 'intellectual' and a superior person generally. For it is brought home to you, at least while you are watching, that it is only because miners sweat their guts out that superior persons can remain superior. You and I and the editor of the Times Lit. Supp;, . . . and Comrade X, author of *Marxism for Infants* – all of us *really* owe the comparative decency of our lives to the poor drudges underground, blackened to the eyes, with their throats full of coal dust, driving their shovels forward with arms and belly muscles of steel. (35)

This passage deserves its fame: its sharp colloquial wit cuts through to uncomfortable if common truth, while rising and opening out at the end to an eloquence of tribute that still remains within the colloquial flow. Orwell's sharpest jabs here are directed at the general state of oblivion that characterises even political radicals, an insult only slightly softened by the prominent inclusion of himself. 'You', 'I', 'all of us', including the editors and intellectuals and reformers who write and read and prescribe while sitting by a comfortable coal fire, only rarely make any mental connection between that underlying condition of our functioning life and the 'black stuff that arrives mysteriously from nowhere, in particular, except that you have to pay for it' (34). The first responsibility of social reportage, this argument implies, is to break through that oblivion, to bring such connections up from the social unconscious where lower class realities are ordinarily consigned.

From the perspective of social science, Orwell's social reportage is vulnerable to many charges: for example, of sympathy unsupported by adequate data. Orwell quite blithely releases the term 'fact' from statistical or theoretical rigour. Still with the miners, there is the example of dirt. 'Middle-class people', he generalises, 'are fond of saying that the miners would not wash themselves properly even if they could, but this is nonsense, as is shown by the fact that where pit-head baths exist practically all the men use them' (38). The term 'fact' here is not a matter of statistics, but works more loosely as the corrective that direct observation brings to prejudice and received opinion. The usage is respectable in ordinary speech: 'As a matter of fact', he goes on to note, 'it is surprising that miners wash as regularly as they do, seeing how little time they have between work and sleep' (38). Orwell's 'matter of fact' is a colloquial synonym of 'actually', 'in truth', 'really', 'the way it really is' if you go to see for yourself and then think it over intelligently.

Other examples of Orwell's idiomatic version of 'fact' appear in his account of the caravan colonies, the extensive clusters of converted buses and covered wagons that had appeared after the Great War in response to supposedly temporary housing shortages, but had by 1936 become quasi-permanent slum housing for about 1000 people in the area of Wigan alone. 'Anyone who wants to see the effects of the housing shortage at their very worst' (61) should, Orwell suggests, go visit a caravan colony. Orwell eschews pretensions to expertise or specialised knowledge. 'Go see for yourself' is the sub-text of his colloquial exhortations; although he includes some numbers and measurements, data rather quickly yields to qualitative description: 'the dirt and congestion of these places is such that you cannot well imagine unless you have tested it with your own eyes and more particularly your nose'. Visual images bear most of the burden of imaginative authority in his descriptive language: 'one woman's face stays by me, a worn skull-like face on which was a look of intolerable misery and degradation. I gathered that in that dreadful pigsty, struggling to keep her large brood of children clean, she felt as I should feel if I were coated all over with dung' (63).

This picture, in almost the same words, already appears in 'The Road to Wigan Pier Diary', the notebook Orwell kept on his tour and used as his aid to memory and composition. The diary entry for 15 February makes clearer than the later narrative that Orwell toured the caravan colony with NUWM (Northern Union of Working Men), collectors of facts about housing conditions, for the purpose of what Orwell reports as repeated but up to that point futile public complaints and appeals about intolerable living conditions. After mentioning in the diary that he has taken some notes on these facts, Orwell proceeds in the Diary, also, from facts to faces: first the face of misery already cited, then another, seen while passing up a 'horrible squalid side-alley': 'youngish but very pale and with the usual draggled exhausted look, kneeling by the gutter outside a house and poking a stick up the leaden waste-pipe, which was blocked. I thought how dreadful a destiny it was to be kneeling in the gutter in a back-alley in Wigan, in the bitter cold, prodding a stick up a blocked drain. At that moment she looked up and caught my eye, and her expression was as desolate as I have ever seen; it struck me that she was thinking just the same thing as I was'.[4]

Intimate identification with expressively suffering faces produces Orwell's most intense writing in *The Road to Wigan Pier*, and often occurs as the pivot of profound changes in his social perspective. In the book's autobiographical second section, he recalls the images that displaced the official benevolent version of British rule that had allowed him to join the police force in Burma. As an ordinary person not 'trained . . . to be indifferent to the expression of the human face', the particulars of Indian suffering under imperial rule came to haunt his imagination and conscience: 'The wretched prisoners squatting in the reeking cages of the lock-ups, the grey cowed faces of the long-term convicts . . . the women and children howling when their menfolk were led away under arrest' (146). Orwell ascribes his flight from the Burmese police service to the intolerable burden of conscience stirred by such visions. As a travelling reporter in the north of England, Orwell is not of course directly administering the system of social victimisation as he was in his role of policeman in Burma. But, he repeatedly insists, if you allow yourself to *see* such faces, you *will* feel directly implicated; at the least you will be stripped of the outsider's illusion (or rationalisation) that other kinds of people somehow don't mind their poverty or imprisonment, that unlike yourself, they prefer to live that way.

A presumption of authority to interpret faces, however, carries its own partiality and likelihood of error. The dramatic moment of eye contact with the woman poking the stick up the blocked drain-pipe in the diary may represent an illusory intimacy occurring largely in Orwell's own imagination. The impression of fiction is increased when one knows that, in the published book, Orwell moved this particular face to a more prominent place, out of the housing chapter to the end of Chapter 1, where it acquires emblematic meaning as the parting vision from his train slowly moving out of Wigan at the end of his tour. Other details also change in this transposition. The dramatic eye-contact disappears, replaced by a clearer argument about interpretation itself: 'It struck me then that we are mistaken when we say that "It isn't the same for them as it would be for us", and that people bred in the slums can imagine nothing but the slums. For what I saw in her face was not the ignorant suffering of an animal. She knew as well as I did what was happening to her – understood as well as I did how dreadful a destiny it was to be kneeling there in the bitter cold, on the slimy stones of a slum backyard, poking a stick up a foul drain-pipe' (18).

The historian, Robert Pearce, disparaging Orwell's status as an 'objective' reporter in *The Road to Wigan Pier*, selects this passage to illustrate Orwell's unconvincing 'mind-reading' and recommends that we should doubt Orwell's 'ability to find the mind's construction in the face and to empathize with people from backgrounds very different from his own'.[5] But if one accepts that the book is *not* to be assessed as the detached, objective document that historical scholarship might prefer, Orwell's visions have their own value in the search for truth. Orwell is consistently arguing against the self-assuaging middle and upper class opinion that the poor are not really that conscious of their misery, a view that is in itself a form of mind reading (or mind denying) since, whether from distance or trained indifference, it denies consciousness to people from other backgrounds. Orwell's visions break through that denial: the crouching miners are not dogs; the woman kneeling on the slimy stones in the cold is not ignorant of her suffering, like an animal. Yet the issue of how far Orwell can presume to use his own feelings and judgements in the interpretation of Wigan appearances remains an important if unresolved issue for him, and this uncertainty is a provocative feature of the book, one of its unsettling challenges to all social and political interpretation.

The Wigan poor force on Orwell not only consciousness of their humanity, but also even sharper self-consciousness about his own middle class prejudices than did the tramps and social outcasts befriended on the expeditions reported in *Down and Out*. He explores this difference by remarking that tramps and derelicts tend to be 'exceptional' beings, and in that sense more akin to the masquerading dropout that Orwell himself was at the time he selected them for his companions. 'Nothing is easier than to be bosom pals with a pickpocket, if you know where to look for him; but it is very difficult to be bosom pals with a bricklayer' (154). Therefore, although industrial unemployment during the Depression had cast out large portions of north-ern industrial England from any normal working class life, the more 'normal' the life, the more difficult did Orwell find any real intimacy to become, as he observes in relation to the coal miners: 'For some months I lived entirely in coal-miners' houses. I ate my meals with the family, I washed at the kitchen sink, I shared bedrooms with the miners, drank beer with them, played darts with them. . . . But though I was among them . . . I was not one of them, and they knew it even better than I did' (156).

Orwell on his trip to the north ends up resigned to aspects of his own class identity more difficult to discard than he had earlier thought: 'It is easy for me to say that I want to get rid of class-distinctions, but nearly everything I think and do is a result of class-distinctions. All my notions – notions of good and evil, of pleasant and unpleasant, of funny and serious, of ugly and beautiful – are essentially *middle-class* notions' (161). For Orwell, acceptance of this unsheddable middle-class identity is far from the complacent self-indulgence that it might be for others, since he openly dislikes many of the 'sickly and debilitating' features that 'a working-class angle' (116) exposes in middle class life.

II

Homage to Catalonia records Orwell's most perilous journey away from 'normal' middle class England and into the action of a very direct struggle against tyranny – that being waged by Spanish government (Loyalist) forces and international volunteers against the invasion in 1936 by Franco's ultra-nationalist army in Spain. The Spanish War further widened Orwell's circle of experience; at the same time, the awkward narrative organisation of the book shows him groping to integrate the complexity of this new experience into his earlier ways of thinking and writing about the individual's relationship to public and political events.

Orwell arrived in Barcelona in December 1936; like many other intellec-tuals and literary visitors, he intended to write some articles as an observer but he also came to Spain to participate in what looked like a worthy, early battle against fascism. The atmosphere in Barcelona was festive with revo-lutionary expectation; the most radical wing of the Loyalist movement was dominant in the city; the anti-Franco struggle carried the promise of further social equality and defeat of feudal and bourgeois oppression. Orwell describes the streets as full of revolutionary music, Anarchist declarations, and workmen already behaving as though the class system had been erased. Without scrutinising the exact politics of the situation too closely, Orwell was intoxicated by its high spirits. He willingly accepted his assignment to the workers' militia, even while also noting (with as yet unregenerate bourgeois scepticism) the dilapidated, untrained, ill-equipped condition of the mostly very young and illiterate recruits who were to be his comrades in battle. Orwell's personal narrative of his early days in Barcelona, followed by five months on a not-very-active fighting line, is continuous with his earlier vivid notations of the look and feel of mundane human experience even in quite extraordinary circumstances – war as well as poverty.

A different, more covert and sinister kind of warfare forced itself on his attention, however, during his final month back in Barcelona when he landed in the midst of the fierce internecine struggle between anti-Franco factions. It was not until his return to Barcelona in May 1937 that he became confusedly caught up in a more deadly struggle than any he had encountered on the front. This was the battle for power being waged by the Soviet-backed Communist Party (known as PSUC) against the Catalan workers' militia (known as POUM).[6] The aspect of the Spanish situation that Orwell was slow to understand – and that remains confusing even now – was the animosity toward social revolution on the part of the Soviet-backed Spanish Communist party, which in 1937 became committed to alliance with bourgeois liberal groups in a Popular Front against Franco. The Catalan workers' militia became the enemy of the Popular Front in Barcelona; Orwell's comrades and their leaders in POUM had social revolution within Spain at the top of their agenda; the Spanish Communist Party and their new allies in the Popular Front rejected this goal as a distraction from the war against Franco, and more particularly as a threat to the Soviet power that had increasingly come to control the Loyalist campaign. PSUC used brutal methods to suppress the workers' groups: Orwell's comrades in the militia were vilified as Trotskyites and even fascist collaborators; its leaders were imprisoned or killed, and the entire takeover of power disguised and misrepresented to the world outside through Communist Party propaganda. Orwell's initial commitment to the fight against Franco's fascism eventually became overshadowed by his revulsion from these brutal tactics that in retrospect he came to call totalitarian – secret police, house searches, arrests, surveillance, propaganda. In this conflict, the Soviet-backed Spanish Communist Party was the aggressor and eventual victor; the workers' militia with which Orwell was affiliated became the defeated object of attack.

Upon his return to London, Orwell's horror at the hidden and vicious character of PSUC's power grab led to his insistent publicising of it – through essays and book reviews, as well as in the writing of *Homage to Catalonia*. Thus began Orwell's preoccupation with the nature of totalitarianism – under whatever party label – and his loss of favour with the 'official' Left in England and America who heard his criticism of Soviet power in Spain as betrayal of what they continued to regard as a clear cut battle between good and evil.

Barcelona in 1938 initiated Orwell's 'transformation' into the political satirist and critic later to target Stalinist Communism in his Cold War parables, *Animal Farm* and *1984*. In some circles this 'transformation' of Orwell's understanding of mid-twentieth century political distinctions and alignments remains his most important testament to truth.[7] The recent opening of Soviet state archives has tended to validate further Orwell's insight against the charges of his detractors. George Packer, looking back now at the more confused and sentimental infatuation of writers such as Ernest Hemingway and W. H. Auden singles out Orwell as one of the few literary figures of the 1930s who was able to sustain 'the pressure of ambiguous reality' in the Spanish war: 'Orwell was always able to sustain two ideas about it; one of betrayal, the other of hope. His encounter with reality in Spain was steady enough that these didn't have to cancel each other out'.[8]

Yet Orwell's double perspective created serious problems for the narrative organisation of *Homage to Catalonia*. Orwell was reluctant to allow his last bad month, or subsequent political insights, to supplant the mood of his earlier, longer, and more substantial experience in Spain – the five months when he was barely aware of the mounting political strife within the anti-Franco movement. In the story of his direct experience of the war on the Aragon front, Orwell's brief references to factional conflicts mainly serve to emphasise how little these political complications meant to him at the time. While on the front with the workers' militia, the prospect of becoming the victim of vicious Communist Party attack was outside his vision. More simply, he explains, reflections about politics characteristically played little part in his experience while events were occurring. Even long after writing his book, with the heightened political consciousness of retrospection, he remained so attached to his initial direct experience in Spain that he instructed his literary executor to remove the two main chapters of political explanation (chapters v and xi) from inside the text to appendices at the end.[9] Although this directive guided the French translation of 1955, English-language editions continue to interrupt the narrative with the chapters of political analysis. This arrangement is partially justified by the degree to which the intelligibility of Orwell's final account of danger, violence and flight from Barcelona depends on more

coherent understanding of the Spanish political situation than the brief inter-
mittent comments within the narrative alone provide. The very fact that the
politics which Orwell hardly understood while on the line later came to so
determine the outcome of his experience in Spain in itself becomes an important if confusing truth conveyed by the book's double narrative. Sentences
such as 'But at the time I was not interested in that aspect of things' register
the narrow awareness and bewilderment that remained important truths for
him about the extremely limited relationship of individuals to history, even
as they participate in it as actors.

The totalitarian impulses within the Spanish Communist movement constitute only one among other truths registered by Orwell in *Homage to
Catalonia*; equally important to the book are the feelings, so often frustrated
in his earlier experiments in downward social mobility, of intimacy with his
young and mostly illiterate comrades in the workers' militia, feelings which
acquire further import because they also join him to other men on other battlefields of history, all preoccupied with the small physical sensations of dis-
comfort and desire, and with the emotions – hardly more than sensations –
of boredom, fear, futility, desire for active engagement and simultaneous
desire for safe release from it.

Homage to Catalonia thus participates in the tradition of anti-heroic
deglorifications of warfare: momentous battles and insignificant skirmishes
become alike in the vulgar commonality of the human body's needs, wants
and vulnerability. What is important in the *experience* of combat are the
physical details: the 'smell of war'; the urgent need for candles, matches,
cigarettes, firewood, with 'lice' the great equaliser across boundaries of politics, social class and history itself: 'Glory of war, indeed! In war *all* soldiers
are lousy, at least when it is warm enough. The men who fought at Verdun,
at Waterloo, at Flodden, at Senlac, at Thermopylae – every one of them had
lice crawling over his testicles' (76). It is from this perspective that Hugh
Thomas, in his monumental history, *The Spanish Civil War*, comments that
Homage to Catalonia 'is a better book about war itself than about the Spanish war'.[10]

Orwell's assignment to the workers' militia made the inglorious experience of war also an experience of liberation for him. Although initially
disappointed to find himself marginalised in a remote mountain area with
an ill-equipped and untrained 'mob' of illiterate recruits, his reflex snobbery
about how a proper army ought to look and act soon yielded to pleasurable
interest in the unfamiliar egalitarian atmosphere within the workers' militia.
Here was a new opportunity for the release from middle-class expectations
and prejudices that he had earlier sought in Paris, London and Wigan: 'Up
here in Aragon one was among tens of thousands of people, mainly though

not entirely of working-class origin, all living at the same level and mingling on terms of equality . . . the ordinary class-division of society had disappeared to an extent that is almost unthinkable in the money-tainted air of England; there was no one there except the peasants and ourselves, and no one owned anyone else as his master' (104). To be sure, all hierarchical distinctions were not dissolved. He was soon made a 'cabo' (corporal), by virtue of his age (most of his comrades were mere teenagers) and slightly greater familiarity with the use of weaponry (not that they were equipped with much). And he did not submerge himself into the equality of deprivation to the extent of rejecting the packets of tea and cigarettes that his wife regularly managed to send him from Barcelona. These small privileges, he insists, did not mar 'the essential point' of social equality in the system: 'Of course, there was not perfect equality, but there was a nearer approach to it than I had ever seen or than I would have thought conceivable in time of war' (27).

Detailed descriptions of experience on the Aragon line make palpable Orwell's unusual feeling of solidarity across class lines in the workers' militia. As in the famous coal mine visit in *The Road to Wigan Pier*, Orwell instructs the reader to appreciate the importance of the physical details: 'Later on the famine of matches and candles made life a misery. You do not realize the importance of these things until you lack them' (32). Orwell's 'you' draws the reader into the minute physical experience of approaching the enemy for an attack through the forest before dawn: 'When you are creeping at that pace you are aware as an ant might be of the enormous variations in the ground, the splendid path of smooth grass here, the evil patch of sticky mud there, the tall rustling reeds that have got to be avoided' (89). Orwell goes even further to a communal sense of 'we' that he virtually never achieves across class lines in his English reportage: 'Once I raised my head; in silence Benjamin put his hand behind my neck and pulled it violently down. . . . Our breathing was enough to give us away. Yet somehow we did get there' (89); 'We climbed out. Paddy held the wire aside for me. As soon as we got away from the shelter of the Fascist parapet we were under a devilish fire that seemed to be coming at us from every direction' (98).

Orwell does not entirely avoid the sentimentality endemic to the genre of war fiction and memoir, though he does eliminate its usual patriotic refrain – 'brothers united in a cause' – by mentioning the 'curious vividness' of feeling nearly similar intimacy with the fascist enemy. Although in the only nighttime skirmish of his whole service, he was eager enough to kill one of the enemy, in the present tense of his memory the Andalusian dawn survives mainly as a scene of tranquillity, idyllic in a crude way. Personal and political enmities – and even the beastly enmity of rats – come together in a harmonious music:

At a table nearby a bearded man with a huge automatic pistol strapped to his belt is hewing loaves of bread into five pieces. Behind me a cockney voice (Bill Chambers, with whom I quarreled bitterly and who was afterwards killed outside Huesca) is singing:

> There are rats, rats,
> Rats as big as cats,
> In the . . .

I am walking up and down the line of sentries, under the dark boughs of the poplars. In the flooded ditch outside the rats are paddling about, making as much noise as otters. As the yellow dawn comes up behind us, the Andalusian sentry, muffled in his cloak, begins singing. Across no man's land, a hundred or two hundred yards away, you can hear the Fascist sentry also singing.

(106)

There is a lyricism to Orwell's memories of the Andalusian line that explains how, at the end of the book, he can affirm the value of the total experience, even in the face of the futility of POUM's military skirmishes and the brutal political machinations of PSUC, to say nothing of the ominous approach of a wider, catastrophic European war: 'Curiously enough the whole experience has left me with not less but more belief in the decency of human beings' (230). Although 'decency' may seem a weak concept to set against the violent political realities evoked by the book as a whole, it here comes to designate a recognition of shared physical and emotional humanity distinct from politics and propaganda – all that is not 'official', in the sense that every form of politics soon becomes.

By the end of *Homage to Catalonia*, Orwell associates 'evil' less with the fascists (whom he has hardly encountered) than with the 'atmosphere of suspicion, fear, uncertainty, and veiled hatred' (195) that creates an 'evil feeling' in the air of Barcelona as the Communists set about liquidating all who dissent from their claim to power. This 'nightmare atmosphere' of political suspicion, persecution and surveillance is the force that most directly threatens Orwell's idea of 'decency', and it ultimately crosses over official ideological distinctions and affiliations. In the hospital outside Barcelona, waiting to be checked out for discharge by his medical board, Orwell became friendly with a wounded Assault Guard from the unit charged with hunting down Orwell's group: 'He was friendly and gave me cigarettes. I said: "In Barcelona we should have been shooting one another", and we laughed over this. It was queer how the general spirit seemed to change when you got anywhere near the front line. All or nearly all of the vicious hatreds of the political parties evaporated' (202). In *Homage to Catalonia* 'decency' becomes peculiarly apolitical, basically set against the deliberate falsity and violence perpetrated in the name of whatever politics are in question.

Orwell's experience of 'decency' in Spain seems to increase the closer he is to battle lines. Orwell helps us understand this seeming paradox by acknowledging his limited experience of the war – on a 'front' where there was so little action as to make boredom or a sense of futility almost as much a danger as bombs or gunfire: 'the things that one normally thinks of as the horrors of war seldom happened to me . . . I do not think a shell ever exploded within fifty yards of me, and I was only in hand-to-hand fighting once (once is once too often, I may say)' (23). Most of the time, Orwell's 'front line' is hardly a place of real war. At times its quietude, broken only by shells softly exploding at a distance, has a semi-real quality of pantomime or dream; it stays in his mind with a 'magic quality' as 'a good patch for my mind to browse upon' (105). Its truth therefore does not represent the truth of war in general any more than it represents the whole truth of the Spanish war. It is another of the partial truths that circulate dynamically within the complex narrative of the book.

III

Orwell's 'good patch' of battlefield has the fertility for the mind associated with pastoral: a special place apart that realises ideal possibilities of human character and relationships commonly hidden or deformed by political and social constructions. But the 'magic quality' of pastoral writing tends to make its truths subject to contrary realities, and calls for nimbleness of mind and language to move between contraries.

The plain style that Orwell made his hallmark in his three nonfiction books of the 1930s is not to be confused with what some might call a simply natural or artless voice. It is a composed and produced instrument to achieve flexibility and power in relation to multiple truths, none of which he comfortably accepted as a total commitment. 'The truth is', he remarks in a praising review of James Joyce's Ulysses in 1936: 'the written word loses its power if it departs too far, or rather if it stays away too long, from the ordinary world where two and two make four'.[11]

This seemingly assured common sense may seem to fit as awkwardly with the complexities of Down and Out in Paris and London, The Road to Wigan Pier and Homage to Catalonia as it does with Joyce's work, but the incongruity diminishes if you take the whole sentence, with its emphasis on motion, words in motion, travelling towards or away from one 'patch' of experience to another. It is this mobile quality that enables Orwell to keep his voice dynamic in his nonfiction of the 1930s. Orwell's style teaches us to approach truth equipped with never fewer than two minds – qualifying parentheses, disclaimers, abrupt shifts of perspective add and subtract partial truths in an open ended process that requires us to calculate the final sum with more than ordinary circumspection.

NOTES

1. *The Road to Wigan Pier*, with foreword by Victor Gollancz (New York: Harcourt Brace Jovanovich, 1958). Quotations refer to this edition by page number within the text.
2. 'Welcome to the Orwell at Wigan Pier', http://www.theorwell.co.uk/content/home; see also 'The Wigan Pier Experience', http://www.museumsunited.org.uk/wiganpier; 'The Borough of Wigan' (1): http://www.manchester2002-uk.com/towns/wigan1; 'Wigan Ancient and Loyal': http//freepages.genealogy.rootsweb.com/-anderton/places/wigan.
3. *Down and Out in Paris and London* (New York: Harcourt Brace Jovanovich, 1961). Quotations refer by page number within the text to this edition.
4. *The Road to Wigan Pier* Diary, 170–214, in *An Age Like This: 1920–1940*, vol. 1 of *Collected Essays, Journalism, and Letters of George Orwell*, ed. Sonia Orwell and Ian Angus (New York: Harcourt Brace and World, 1968), 178.
5. Robert Pearce, 'Revisiting Orwell's Wigan Pier', *History: the Journal of the Historical Association*, July 1997. http://www.seas.upenn.edu–allport/chestnut/wwigpier.htm.
6. PSUC stood for Partido Socialista Unificado de Cataluna, known as the Catalan Communists; POUM was the acronym for Partido Obrero de Unificación Marxista, associated with Anarchist, anti-Stalinist socialists.
7. Peter Stansky and William Abrahams emphasize this radical shift in *Orwell: The Transformation* (New York: Knopf, 1979), 235. See also Christopher Hitchens, Introduction, *Orwell in Spain*, ed. Peter Davison (London: Penguin, 2001), ix–xviii.
8. George Packer, 'The Spanish Prisoner', *New Yorker*, 31 October 2005, 87. Packer is reviewing Stephen Koch, *The Breaking Point: Hemingway, Dos Passos, and the Murder of José Robles* (New York: Counterpoint, 2005).
9. See *Orwell in Spain*, ed. Peter Davison (London: Penguin, 2001), 29.
10. Thomas, *The Spanish Civil War* (revised), (New York: Random House [Modern Library], 1999), 635 n.2.
11. Review of recent fiction in *New English Weekly*, 24 September 1936, in *An Age Like This*, 231.

5

MICHAEL LEVENSON

The fictional realist: novels
of the 1930s

I

George Orwell's four novels of the 1930s could only have been written in
that decade. As he left them behind, he often wondered how they could have
been written at all. Orwell composed the books – *Burmese Days* (1934), *A
Clergyman's Daughter* (1935), *Keep the Aspidistra Flying* (1936) and *Coming
Up for Air* (1939) – with an intense consciousness that he was writing after
the heady days of modernism and beneath its shadow. At the same time he
never allowed himself to forget the degraded social reality that surrounded
his literary work, a recognition of imminent catastrophe. This double sense –
literary belatedness, social emergency – pervades the novels. It accompanies
a third condition, which is simply Orwell's conviction that novel-writing
should be his vocation. This point should not be taken for granted. Orwell
holds to his vocation despite the fact that his early fictions continually failed,
especially in his own estimation, and that he had a successful parallel career as
a documentary journalist. The book-length journalism of the 1930s – *Down
and Out in Paris and London* (1933), *The Road to Wigan Pier* (1937) and
Homage to Catalonia (1938) – has had a far more prominent afterlife than
the fiction, and the first two of these books gained significant recognition
when they first appeared. Yet Orwell continued to write novels in the face
of his failure, or at best quite limited success.[1] Moreover, the novels all
take failure as their central subject. These circumstances – four failed novels
about failure – have discouraged the attention of both scholars and common
readers. When the books have been addressed, they have usually been taken
as distractions from the journalism or as false starts toward the triumphs of
Animal Farm and *Nineteen Eighty-Four*. In the view offered here, the novels
have a claim in their own right. They represent the determined, even wilful
attempt of a young professional author to sustain a career after modernism
and in the teeth of social collapse.

Orwell became a published author during an unsteady transition in British literature. The consolidation of modernism had been achieved, and while its achievements were not universally accepted, its cultural visibility was incontestable. Yet, even as an experimental modernism was conspicuous, by the early and middle 1930s it had lost its inevitability. Eliot's conversion, Lawrence's death, and Joyce's turn toward *Finnegans Wake*, made the work of the early 1920s look historical. When he settled on a commitment to literary realism at the beginning of his career, Orwell was not making a naive or unconscious gesture. Even as he disdained the 'highbrow' taste of an educated elite, he was unable simply to set it aside. Although they look at the world from opposing perspectives, both highbrow and lowbrow enclose themselves in a consoling unreality and deny the claims of ordinary life. Realism is understood as the representation of the 'ordinary', a term whose meanings Orwell considers self-evident; it is not one literary method among others but the only acceptable aesthetic in an epoch of self-delusion.

II

The opening paragraph of Orwell's first novel does not have the look of a manifesto, but it does establish the tonality of a resolute literary programme.

> U Po Kyin, Sub-divisional Magistrate of Kyauktada, in Upper Burma, was sitting in his veranda. It was only half past eight, but the month was April, and there was a closeness in the air, a threat of the long, stifling midday hours. Occasional faint breaths of wind, seeming cool by contrast, stirred the newly-drenched orchids that hung from the eaves. Beyond the orchids one could see the dusty, curved trunk of a palm tree, and then the blazing ultramarine sky. Up in the zenith, so high that it dazzled one to look at them, a few vultures circled without the quiver of a wing.

All six of Orwell's novels begin by indicating the time of day, as much to imply that to enter a fictional universe must be to orient ourselves within the scale of dailiness. To name the time is to acknowledge the difficult exactions of the clock – 'As the alarm clock on the chest of drawers exploded like a horrid little bomb of bell metal . . .' (*A Clergyman's Daughter*) – but it is also to establish the world of work: 'Mr. Jones, of the Manor Farm, had locked up the hen-houses for the night, but was too drunk to remember to shut the pop-holes' (*Animal Farm*). The reflex to tell the time is so marked presumably because Orwell's view is that before we belong to the sweep of decades or centuries, epochs or ages, we are creatures of immediacy. To be located within daily time is to be located within the space of work and the rhythm of routine. Here at the opening of *Burmese Days*, the specification of time inaugurates a carnival of particularity: a name, a title, a nation, a place, but also the vegetation, the vultures and the weather. The realist conviction invites a democracy of attention. The scanning eye at the opening of *Burmese Days* might serve as an image of the author at the moment of composition. The impulse is to survey the miscellany of concrete objects, nameable and countable, and then to reflect the material array within the structure of a sentence.[2] Indeed, the sentence offers itself, not simply as a representation of the real, but as its re-enactment: the unfolding of a precise sentence repeats the clarity and dignity of the world.

But the act of representational transcription is not a neutral regimen. It will become a form of politics, and it will never cease to be what it is at the start, namely an ethics.[3] To register the world of fact, in its precise givenness and its radical multiplicity, is to establish an ethical standard. Realist truth-telling is a rejoinder to the culture of fantasy and escape. In *Burmese Days*, it also gives a basis for the critique of empire. The timber merchant John Flory lives in demoralisation, even despair, because he has seen through the deception of the imperialists. He is lonely and miserable, because he 'had grasped the truth about the English and their Empire'; it is 'a despotism with theft as its final object'. On the ground of its stringent realism *Burmese Days* exposes brutality and, what is seen as still worse, deception and self-deception.

Drifting toward nihilism, Flory entertains a single hope: that he will find someone to love, so that the loneliness of the truth-telling life will be mitigated in personal communion. It is a sentimental dream out of the novels that Flory has mocked. But when he meets Elizabeth Lackersteen and talks to her about books, he lets himself be carried along in the dream-vision. In fact, as the reader (though not Flory) will soon learn, Elizabeth had been raised in circumstances that make her entirely unsuited to Flory. She is only susceptible to him when he assumes the role of 'manly man', as in a scene where he shoots a leopard and she swooningly admires his prowess with the gun. But whenever Flory shows his hatred of empire, his love of books, his interest in Burmese culture, or his contempt for the Anglo-Indians at the Club, Elizabeth withdraws. The romance is doomed from the start. The course of events – her recoiling from Flory when the dashing soldier Verrall arrives in the village, her mortification when Verrrall leaves without notice, her drift back toward Flory and then the conclusive break when his Burmese mistress stages a scene in church – all this follows the trajectory of disenchantment. Immediately after the public disgrace, Flory makes a desperate appeal to Elizabeth. Even as she pulls from his grip, he summons the dream of a saving domesticity: garden, watercolours on the wall, bookshelves and a piano. "You should have a piano', he said despairingly' – to which she responds, 'I don't play the piano'. It's the last of Flory's mortifications and leads directly to his suicide.

Flory is the only Anglo-Indian to understand the illusions of Empire: the way it demeans the natives whom it pretends to uplift, and the way it corrupts the imperialists who sustain its false image. And yet the man of disenchanted political clear-sightedness is precisely the one who becomes lost within the infatuation of love. Even when he is able to see Elizabeth 'almost as she was – silly, snobbish, heartless', still, 'it made no difference' to him; he remains caught within the mirage of his desire. Flory, that is to say, loses his standing as a voice of reason and critique. The unmasker of Empire needs to be unmasked himself. We should recognise this turn as part of the radical irony, even the nihilism, of *Burmese Days*. The stern realist demand is for a life without illusion. As the politically sceptical Flory succumbs to the infatuation of love, it is the voice of the narrator that alone remains free of illusion.[4] But the narrator speaks out only intermittently, with an eruption of authoritative judgement that quickly subsides. When Elizabeth overpraises Flory for his reaction to the harmless water-buffaloes, we are briskly told that 'When one does get any credit in this life, it is usually for something that one has not done'. After Flory's death we read that 'There is a rather large number of suicides among the Europeans in Burma, and they occasion very little surprise'. Such gnomic utterances confirm the unconsoling view, but they are rare and far between. Although the sceptical burden of the novel is unmistakable, it remains almost entirely implicit. The narrator prefers not to speak in propria persona but to leave characters to discover and to disclose their hopelessness.

III

In the essay 'Why I Write', Orwell confesses that he began by wanting 'to write enormous naturalistic novels with unhappy endings, full of detailed descriptions and arresting similes, and also full of purple passages in which words were used partly for the sake of their sound'.[5] He offered *Burmese Days* as 'rather that kind of book', and in fact much of this original impulse – including a broadly naturalistic standpoint, a careful descriptivism, and the refusal of happy endings – persisted through the 1930s, though in a strikingly changed form. The changes are at least in some measure a product of Orwell's reading in Conrad, Joyce, Lawrence and Woolf. For all his resistance to modernist disengagement, he clearly accepted much of the critique of nineteenth-century novelistic form. He gave up the dream of the 'enormous' fiction that would tell a total truth; he embraced the discipline of a prose in which every word counted; and above all, he resisted the lure of a garrulous, omniscient narrator in favour of the rigorously limited perspective of his characters.

Although Orwell would eventually come to negative judgements on all his fiction of the 1930s, he was sharpest toward *A Clergyman's Daughter*. 'There are whole wads of it', he wrote, 'that are so awful that I really don't know what to do with them'. I concur. But for all its failures – the turgid writing, the awkward plotting, the unconvincing characterisation – the book retains an interest, simply because of its place in an unstable phase of Orwell's career. He was always blunt in making distinctions between form and content, technique and subject-matter; he was also unembarrassed in offering the strongest claims for content. He lampooned the cultured circles who saw literature as only 'the manipulation of words'; for them, 'subject-matter was the unforgivable sin, and even to be aware of . . . subject-matter was looked upon as a lapse of taste'. Orwell's fiction of the 1930s is a reassertion of the claims of content.

In all four novels of the decade Orwell identifies events that are, or should be, familiar to his contemporaries. Yet, at the same time, his impulse – with an important qualification that will appear later – is to show states of emergency within the familiar situations. *Burmese Days* insists on the daily work of Empire as a constitutive fact of British life; much of its critique is directed at the failures of the ordinary imperial machine. Yet, its narrative depends on the total breakdown of its protagonist: his rage, his nihilism, his suicide. Even as the novel claims that suicides are more common than one thinks, it insists on the extremity of Flory's end. In *A Clergyman's Daughter*, the 'subject' is religious crisis, which Orwell locates within a familiar small country town. Dorothy Hare is a recognisable portrait, from literature if not directly from life: the hard-pressed child of a selfish parent, repressed and pious, the one who carries on the real work of the parish while her father drifts in protective fantasy. The novel insists on the obsolescence of both the Anglican faith and its social / institutional practice. Reverend Hare, the clergyman of the title, is 'an anachronism' who 'ought never to have been born into the modern world'. The younger son of a baronet, he went into the Church according to the out-moded habits of the aristocracy, but now, 'tethered by his poverty to the age of Lenin and the *Daily Mail*, [he] was kept in a state of chronic exasperation', which discharges itself in the endless demands made upon his daughter.

The donnée of the novel is that Dorothy will enact the collapse of an anachronism; she will live out the experience of an unsustainable faith. The difficulty is that the novel has a second, unstated premise, namely that the protagonist is a pious, selfless and obedient woman, who would never resist the tyranny of her father. Orwell's notorious solution is to have Dorothy lose her memory and to wake up in London not knowing who or where or what she is. When he admitted 'an inherent fault of structure' that he could find no way to address, Orwell was surely thinking of this awkward device.[6] Still, as awkward as it is, it secures the effect that he needs. It creates a kind of Rousseauist condition of radical innocence. Lacking any assumptions or traditions, Dorothy engages with the root needs of any human creature: to eat, to find shelter, to enjoy companionship. For the six weeks of her amnesia, the novel follows her through the primitive gestures of survival that Orwell had tested in his own life.

Within the argument of *A Clergyman's Daughter*, Dorothy Hare's existence outside the sphere of her father, her town and her faith, allows her to put all those necessities in question.[7] When she recovers her identity – no more plausibly than she lost it – she discovers that her faith is gone. It's a mysterious thing to lose faith, comments this narrator, 'as mysterious as faith itself. Like faith, it is ultimately not rooted in logic; it is a change in the climate of the mind'. Within the urgency of her life, the urgency of pleasure as well as need, religious belief simply drops away for her. We may take this as a key 'thesis' within a novel that aims to work toward metaphysical, or at least ethical, conclusions. Faith is anachronistic; it is an effect of habit and convention; it will not withstand the encounter with basic needs. However this is not the end of the argument.

When the cloud over Dorothy's disappearance has lifted, she sees no choice but to return. She has no faith, but she has a routine, a context, a pre-given world. On the one hand, she recognises that there is no solution: 'There was, she saw clearly no possible substitute for faith; no pagan acceptance of life as sufficient to itself, no pantheistic cheer-up stuff, no pseudo-religion of "progress" with visions of glittering Utopias and ant-heaps of steel and concrete. It is all or nothing'. On the other hand, she intuitively grasps that 'the solution to her difficulty lay in accepting the fact that there was no solution; that if one gets on with the job that lies to hand, the ultimate purpose of the job fades into insignificance; that faith and no faith are very much the same provided that one is doing what is customary, useful and acceptable'. Dorothy will resume her old life with all its stress and anxiety, and the routines of work will take the place of faith. She will even attend church again, because 'however absurd and cowardly' it may be, 'there is something – it is hard to define, but something of decency, of spiritual comeliness – that is not easily found in the world outside'. Even when belief is gone, the 'customary, useful and acceptable' provide all the consolation that we should ever have expected.

In the middle 1930s, Orwell held to the work of the 'normal decent person' as the one integrity amid unavailing alternatives. Yet, this ideal turned out to be an unsteady foundation. It was one thing to make an ethical / political commitment to normality and another to articulate its literary form. Each of the four novels takes pains to invent a plausible stage for its 'ordinary' characters. The stage is plausible because it belongs to the immediate social world, and the characters are ordinary insofar as they have no special gifts or powers; they are mixed and erring creatures who might stand on any street corner. To honour this realist demand is to keep faith with the community of the normal and the decent. And yet as I have suggested, the fiction of the ordinary world moves repeatedly toward exceptional events and states of mind. Dorothy Hare's breakdown and amnesia is one sign. Another is the 'surrealist' theatre in Trafalgar Square at the beginning of part three of *A Clergyman's Daughter*, a scene openly indebted to Joyce's Nighttown sequence in *Ulysses*.

A paradox inhabits these novels, which articulate an ethic of workaday routine that can only be understood through a radical recognition. The goal is to disclose the truth about a contemporary social emergency, whether in the outposts of Empire or in a sleepy country town, but the disclosure can only take place through a collapse of routine. The violence within the first two novels – the violence of Flory's suicide and the formal rupture in *A Clergyman's Daughter* – reflects the attempt to lay bare the rickety structure of an obsolete social form by taking it to its limits. This makes for an unsteadiness of tone, especially in the second novel, when the fiction moves from ordinary life to the extreme vantage point from which it can be seen. But then that extremity (suicide, amnesia, social degradation) is reabsorbed within the tones of realism.

IV

Raymond Williams came at these questions another way. In a suggestive reading of the early work, Williams proposed that the two forms of Orwell's writing in the 1930s, the 'fiction' and the 'documentary journalism' should be seen as pondering the same difficult relationship between fiction and fact.[8] Williams reminds us of how events in Orwell's diaries, letters and reportage reappear as incidents in the novels. Elephants are shot, church services are attended, and hops are picked in both genres. However in the fiction, argues Williams, Orwell relies on central characters as his 'intermediaries', imaginary representatives of the author, who capture only a part of his experience. They represent it in the passive mode, as an *enduring* of history without the possibility of genuine response. The result for Williams is the 'artistic failure' in the novels, their inability to produce coherent identities that respond actively to their historical situation. The documentary essays, on the other hand, give up the fictional intermediary and allow Orwell to present 'not only what had happened to him and what he had observed, but what he felt about it and what he thought about it'. An achievement of this 'direct voice', which Williams regards as the triumph of the decade, is the creation of the figure 'Orwell'. It unites both aspects of the exemplary life: the endurance of social crisis and the active response of the writer.

This argument has an unquestioned power. It helps to confirm a consensus on the merits of the documentary writing and the weaknesses of the fiction. But here it's worth asking why Orwell persisted with his novels, even as he offered scathing self-condemnation. What did he think he was doing in these books? Partly, of course, he was simply sustaining a modestly money-earning career, a career that might never become a vocation. Yet the will to succeed as a writer of fiction was strong in Orwell. The letters of the 1930s make clear that he was drawn to the glamour of authorship and that for him the glamour belonged not to journalism but to novel-writing. Joyce and Lawrence, and also Maugham and later Miller, were strong and magnetic images.

Still, it is clear that social hope and political conviction animated the novels from the start. *Burmese Days*, *A Clergyman's Daughter* and *Keep the Aspidistra Flying* each offer politically inflected representations of a complex world. If they are not systematic or theoretical, they are nevertheless strenuous attempts to disclose the mechanism of a failing social apparatus. The workings of Empire, the machinery of capitalism, the conditions of the Church and the schools, the circumstances of the dispossessed – these subjects appear as large-scale problems (and failures) that the novels labour to recreate, even as they develop one sentence, one fact, at a time. Williams sees the logic of the career as driving toward the invention of a complex subjectivity ('Orwell'), that can speak in the first person in order to synthesise experience and critical reflection. But there is another logic, at least as strong. The impulse to articulate a richly textured fictional universe disclosing a truth about the larger world – this is a motive that will carry Orwell on to *Animal Farm* and *Nineteen Eighty-Four*. When he described the power of modernism, especially in the example of Joyce's *Ulysses*, as fabricating details into a 'huge complex pattern', he is at the same time acknowledging his own interest in the illuminations of pattern, not as a merely aesthetic whole, but as a construction that aims to register a social totality. *A Clergyman's Daughter* draws on his own churchgoing, his time in the hop fields, and his experience as a schoolteacher in order to create a composite image of contemporaneity. Even the decision to make his protagonist a woman can be understood as an impulse to escape the limitations of contingent personhood.

The novels aspire to a synthetic account of social contemporaneity. At the same time, all four books sustain the formal commitment to the limited narrative perspective of a focalised individual. If the fiction is an attempt to represent a larger-than-personal world, it nevertheless assumes an almost entirely personal standpoint. The thin judgements of a detached narrator, as I have suggested, are of limited importance; they mark out a zone of disenchanted, often cynical, reason that surrounds the events; but the work of social interpretation and political engagement is left to the characters, who are most often unsuited to the task. A fissure opens in these novels between their ambition to utter historical truth and the personal limitations on the acts of utterance – those finite, usually visual perceptions constrained by the grammar of the realist sentence.

What we might think of as the 'stain' that Orwell inscribes on his characters is a sign of their limitation. John Flory has a birthmark, 'dark blue' and 'hideous', 'stretching in a ragged crescent down his left cheek, from the eye to the corner of the mouth' (16). All through his erratic courtship of Elizabeth Lackersteen, he struggles to keep it out of sight, but it always returns to view, haunting Flory and eventually appalling Elizabeth. During the final romantic cataclysm, it 'was, finally, the birthmark that had damned him'. As Alex Zwerdling has noticed, the corresponding 'stain' in *A Clergyman's Daughter* is Dorothy Hare's revulsion from sexuality. 'To be kissed or fondled by a man – to feel heavy male arms about her and thick male lips bearing down upon her own – was terrifying and repulsive to her. Even in memory or imagination, it made her wince. It was her especial secret, the especial, incurable disability that she carried through life' (80).[9] Like Flory's birthmark, Dorothy's repulsion is offered as a primal wound, an originary flaw, beyond responsibility or comprehension. The novels decline to explain these wounds as an effect of social or psychological causes; they appear instead as sheer brutal contingencies, defects at the heart of things. They also interrupt the social ambitions of the novels, because they stand as vivid signs of constraint for the very characters entrusted with social representation. What is enacted formally as limited point of view is enacted thematically in the 'stain'.

Keep the Aspidistra Flying offers a significant variant on the pattern. Gordon Comstock does not have a physical or physio-psychological flaw, but he enters the novel equally marked by trauma.[10] In his case the trauma is fully social; it is the experience of the cash-nexus within capitalist society; and its effect on Gordon is to create a fixity as conspicuous as Florys' birthmark and as deeply rooted as Dorothy's sexual repugnance. Constantly reiterated through the length of the novel is Gordon's complaint that money has degraded life in every aspect, including its most intimate aspects. He looks out at the advertising posters on the 'graceless street' where he sees,

'Desolation, emptiness, prophecies of doom', the 'great death-wish of the modern world' (586) – a world in which 'money is virtue and poverty is crime' (603). Poverty kills thought, poverty destroys love. No exchange within the money economy is free from the circulating poison.

Part of what makes Gordon's vehemence attractive to his author is that it refuses the consolation of the usual solutions. Most strikingly, he mocks the reassurances of socialism, offered here by way of Ravelson, a wealthy friend and would-be patron, the editor of the literary journal *Antichrist* and the cheerful exponent of a revolutionary future. 'Read Marx' is his advice to the demoralised Gordon. Ravelson is a counterpart to Warburton, the comfortable aesthete in *A Clergyman's Daughter*. Both figures emit the affirmations that depend on their prosperity; they can afford to be cheerful. There are sharp differences, of course, in the two solutions, but for Orwell in 1935 Warburton's aestheticism and Ravelson's politics come to much the same thing: they are merely theoretical and evasive approaches to the problems of life. Their positions are only possible for those who don't suffer from the brutality of the historical moment. They are 'ideological' in the worst sense for Orwell; they are not only lies and distortions; they are also soothing and pleasurable. Indeed one of the strengths of these two novels of the mid-1930s is the recognition that virtues like generosity and kindness are all too easy for the emancipated sensibilities of the well-to-do.

But if Gordon Comstock is a trenchant critic of middle-class socialism and the delusions of ideology, he too is caught in the trap of theory. His nihilism poses questions still more difficult than Ravelson's socialism. His loathing of the money society is an *idée fixe*, which interrupts friendships, family ties and his fragile romance with Rosemary. Yet, within Orwell's frame of values, Gordon's obsessive beliefs – his 'hatred of modern life, the desire to see our money-civilization blown to hell by bombs' – have the merit of emanating from lived experience. Because he exists on two pounds a week, his hatred for money is 'a thing he actually felt'. Belief brought close to feeling, theory as experience, this is something that Orwell thinks intellectuals fail to achieve and that he always admires. Moreover it's clear that Orwell stands close to this relentless critique. Gordon Comstock offers a savagely disenchanted view of social failure; in so doing, he sinks into physical and mental misery: what then is to be done?

That something *can* be done is due to Orwell's re-visioning of the 'stain' that marks character. Like John Flory and Dorothy Hare, Gordon is an exile within, one who is unable to coincide with social norms, indeed unable to establish secure personal ties at all. The isolation of the blighted protagonist is the condition of all three fictions. But because Gordon's stain is 'intellectual', it is open to change as the others were not.[11] He is held in the grip of a picture: a fully corrupted world to which the only honourable response is refusal; if this means the degradation of friendless poverty, then so be it: 'He had lived thirty years and achieved nothing except misery. But that was what he had chosen. It was what he *wanted*, even now. He wanted to sink down, down into the muck where money does not rule'. *Keep the Aspidistra Flying* acknowledges the deadly consistency of this position and then labours to overcome it. Given its assumptions, the solution cannot be merely intellectual; it's important to the novel that no one can *persuade* Gordon out of obstinate death-tending conclusions. Ideas are embedded in experience. They will only change as the experience changes: to this extent Orwell accepts a 'materialist' theory of mental life.

The melodramatic risk in *Keep the Aspidistra Flying* is greatest in Rosemary's unbroken love for Gordon and her loyalty in the face of insult. At the point of his deepest decline she comes to him in the garret, and for the first time the two make love. The act is neither emotionally nor physically exalted; it is done in the stink. But the melodramatic result is Rosemary's pregnancy, and Gordon's decision to return to the world – to marriage, his job in advertising and lower-middle-class life. The novel's close, which has embarrassed many readers, leaves the couple in their modest new flat, excited by every stick of furniture, from the double bed 'with pink eiderdown!' to the kitchenette, the bookcase and 'the chest of drawers!' This is love and domesticity in exclamation points, recalling, perhaps self-consciously, the sentimental Dickens of the Christmas books.

Yet the melodrama and the sentimentality, however awkward, need to be placed within the austere conditions of the novel. Gordon Comstock's argument is one that Orwell struggles to counter, largely because he recognises its force. If you accept that social degradation is 'endemic', then it is difficult to refute the claim that integrity lies in a total refusal. In the mid-1930s, Orwell's burden was to articulate an alternative to the death-seeking logic of history. If that seems melodramatic, it is no less so than a contemporaneous work that enacts a similar struggle, Freud's *Civilization and its Discontents*. The struggle between Eros and Thanatos, 'this battle of the giants' memorably rehearsed in Freud's book, is also performed in *Keep the Aspidistra Flying*, a fact that should not be obscured by its realist manner and its lower middle class milieu.

Because the problem is so deeply rooted, the novel looks to a deep solution, which indeed risks sentimentality. The device of Rosemary's pregnancy and Gordon's recognition of stubborn human persistence return him to the 'stream of life'. Within his view of civilisation's discontents, Orwell also holds to a fundamental distinction between two streams. The final celebration of lower middle class domesticity, for all its notorious mawkishness, emerges from his refusal of escape as an appropriate response. Gordon Comstock had imagined that he could somehow get outside the decay. But for Orwell the only adequate response is to refuse the temptations of escape and to find the life-stream that is not beyond but only within the workaday routines of common existence.

The strain in the rhetoric reflects the struggle of radical decency. However it may be taken by readers, this ordinariness is offered as a rooted ethic, profound enough to contest the 'awful thraldom of money'. It's notable that even in the midst of its sentimentality, the novel accepts the claim that money pulls the strings of human puppets. Radical decency is an alternative, not because it challenges the rule of money, but because it sustains a recognisably human life. It depends not simply on an idea of 'average character', but on an engagement with the conduct of daily existence. Ordinariness is not a state of mind, but a social practice.

V

The experience with the miners in 1936, leading to the publication of *The Road to Wigan Pier*, and the time spent in the following year with the anarchist brigade POUM during the Spanish Civil War, which led to *Homage to Catalonia*, were decisive to Orwell's political transformation. A few years later, in 'Why I Write', he would say that 'Every line of serious work that I have written since 1936 has been written, directly or indirectly, *against* totalitarianism and *for* democratic Socialism, as I understand it'. This statement accurately captures the political commitment that Orwell undertook in the mid-1930s, and it acknowledges the embrace of Socialism, which he criticised and parodied up to the moment of change. But the passage ignores a rival strain in thought, one significant for the ending of *Keep the Aspidistra Flying* and central to his last novel of the decade, *Coming up for Air*. This current was a product of reading Henry Miller: indeed Orwell's encounter with the novels, especially with *Tropic of Cancer*, was as transformative as his political conversion. Furthermore, it unsettled the political convictions with which it coincided.

Orwell reviewed *Tropic of Cancer* when it appeared in 1935, but his reaction was cautious and uncertain. He called the novel 'remarkable', especially in its sexual descriptions, though not because of their 'pornographic appeal', but 'because they make a definite attempt to get at real facts'. In an age of sentimentality which idealises physical life, Miller brutally insists on 'ugly things'. Orwell is unsure whether the book should be taken as a pessimistic vilification of humanity or as a celebration of life without the veil. Almost exactly a year later in a review of Miller's *Black Spring*, he referred to the caution of his earlier essay and admits that he had underpraised *Tropic of Cancer*. For a second time he compares it to *Ulysses*, and while he again affirms that Joyce's work is much grander, he insists that Miller's novel too is able to 'cast a kind of bridge across the frightful gulf which exists, in fiction, between the intellectual and the man-in-the-street'.

Orwell's first three novels had been written in quick succession, and for all their differences, they made a continuous and largely coherent phase of the career. *Coming up for Air*, however, appeared after the momentous encounters in Wigan and in Spain, after the avowal of Socialism, and also after a reconsideration of the function of literature. Appearing at the end of a stage of development, the novel revises the very project it brings to completion. Although its surface appears casual, *Coming up for Air* is the product of a deliberate, even polemical design. George ('Tubby') Bowling is Orwell's rendering of the average sensual man, a figure who had been preoccupying him all through the 1930s and especially after his encounter with *Ulysses*. Bowling, like Leopold Bloom, always lives near his body. Food, drink, sex are pleasures that he admits and enjoys; he amuses himself with his daydreams; he is insatiably curious (though anything but a scholar). Bowling is also free from the stains that had blighted the lives of his predecessors; he has no birthmark, no sexual neurosis, no obsessive social resentment. His one distinguishing mark is his corpulence. But for Orwell, as for Bowling himself, being fat has all its clichéd virtues: it 'keeps you from taking things too hard' and 'one of the advantages of being fat [is] that you can fit into almost any society'. The earlier protagonists had endured disaffection and alienation, but Bowling is prepared to enjoy his desires.

History, however, has interrupted his instinctive course of happiness. Orwell conceives his character as the ordinary self on which civilisation was founded and on which it could thrive again. But Bowling is hemmed in by the disasters of his century. The prospect of a catastrophic war looms in front of him, but so too does the hopelessness of what he calls 'the realities of modern life', including the 'everlasting frantic struggle to sell things. With most people it takes the form of selling themselves . . .' In its critique of contemporary life, *Coming up for Air* belongs within the lineage mapped by the previous novels. Its difference lies in a standpoint – a character, a voice – founded on affirmation and acceptance. Constrained by a narrow life and a bad marriage, Bowling is still capable of pleasure. He tends toward a 'joy in life', an 'interest in things for their own sake'. Even in bad times he sustains the image of a flourishing existence.

What makes *Coming up for Air* Orwell's most deliberate novel of the 1930s is that it owes so much to a coherent body of thought that also informs the important essay 'Inside the Whale', an essay in which Orwell consolidates a view of modern literary history and also a programme for fiction. Within this account the members of the 'Joyce-Eliot' generation, including Pound, Lewis, Lawrence, Huxley and Strachey (but not Woolf), differed in many respects, but their works converged in a 'tragic sense of life'. They abandoned a notion of progress; they saw through the sentimentality and pretensions of their age. Yet despite their seriousness, the modernists remained oblivious to political life. Then the pendulum swung. A new movement, even more coherent, emerged abruptly in the early 1930s. Auden, Spender, Day-Lewis, MacNeice and Upward, asserted the responsibility of literature and addressed the crises of the age; they broke free of tragic pessimism and saw literature as political engagement. So far, so straightforward. But the brisk turn in the essay comes when Orwell refuses the politics of the literary 1930s – and this despite his own recent turn to socialism. Notoriously, he represented the writers around Auden as lost within a self-indulgent fantasy: lacking other forms of conviction, they had assumed a Marxist faith, substituting Communist orthodoxy for the Church. Now, at the end of the 1930s, their weakness has been exposed.

The lesson of this history, writes Orwell, is 'that a writer does well to keep out of politics'. In itself, this is a startling remark, especially for one who would claim that all his work since 1936 was composed '*for* democratic Socialism'. But in 1939 Orwell was pursuing an alternative to both the tragic disengagement of the high modernists and the failed political commitments of their successors. Within this context Henry Miller stood by himself as the telling alternative. He had set aside the political imperatives of literature; he guiltlessly refused any appeal to obligation; he is 'inside the whale', in the 'final, unsurpassable stage of irresponsibility'. Miller can see what is happening in the world, but 'he feels no impulse to alter or control the process that he is undergoing. He has performed the essential Jonah act of allowing himself to be swallowed, remaining passive, *accepting*' – even when this means accepting 'concentration camps, rubber truncheons, Hitler, Stalin, bombs, aeroplanes'. The voice of acceptance is irresponsible, but it is a human voice.

George Bowling is Orwell's Jonah, and *Coming Up for Air* is in significant respects a contribution to the 'school of Miller'. Even his corpulence can be read as a punning version of the 'yards of blubber' that Miller finds inside the whale. Hemmed in on every side – by job, home, history – Bowling neither comprehends the political world nor tries to change it. He merely wants to rediscover the ground of happiness. In its central movement, *Coming Up for Air* is an unembarrassedly affirmative recovery of early-century innocence: boyhood, family life and country rambling in the town of Lower Binfield. Bowling is frankly sentimental about 'the civilization which I grew up in':

a time of better beer, simpler emotions, and above all fishing, an immediate pleasure and also typical of the civilisation that is gone. Fishing in *Coming Up for Air* is what sex was in *Tropic of Cancer*. 'Fishing', as Bowling puts it, 'is the opposite of war'.

The open nostalgia of *Coming Up for Air* needs to be seen as a determined imaginative act. Orwell takes from Miller the figure of the 'accepting man', who looks for whatever joy the world can offer and evokes the past because its satisfactions were greater than the miseries of the present tense. The turn to the first person is at once homage to Miller and a refusal of the detached narrator who had managed the previous novels. George Bowling speaks to us directly and presents himself as the ordinary man of appetite; the ideal reader of the book would be such another. *Coming Up for Air* aims toward a literary populism that had shown itself in *Ulysses* and had achieved a demotic flowering in *Tropic of Cancer*. But Orwell's novel makes a notable attempt to revise the tradition that it constructs. The difficulty with Joyce was that his sense of ordinary life was entangled with 'horror and repentance'. Miller escapes those emotions, and yet his work too suffers a deflection from common experience. As it takes up the threshold-testing lives of expatriates in Paris, *Tropic of Cancer* concerns itself with 'people drinking, talking, meditating and fornicating, not [with] people working, marrying and bringing up children'. The latter, of course, are Orwell's subject in *Coming Up for Air*, his attempt to establish a novel fully on the ground of common life.

'Tubby' Bowling goes in search of lost time, the rooted organic community of pre-war England before it was devastated by capitalism. But in the novel's other significant gesture Bowling contemplates future time, the prospect of a devastating and imminent war. Time future, like time past, has been obliterated by a present tense dominated by vacuous work, empty routine, the oppressions of the Bank of England, the Home Secretary, the Pope, Hitler and the Temperance League. The present is lurching toward catastrophe; the only hope is to break its grip and to recover both past and future. This is Tubby Bowling's vocation, and it's the gift of his commonness. Just to the extent that his desires are average and sensual, he can see clearly what intellectuals, like his old school-master Porteous and the Left Book Club, can never bring into focus.

> I'm not a fool but I'm no highbrow either, and God knows that at normal times I don't have many interests that you wouldn't expect a middle-aged seven-pound-a-weeker with two kids to have. And yet I've enough sense to see that the old life we're used to is being sawn off at the roots. I can feel it happening. I can see the war that is coming and I can see the after-war, the food-queues and the secret police and the loudspeakers telling you what to think.

Beneath its leisurely manner, *Coming Up for Air* articulates a stubborn vision of constrained possibility. The present tense is trapped within the logic of disaster. The only way to recognise the danger ahead is by opening up to the organic past that offers a standard of decency. Simply by keeping close to his ordinary desires, interests and hopes, Bowling can see more clearly than those around him.

And yet, he does nothing with his recognition. By his lights and the lights of his author, we are entering an age of terror: even the clear-sightedness of ordinary vision cannot avert the war. George Bowling goes home to his unhappy marriage; is caught in his lie; and resigns himself to endure his unavailing life. He ends in resignation: 'Why had I bothered about the future and the past, seeing that the future and the past didn't matter? Whatever motives I might have had, I could hardly remember them now'. At the end, there subsists merely a voice that has not yet gone quiet. Orwell does not see capitalism and its progeny (fascism, empire, advertising) as the preconditions for humane socialism. He sees them as violent eruptions blocking the restoration of the 'stream of life'. Bowling has nothing to do but to accept his condition, but if he can do that with his average sensual humanity, then until he falls silent, he will remind us of us.

What is true of Tubby Bowling is true of the modern novel, as Orwell understands it at the end of the 1930s. The form is doomed, as the autonomous individual is doomed, and as 'liberal Christian culture' is doomed – all for the same reason. No matter who wins the war, the age of totalitarianism is imminent; it will obliterate the conditions that made fiction possible: individual freedom, mental honesty, a minimum of censorship. Even at this moment of radical pessimism, Orwell's instinct is to keep writing. For as long as they last, novels sustain a counter-world, a space apart. If he has no belief in their future, still the assumption of failure has been what impelled the literary career from the start.

NOTES

1. A characteristic and influential early judgement came from Q. D. Leavis, who at the end of the decade wrote that 'Mr. Orwell must have wasted a lot of energy trying to be a novelist – I think I must have read three or four novels by him, and the only impression those dreary books left on me is that nature didn't intend him to be a novelist. Yet his equivalent works in non-fiction are stimulating'. Q. D. Leavis, *Scrutiny* (September 1940), 173.
2. Compare here Carl Freedman's discussion of the 'empiricist and externalizing problematic of Orwellian naturalism'. *George Orwell: A Study in Ideology and Literary Form* (New York: Garland, 1988), 50.

3. Naturalism, as George Woodcock, has put it, 'permeated every aspect of his outlook'. *The Crystal Spirit: A Study of George Orwell* (London: Fourth Estate, 1967), 56.
4. Eagleton writes that '"ordinary" living is mocked and caricatured through the dehumanizing eye of a more intelligent observer, who is himself deflated – reduced to normality – by his own or others' scepticism', but here is exactly where we need to consider the eye of the narrator, who exists at the limit of fiction and remains invulnerable to deflation. Terry Eagleton, 'Orwell and the Lower-Middle-Class Novel' in *George Orwell: A Collection of Critical Essays*, ed. Raymond Williams (Englewood Cliffs: Prentice-Hall, 1974).
5. *The Collected Essays, Journalism and Letters of George Orwell*, vol 1., *An Age Like This*, eds. Sonia Orwell and Ian Angus (London: Secker & Warburg, 1968), 3.
6. Eagleton persuasively argues that 'The loss-of-memory gambit simply effects a neat transition from rectory to common lodging-house without raising the complicated issues of motive and purpose which, as a *conscious* process, this would inevitably involve'. 'Orwell and the Lower-Middle-Class Novel', 22.
7. Lynette Hunter notes a difference in the representation of institutions in *Burmese Days* and *A Clergyman's Daughter*. The latter novel, she writes, 'shows the "constructed" character of institutions'. While Flory 'views the state not even as monolithic but as natural', Dorothy Hare 'is shown in the process of recognising it as artificial'. Lynette Hunter, 'Blood and Marmalade: Negotiations between the State and the Domestic in George Orwell's Early Novels', *Remembering the Thirties: Modernism and After*, eds. Keith Williams and Steven Matthews (London and New York: Longman, 1997), 20.
8. Raymond Williams, *George Orwell* (New York: Viking, 1971), 39.
9. Alex Zwerdling, *Orwell and the Left* (New Haven and London: Yale University Press, 1974), 156.
10. Although Zwerdling speaks of Gordon Comstock's poverty as the corresponding 'disability', it seems clear that Orwell regards his 'theory of poverty' as the traumatic fixation. *Orwell and the Left*, 157.
11. Here is where we need to resist the generality of Woodcock's strong early formulation. 'The central figure of every Orwell novel is a solitary, detached by some scar in his past from the world in which he finds himself, compelled to live the double existence of the misfit and, after inevitable and ineffectual rebellion, doomed to fail and be destroyed or finally and hopelessly to be enslaved'. *The Crystal Spirit*, 53.

6

WILLIAM E. CAIN

Orwell's essays as a literary experience

The experience of reading George Orwell's essays is special – bracing, illumi-
nating, invigorating. It is not the specific judgements Orwell makes as much
as the action of his thinking and the movement of his feeling that distinguish
him. He took stands on issues; he had convictions and expressed his principles. But this is not the defining fact about Orwell as a literary figure, as
an artist. He is a great essayist because of the experience he creates for readers – a provocation of the intellect, an education of the intelligence, which
includes but exceeds the positions he advocated. Orwell aims in his essays
to make readers more self-conscious, more aware of how we think and feel.

A demanding writer, Orwell requires close attention and incites self-
scrutiny. In his literary enterprise, if not in his style, he is akin to Ralph
Waldo Emerson, for in his essays Orwell exhibits 'man thinking' (Emerson's
phrase in 'The American Scholar', 1837), and the Emerson-like creation of
unorthodox thinking is his goal.[1] Self-reliance and non-conformity: these
are Emerson's central terms, and they signify Orwell's ambition and activity
as a writer of essays as well.

The immediate impact of Orwell's sentences and paragraphs is not
Emersonian: Emerson is more allusive and harder to fathom from line to
line. But an intention as essayists unites them: like Emerson, Orwell shapes
sentences that disconcert and surprise readers; he impels us to feel discon-
tented with stock ideas and conventional opinions. Orwell resolutely believed
in common sense (he called this his 'belly-to-earth attitude'), but at the same
time he recognises that common sense is hard to acquire, and this is because
false kinds of common sense saturate society, culture and politics. Genuine
common sense is needed to counter what we have come unthinkingly to
accept as 'common sense' – the received views that all of us are accustomed
to and that we tell ourselves we know are true.

'Till recently it was thought proper to pretend that all human beings are
very much alike', Orwell states in 'The Lion and the Unicorn' (19 February
1941), 'but in fact anyone able to use his eyes knows that the average of

human behaviour differs enormously from country to country'.[2] The sentence sounds straightforward: simply look, and you will see differences in behaviour. But the significant point is the one that Orwell implies – few people have made keen use of their eyes or, if they have, have admitted to what they see.

Everyone has the capacity to see something that is there and to say what it is; hardly anyone has done so. 'There is no question about the inequality of wealth in England', Orwell maintains. 'It is grosser than in any European country, and you have only to look down the nearest street to see it'.[3] Again what is striking is less the capacity of each person than the fact that the obvious is not being seen. Only a readjusted vision, the acquisition and application of true common sense, will make visible something plainly in view.

Resistant to any type of corporate mentality, Orwell crafted essays to prompt and press readers toward independence of vision, uncommon common sense, and integrity of mind. This motive informs Orwell's best novels, his political satires *Animal Farm* (1945) and *Nineteen Eighty-Four* (1949), which secured his place in literary history. But his achievement as the author of these novels has prevented us from gauging the full power and richness of the work he produced in the same decade in essays, newspaper columns, review articles and book reviews. It is this decade that I will examine here: what Orwell did in these years as an essayist is one of the major achievements of modern literature.

This is not to sell short Orwell's essays of the 1930s, which include such classics as 'A Hanging' (1931) and 'Shooting an Elephant' (1936). Combining vivid personal experience with cultural, social and political commentary, there is also in this decade 'The Spike' (1931), which describes a boarding-house for the homeless, 'Bookshop Memories' (1936), which deals with second-hand bookshops, and 'Marrakech' (1939), which portrays Moroccan life. During the 1930s Orwell in addition wrote articles on Melville, Pope, Carlyle and others. But it was during the 1940s, as the Second World War raged and later as the Cold War heated up, when the essayist Orwell became 'supreme' among his contemporaries.[4] This body of writing, as Irving Howe has noted, established Orwell as 'the best English essayist since Hazlitt, perhaps since Dr Johnson,' the 'greatest moral force in English letters'.[5]

In his essays of the 1940s, Orwell writes with such lucidity and ease of expression that we might imagine we could write like him ourselves. But because his style is guided by a distinctive action of mind, Orwell is impossible to imitate. It is sharpness of thinking, not elements of style, which Orwell intends to enact for and instill in readers. This feature of his essays makes them rewarding for readers now – not primarily the content of the essays (however interesting that is), but the experience of them, our response to Orwell's sentences, above all in the work from 1940 to his death.

In 1940 Orwell published 'Charles Dickens', which remains a first-rate survey; 'Boys' Weeklies', a pioneering foray in cultural studies; and 'Inside the Whale', a survey of modern literature keyed to Henry Miller, the controversial author of *Tropic of Cancer*. Also in 1940, Orwell reviewed *Mein Kampf* and wrote 'My Country Right or Left', his call for patriotism as England faced the Nazi threat. For 1941 Orwell's work includes: 'The Lion and the Unicorn: Socialism and the English Genius', 'Tolstoy and Shakespeare', 'The Meaning of a Poem', 'Literature and Totalitarianism', 'Wells, Hitler, and the World State', and 'The Art of Donald McGill' (a study of comic postcards), and 'No, Not One' (an analysis of the case for pacifism). Among the essays from 1942, there is 'Rudyard Kipling' and 'Looking Back on the Spanish War', which reviews Orwell's own experiences of that time and place and explores the difficulty of writing the war's history.

In November 1943, after resigning from his post on the staff of the BBC, Orwell began an association with a weekly Socialist newspaper, *Tribune*, serving as its literary editor and writing for it a weekly 'personal' column; he wrote eighty of these columns from December 1943 to April 1947. For 1944, his essays include 'The English People', 'Benefit of Clergy: Some Notes on Salvador Dali', and 'Raffles and Miss Blandish' (a study of crime novels). For 1945: 'In Defence of P. G. Wodehouse', 'Anti-Semitism in Britain', 'Poetry and the Microphone' (on the radio broadcast of literary programs), 'Notes on Nationalism', 'The Freedom of the Press', 'Revenge is Sour' (on Nazi war-crimes), 'The Prevention of Literature', and 'Politics and the English Language'. In 1946: 'James Burnham and the Managerial Revolution', 'Why I Write', and 'Politics vs. Literature: An Examination of *Gulliver's Travels*'. For 1947: 'Lear, Tolstoy, and the Fool', 'Burnham's View of the Contemporary World Struggle', and 'In Defence of Comrade Zilliacus', on the need to uphold freedom of speech even for one's enemies.

During 1948–49, as Orwell suffered from illness and struggled to complete *Nineteen Eighty-Four*, he wrote 'Writers and Leviathan', which considers the relationship between creative writing and political commitment, 'George Gissing', 'Such, Such Were the Joys', which recalls his schooldays (this essay may have been drafted earlier), and 'Reflections on Gandhi'. At the time of his death in January 1950 at age forty-six, Orwell was gathering notes for a piece on Evelyn Waugh and for a long short story, planning essays on Gissing and Joseph Conrad, looking ahead to a long essay or a short book on Mark Twain, and considering 'a novel dealing with 1945'.[6]

Listing the high points of Orwell's production in the 1940s is not, however, the same as reading him and thereby exposing oneself to the dislocations and renewals of mind that he intended to generate. It is a puzzling aspect of Orwell biography, criticism and scholarship that for all of the esteem bestowed upon his essays – their astutely chosen details, directness of expression, and against-the-grain perspectives – few have articulated the reader's experience of them and described the perpetually stimulating activity of mind that this writer's organisations of language provide. Statements like this one by Julian Symons are common: 'I have always believed that what Orwell wrote is less important than what he was'.[7] And there is this, by the critic Stefan Collini: Orwell is 'more important as a symbol than for what he actually wrote'.[8]

Critics, furthermore, seem eager to approve or disapprove of Orwell's social and political positions, and the result is that they make the writing less effectual, less of a complex experience, than it is. The Marxist critic Terry Eagleton, for instance, has rebuked Orwell for his 'empiricism' and lack of interest in theory:

> 'In order to hate imperialism, you have got to be part of it', Orwell wrote, which is plainly false: being part of it in the way he was is as likely to blunt your hatred as to sharpen it. This, in fact, is just the kind of slipshod generalization that Orwell's cult of the particular is supposed to resist.[9]

Too quick to judge, Eagleton misses Orwell's subtlety. Orwell is asserting that someone who is involved (as he was) in colonial administration and policy has a deeper understanding than someone who is not. But he also seeks in the sentence to move us to realise that we are inside the colonial experience even when we may tell ourselves we are not. Everyone is implicated in colonial experience, those who dwell in India and Burma and those who live in England: it is not merely a question of where we are, but how we think, and what we are willing to admit to being part of. Orwell thus is making a distinction that his sentence endorses (you have to be in it to understand it) and contests (you are already in it – *that* is what you must grasp, what you must feel). Eagleton's response shows what Orwell was (and is) up against.

Orwell acknowledged that writers have designs on their readers; there is a political dimension to all forms of writing. 'Every piece of writing', he claims, 'has its propaganda aspect'. 'And yet', he adds, 'in any book or play or poem or what not that is to endure there has to be a residuum of something that simply is not affected by its moral or meaning – a residuum of something we can only call art'.[10]

Orwell is an artist: he embeds in sentences the 'something' that will make his work more than propaganda and position-taking and that will ensure it lasts. His intention is to write not only for his own generation, but also for later generations: he intends the effect of his sentences to be permanently present in his prose. It is the reader's responses that Orwell has in view all of the time; he anticipates them and coaxes and coerces adjustments in our pathway through them. Orwell writes sentences that reveal his thoughts and feelings and that provoke acts of analysis and reflection in us, decades after the immediate positions he treated.

Here is the opening of 'Why I Write' (summer 1946):

> From a very early age, perhaps the age of five or six, I knew that when I grew up I should be a writer. Between the ages of about seventeen and twenty-four I tried to abandon this idea, but I did so with the consciousness that I was outraging my true nature and that sooner or later I should have to settle down and write books.[11]

'Outraging my true nature' is the strong phrase Orwell uses to express his self-violation. Used as a transitive verb, 'outrage' means to rape; to subject to violent injury or gross insult; to do violence to; to cause a feeling of anger or violent resentment in. But the phrase is placed to disturb the reader too: Orwell is making a point about himself and pointing at the reader, who is prompted through it to assess his or her own life-choices – the outrage that one might be doing to one's true nature.

Orwell's friend Richard Rees rightly said, 'it was easy to underestimate the acuteness and power of Orwell's mind; and his readers are equally likely to be misled by his unpretentious and straightforwardly simple style'.[12] Orwell does possess a powerful mind, and his clear-seeming style in his essays is the result of deliberate craftsmanship; he is the practitioner of an artful set of techniques, a complicated strategy for engaging the minds of readers. In all of his essays, especially those in the 1940s, Orwell is examining and clarifying what he thinks, what everyone thinks, and what the reader thinks now but ought to be thinking instead. He is creating the means through which we can learn to think about how our minds operate.

Orwell was intrigued by, and invested in, the English language as the resource through which to manage these extensions of the reader's consciousness. As *Animal Farm*, *Nineteen Eighty-Four*, and the essay 'Politics and the English Language' bear witness, he understood and protested against dishonest, manipulative uses of language in totalitarian regimes. He knew the limits of language, saying, for example, in 'New Words' (probably written in early 1940): 'Everyone who thinks at all has noticed that our language is practically useless for describing anything that goes on inside the brain'.[13] In the same essay he says:

All likes and dislikes, all aesthetic feeling, all notions of right and wrong (aesthetic and moral considerations are in any case inextricable) spring from feelings which are generally admitted to be subtler than words. When you are asked 'Why do you do, or not do, so and so?' you are invariably aware that your real reason will not go into words, even when you have no wish to conceal it; consequently you rationalise your conduct, more or less dishonestly.[14]

But elsewhere Orwell stressed that there is more to language than the failure of words to give adequate explanations. 'The greatest quality of English', he contends, 'is its enormous range not only of meaning but of *tone*'. 'It is capable of endless subtleties', he maintains, 'and of everything from the most high-flown rhetoric to the most brutal coarseness'.[15]

We might object that language cannot be both limited and inexhaustible. But such an objection fails to demonstrate a capacious understanding of what language is and does. Orwell believed that a writer has to think his or her way through the limitations that language imposes: we should never forget how much can be done with it. Writing, he concludes, is disciplined work:

Whoever writes English is involved in a struggle that never lets up even for a sentence. He is struggling against vagueness, against obscurity, against the lure of the decorative adjective, against the encroachment of Latin and Greek, and, above all, against the worn-out phrases and dead metaphors with which the language is cluttered up.[16]

To see clearly, write plainly, and think honestly: these have to be fought for and sustained. As Orwell declared of common sense: 'To see what is in front of one's nose needs a constant struggle'.[17] The struggle is a political necessity and, as Orwell suggests in another passage in 'Why I Write', an aesthetic duty with its own rewards:

What I have most wanted to do throughout the past ten years is to make political writing into an art. My starting point is always a feeling of partisanship, a sense of injustice. When I sit down to write a book, I do not say to myself, 'I am going to produce a work of art.' I write it because there is some lie that I want to expose, some fact to which I want to draw attention, and my initial concern is to get a hearing. But I could not do the work of writing a book, or even a long magazine article, if it were not also an aesthetic experience.[18]

When Orwell says 'aesthetic experience', is he referring to something that happens to him as he writes or to something he hopes to make happen for the reader? The answer is both. For Orwell there is political writing and there is political writing that is a form of art experienced by the writer and the reader.

In political terms, Orwell may have gotten a hearing and brought a lie to light, and as readers we may have been directed toward a new viewpoint. But in aesthetic terms, it is the sphere of thinking and feeling where the essential action is.

In a sense, then, Orwell's position on an issue is not the primary thing. Issues change, and positions change with them. What is ongoing, and imperative, is the meaning of taking a position, the coming to consciousness of how and why positions are taken. This theory and practice makes the essayist Orwell an authentic artist, a great writer.

As an artist Orwell is an attention-seizer, and through his opening sentences he means to surprise us into a shift in our thinking as we encounter a point that is new or a familiar point given an uncommon expression. He makes us aware of being acted upon by an organisation of words, and he mastered this strategy in his essays of the 1940s:

> Dickens is one of those writers who are well worth stealing.[19]
>
> As I write, highly civilised human beings are flying overhead, trying to kill me.[20]
>
> Incoherent and, in places, silly though it is, this book raises a real problem and will set its readers thinking, even if their thinking only starts to be useful at about the place where Mr. Noyes leaves off.[21]
>
> Considering how likely we all are to be blown to pieces by it within the next five years, the atomic bomb has not roused so much discussion as might have been expected.[22]

Next, at greater length, is the opening section of one of Orwell's 'As I Please' columns. The first sentence sets up the second, where the charge is laid:

> When the Caliph Omar destroyed the libraries of Alexandria he is supposed to have kept the public baths warm for eighteen days with burning manuscripts, and great numbers of tragedies by Euripides and others are said to have perished, quite irrecoverably. I remember that when I read about this as a boy it simply filled me with enthusiastic approval. It was so many less words to look up in the dictionary – that was how I saw it.[23]

Orwell recalls a cultural catastrophe, accenting its extreme devastation ('destroyed', 'perished'), holding up an image of treasures in flames while indifferent people enjoyed a warm bath, and underscoring the permanence of the loss ('quite irrecoverably'). The next sentence is, deliberately, the animated opposite ('enthusiastic' heightens the effect) of the lament or indignation we might have expected to hear him voice. The third sentence implies that Orwell has matured beyond this response: 'I saw it that way then, but of course not now'. Yet the tone carries a lingering appeal – if not about the destruction itself, then in the recollection of how young Orwell (i.e., Eric Blair) responded when he initially heard about it.

Through sentences such as these, and the development of the claims and arguments that follow from them, Orwell brings to light realities we do not wish to see: he puts pressure on our typical thoughts, feelings and responses. In the wartime essays of the 1940s, Orwell dared even to express opinions he knew that readers would find shocking. In 1940, he reviewed *Mein Kampf*:

> I should like to put it on record that I have never been able to dislike Hitler. Ever since he came to power – till then, like nearly everyone, I had been deceived into thinking that he did not matter – I have reflected that I would certainly kill him if I could get within reach of him, but that I could feel no personal animosity. The fact is that there is something deeply appealing about him.[24]

This is not a joke gone badly awry: Orwell is being serious and creating an occasion for us to measure our own seriousness. Peer into your soul: what is your response to Hitler? Orwell says he tried to dislike Hitler and failed, only to state next that if he had the chance he would kill Hitler nonetheless. Is it better or worse to kill Hitler without 'personal animosity'? It is not just an absence of animosity: Orwell finds Hitler 'deeply appealing', intensifying the claim with a 'deeply' he could have omitted.

In this passage there is a content to Orwell's words that could be debated and judged. But what makes Orwell, as an essayist-artist, a permanent resource is our interior experience of the content, the discomfiting, exploratory form of thought and feeling that Orwell induces us into. From week to week in the 1940s Orwell assailed imperialism, capitalism, fascism and Stalinism. But he came to realise that his adversary was not a specific ideology or world-system as such. It was a prevailing cast of mind – the mind as it functions on the basis of conformity and habit, the mind detached from and unknowing of its own operations. As a literary artist Orwell wrote to equip readers to name and feel truth.

Orwell was committed to objective truth – a manifest truth out there that he clung to amid totalitarian apologists and truth-deniers. He warned, 'the very concept of objective truth is fading out of the world';[25] and he insisted, 'however much you deny the truth, the truth goes on existing, as it were, behind your back'.[26] 'The really frightening thing about totalitarianism', Orwell said, 'is not that it commits "atrocities" but that it attacks the concept of objective truth: it claims to control the past as well as the future'.[27]

Yet Orwell understood truth in another sense. 'No sermons, merely the subjective truth', he remarks in praise of Henry Miller.[28] There is the truth out there, and the truth one feels within. For Orwell these are not contradictory; they exist in a tense, complementary relationship with one another. He sought to force readers to look inside precisely so that they would come into possession of an accurate vision of what was outside – the crimes that were being committed, the people who were being tortured and murdered.

In his project as an artist, Orwell recognised the complicated, morally necessary tasks of both looking out and looking in, and saying honestly in both instances what one sees. It is an inner and outer process of discovery and witness he undertakes, and these are the revelations of consciousness in the reader that Orwell's art in his essays effects.

'What vitiates nearly all that is written about anti-Semitism'. Orwell observed,

> is the assumption in the writer's mind that *he himself* is immune to it. 'Since I know that antisemitism is irrational,' he argues, 'it follows that I do not share it.' He thus fails to start his investigation in the one place where he could get hold of some reliable evidence – that is, in his own mind. . . . The starting point for any investigation of antisemitism should not be 'Why does this obviously irrational belief appeal to other people?' but 'Why does antisemitism appeal to *me?* What is there about it that I feel to be true?' If one asks this question one at least discovers one's own rationalisations, and it may be possible to find out what lies beneath them.[29]

Orwell expects us not to ponder neutrally the questions he raises but to apply them to ourselves: this is the self-assessing nature of the literary experience of reading one of Orwell's essays. He is the most engaging confrontational writer there is. The pleasure he gives is intended to hurt.

Orwell emphasises the 'courage' that the art of writing requires. 'Good novels', he affirms, 'are written by people who are *not frightened*'.[30] 'The first thing that we ask of a writer', he says, 'is that he shall not tell lies, that he shall say what he really thinks, what he really feels':

> For writing is largely a matter of feeling, which cannot always be controlled from outside. It is easy to pay lip-service to the orthodoxy of the moment, but writing of any consequence can only be produced when a man *feels* the truth of what he is saying; without that, the creative impulse is lacking.[31]

It is not enough for a writer to know the truth. One must also feel the truth one knows, for without that there is no creative dimension to the writing. A writer might hold the correct position on an issue, but if he does not feel it from within, his writing will be hollow. There will be no conviction in the language (it will be something other than art), and there will be no aesthetic experience and ultimately no instruction for the reader.

Orwell knew he risked hostile responses: the hurt he administers is intended to benefit readers, not harm them, but hurt is present in his prose and he was aware that many would dislike being chastened. However, he maintains, 'if liberty means anything at all, it means the right to tell people what they do not want to hear'.[32] Such liberty also means that as an essayist Orwell must be freely willing to feel and say to himself what would be easier for him to ignore or dismiss. Each writer must face truths from which he or she would prefer to turn away.

In this context Orwell makes a distinction between the journalist and the artist:

> The journalist is unfree, and is conscious of unfreedom, when he is forced to write lies or suppress what seems to him important news: the imaginative writer is unfree when he has to falsify his subjective feelings, which from his point of view are facts. He may distort and caricature reality in order to make his meaning clearer, but he cannot misrepresent the scenery of his own mind: he cannot say with any conviction that he likes what he dislikes, or believes what he disbelieves. If he is forced to do so, the only result is that his creative faculties dry up.[33]

We honor Orwell for political positions he held and expressed in his essays about the issues of his time. But even more we should value him as an artist for the literary experience he gives us and that is exhibited in the operations of his language. Orwell wants us to discover how we think, know what we truly feel, and understand who we are.

NOTES

1. Ralph Waldo Emerson, 'The American Scholar', 1837, rpt. *Ralph Waldo Emerson: Essays and Lectures*, ed. Joel Porte, New York: Library of America, 1983, p. 54.
2. Carey, p. 291; *CEJL*, 2:56. Page references are to Orwell's *Essays*, ed. John Carey, New York: Knopf, 2002, and *The Collected Essays, Journalism, and Letters*, 4 vols., ed. Sonia Orwell and Ian Angus (*CEJL*), New York: Harcourt Brace, 1968.
3. Carey, 300; *CEJL*, 2:64.
4. Gordon Bowker, *Inside George Orwell*, New York: Palgrave, 2003, p. 432.
5. Irving Howe, 'George Orwell: "As the Bones Know"', rpt. *Decline of the New*, New York: Horizon, 1970, p. 270.
6. *CEJL*, 4:497, 506, 509.
7. Julian Symons, 'Orwell: A Reminiscence', *London Magazine* 3, September 1963, p. 48.
8. Stefan Collini, 'The Grocer's Children: The Lives and Afterlives of George Orwell', *Times Literary Supplement* 20 June 2003. For a detailed exploration of Orwell's symbolic status, see John Rodden, *The Politics of Literary Reputation: The Making and Claiming of 'St George Orwell'*, 1989, new ed. Somerset, New Jersey: Transaction, 2002.

9. Terry Eagleton, 'Reach-Me-Down Romantic', *London Review of Books* 25:12, 19 June 2003.
10. 'Tolstoy and Shakespeare', 7 May 1941; Carey, 356; *CEJL*, 2:130.
11. Carey, 1079; *CEJL*, 1:1.
12. Richard Rees, *George Orwell: Fugitive from the Camp of Victory*, Carbondale: Southern Illinois University Press, 1962, p. 8.
13. Carey, 260; *CEJL*, 2:3.
14. Carey, 261; *CEJL*, 2:4–5.
15. 'The English People', written early 1944, published 1947; Carey, 634; *CEJL*, 3:25.
16. 'The English People', written early 1944, published 1947; Carey, 634; *CEJL*, 3:25.
17. 'In Front of One's Nose', 22 March 1946; Carey, 1043; *CEJL*, 4:125.
18. 'Why I Write', Carey, 1084; *CEJL*, 1:6.
19. 'Charles Dickens', 11 March 1940; Carey, 135; *CEJL*, 1:413.
20. 'The Lion and the Unicorn', 19 February 1941; Carey, 291; *CEJL*, 2:56.
21. 'Review of *The Edge of the Abyss*', 27 February 1944; Carey, 549–50; *CEJL*, 3:99.
22. 'You and the Atom Bomb', 19 October 1945; Carey, 903; *CEJL*, 4:6.
23. 'As I Please 32', 7 July 1944; Carey, 679; *CEJL*, 3:178.
24. 21 March 1940; Carey 250–51; *CEJL*, 2:13.
25. 'Looking Back on the Spanish War', 1942; Carey, 440; *CEJL*, 2:258.
26. 'Looking Back on the Spanish War', 1942; Carey, 442; *CEJL*, 2:259.
27. 'As I Please 10', 4 February 1944; Carey, 535; *CEJL*, 3:88.
28. 'Inside the Whale', 11 March 1940; Carey, 247; *CEJL*, 1:247.
29. 'Anti-Semitism in Britain', April 1945; Carey, 856; *CEJL*, 3:340–41.
30. 'Inside the Whale', 11 March 1940; Carey, 240; *CEJL*, 1:519.
31. 'Literature and Totalitarianism', 21 May 1941; Carey, 361, 364; *CEJL*, 2:134, 136.
32. 'The Freedom of the Press', 17 August 1945; Carey, 888.
33. 'The Prevention of Literature', January 1946; Carey, 937–38; *CEJL*, 4:65; see also 'As I Please', 68, 3 January 1947; Carey, 1157; *CEJL*, 4:267.

7

JOHN ROSSI

'My country, right or left': Orwell's patriotism

I A Revolutionary in Love With the Past

It is a commonplace observation to say that George Orwell was something of a paradox. A product of the lower upper middle class (he was precise about such matters) who admired the working classes, he also was a socialist who savaged his fellow leftists for their inconsistencies. Most interestingly, Orwell was an internationalist while at the same time a fervent patriot.

Orwell's critical sense of patriotism sets him apart from the generation of English radicals of the 1930s and 1940s, most of whom were Marxists of various stripes. It was his patriotism that inspired Orwell in the grim early days of the Second World War when Great Britain seemed on the brink of invasion and defeat. His patriotism was instinctive, not the result of some philosophical analysis and because of that, it enabled him to reach beyond left wing circles to a wider audience.

In developing his ideas on patriotism Orwell made a major contribution to English thought. In his key writings between 1940 and 1942 'My Country, Right or Left' and especially *The Lion and the Unicorn* Orwell helped rescue the concept of patriotism from the ash heap of history where it had lain since the First World War.

The emotional patriotism of England during the First World War had rendered the concept ridiculous in the eyes of sophisticated thinkers. As nurse Edith Cavell had remarked before her execution by the Germans: 'Patriotism is not enough'. For the young idealists of the 1930s love of country was something to mock. The denigration of patriotism helped pacifism achieve its greatest popularity by the mid-1930s. Novels like Erich Remarque's *All Quiet on the Western Front* (1930), plays like R. C. Sheriff's 'Journey's End' (1929) and memoirs such as Robert Graves' *Goodbye to All That* (1930) reached enormous audiences. The Labour Party rejected rearmament throughout the decade. In fact, a frankly committed pacifist, George Lansbury, led the party until 1935.

In left wing circles by the early 1930s patriotism gave way to pacifism and a vague kind of internationalism, loosely identified with the League of Nations. But despite their pacifism the major direction left wing internationalism took was a deep admiration for the 'Soviet experiment' as Stalin's cruel regime was often described.

Neither pacifism nor idolisation of Communism touched Orwell, who seemed inoculated by a kind of residual patriotism. That the concept of patriotism was part of his intellectual heritage is evidenced in his literary work from the beginning of his career. Partly because of this latent sense of patriotism he began to gain a wide audience in the early days of the Second World War when England's sense of patriotic destiny revived in the face of the Nazi threat.

Orwell's roots were linked to the British Empire. His father held a high level administrative position in the Opium Department of the Indian Civil Service. His mother was from a French commercial family in Burma. Although Orwell was born in India in 1903 he was raised in England. His family's imperial experience helped shape Orwell's outlook. He would spend five years as an Imperial policeman in Burma in the late 1920s, years he considered wasted but filled with memories that inspired some of his best writing such as the essays 'A Hanging' and 'Shooting An Elephant'. Although he would eventually rebel against the idea of Empire, he never rejected the outlook he absorbed as a young man.

Orwell's tendency to romanticise the past, especially the not-too-distant past, gave a certain reactionary aura to some of his writings. This view of his past Orwell refused to give up. As he explained in his essay 'Why I Write': 'I am not able, and I do not want, completely to abandon the world-view that I acquired in childhood'. The operative part of this comment is Orwell's determination not to reject the milieu that shaped him, the age of Edwardian smug self-satisfaction that saw one quarter of the world coloured in the red of the British Empire.

Malcolm Muggeridge once observed that what made Orwell unique among leftists of his generation was the fact he was really a revolutionary in love with the past.[1] In this way Orwell resembled some of the angry non-doctrinaire nineteenth century radicals like William Cobbett more than any contemporary Socialist.

Because the atmosphere in Great Britain in the 1930s, when Orwell began his literary career, was decidedly pacifist there was unwillingness on the part of the governing classes as well as intelligentsia to use force for political ends. The blood-soaked battlefields of the Somme and Passchendaele testified to the futility of war. This fear of war blinded the English to the growing danger from Hitler's and Mussolini's regimes until late in the decade.

For most of the 1930s Orwell, although he was never a pacifist, shared this misjudgement of the dangers of Fascism and Nazism. Until the Spanish Civil War radicalised him, Orwell saw little to choose between traditional capitalism and Fascism or Nazism. They were economic and social systems based on exploiting the lower classes. Despite his careful use of language Orwell rarely distinguished between Fascism and Nazism. As a result his insights into them were pedestrian, even banal. For him these forms of total-itarianism were the final stages of the collapse of capitalism. By contrast, his analysis of Communism was original. Unlike many of his left wing col-leagues, Orwell was enamoured of Communism neither as a theory nor by Stalin's unique perversion of it. He never experienced a Stalinoid phase. The closest Orwell came to Communism was to flirt with what John Newsinger calls being a 'literary Trotskyist'.[2]

Orwell distrusted Communism because of its institutional use of terror and its assault on the idea of human liberty. The fact that Communism was fashionable among the left wing intelligentsia reinforced Orwell's scep-ticism. Orwell viewed intellectuals as nothing more than idea mongers. He believed that the instincts of the working class were more honest and reliable. Orwell's dislike of his fellow intellectuals played a major role in the formu-lation of his ideas. It saved him at times from embracing foolish notions. As he wrote in one of his more memorable observations about the fash-ionable ideas and trendy politics of the intelligentsia: One has to belong to the intelligentsia to believe certain things, 'no ordinary man could be such a fool'.

Orwell's uniqueness among English leftists arose from a residual sense of patriotism, a love of things English that he was never ashamed of. As early as *Down and Out in Paris and London* (1933) while Orwell was still search-ing for a political voice, he articulated this elemental patriotism. 'There are indeed many things in England', he wrote of his return from the continent, 'that make you glad to get home; bathrooms, armchairs, mint sauce, new potatoes properly cooked, brown bread, marmalade, beer made with veri-table hops . . .' Then in a typical Orwell aside he ends this paean of praise to Englishness by saying all these things are splendid 'if you can pay for them'.[3]

Similar expressions of basic patriotism are sprinkled throughout Orwell's early writings. Even in *The Road to Wigan Pier* (1937), a work that had nothing to do with patriotism, Orwell noted that one of the reasons socialism failed to gain a wide audience was its attack on 'certain things (patriotism, religion, etc.) which lay deeper than the economic motive'.[4] He contrasted that with the success of Fascism, part of whose appeal, he argued, was as an upholder of patriotism as well as the military virtues.[5]

About the only contemporary who shared Orwell's attitude regarding patriotism was that equally idiosyncratic master of paradox, G. K. Chesterton. Shortly before his death in 1936 he wrote: 'I believe that patriotism rests on a psychological truth; a social sympathy with those of our own sort, whereby we see our potential in them; and understand their history from within'.[6] Orwell would find little to disagree with in these sentiments.

If Orwell's early writings are examined as a whole they reveal a love of certain English qualities – the countryside, the food, the people's gentle manners, even the climate. What they do not express is hatred or contempt of those not English. Orwell thought it was revealing that the working class found foreigners funny not threatening. In contrast, he noted the intelligentsia was cut off from their own culture: 'they took their cooking from Paris and their ideas from Moscow'.[7]

Orwell found the patriotism of the working class healthy and he differentiated it from vulgar nationalism. He would later carefully spell out this distinction. In his seminal essay, 'Notes on Nationalism' (1945) Orwell argued that patriotism meant 'devotion to a particular place and particular way of life, which one believes to be the best in the world but has no wish to force on other people. Patriotism is of its nature defensive, both militarily and culturally. Nationalism, on the other hand, is inseparable from the desire for power. The abiding purpose of every nationalist is to secure more power and more prestige, not for himself but the nation . . . in which he has chosen to sink his own individuality'.[8]

After his involvement in the Spanish Civil War in 1937 Orwell's writing became more overtly political. Spain taught him many things and converted him into a full-blown socialist. It also convinced him that a terrible war was coming, a struggle that would pit two corrupt systems of government, capitalism and Fascism, against each other. Spain also taught him that there were things worth fighting for. His experiences in Catalonia early in the war gave him the first inkling that the middle class and working class could be united around a kind of revolutionary patriotism. In a letter to Geoffrey Gorer in September 1937 after his return from Spain Orwell argued that it was 'futile to be "anti-Fascist" while attempting to preserve capitalism. Fascism after all is only a development of capitalism . . . I do not see how one can oppose Fascism except by working for the overthrow of capitalism . . .'.[9]

He adhered to these views in a confused way for the next two years. He came to believe that when the war came it would lead to a peculiar English form of Fascism taking hold in the country. After his Spanish experiences he joined the Independent Labour Party in June 1938, the most radical and pacifist of the leftwing political parties in England. By joining the ILP Orwell was distancing himself from the Communist dominated Popular Front argument that a war was necessary to stop Fascism. To him the Popular Front simply was 'an unholy alliance between the robbers and the robbed'.[10]

The last major work he wrote before the Second World War broke out, his novel *Coming Up For Air* (1939), reflects a longing for a lost past which the protagonist, George Bowling, like Orwell, locates in the years before the First World War. The novel, however, is not a reactionary tract, a yearning for some lost utopia. In fact, Bowling's dreams of the destruction wrought by the next war in some ways foreshadow the world of *Nineteen Eighty-Four*.

After *Coming Up For Air*'s publication in June 1939 Orwell believed that war was unavoidable. He lost interest in writing fiction. In his first letter to the influential American liberal journal *Partisan Review*, Orwell wrote of these times: 'only the mentally dead are capable of sitting down and writing novels while this nightmare is going on'.[11] By the summer of 1939 Orwell was beginning to wonder what the coming war would mean for him. Some time that summer of 1939 Orwell underwent a political transformation – he discovered that his martial spirit wasn't dead and that he was a patriot at heart.

In a famous passage in his essay, 'My Country, Right or Left' Orwell traces the rediscovery of his patriotism to a dream he had the night before the Nazi-Soviet Pact was signed on 24 August 1939. In what is most likely a literary device he writes that when he awoke to the news he knew when the war broke out he would be relieved but more importantly, that he would fight. 'I was a patriot at heart, . . . would support the war, would fight in it if possible'. This conviction Orwell links to what he called the long drilling of patriotism in English life. Once England faced a crisis he wrote, 'it would be impossible for me to sabotage it'.[12]

Orwell would return to these views again and again in the coming months. Shortly before Hitler launched his Blitzkrieg against the West, Orwell reviewed Malcolm Muggeridge's portrait of recent English history, *The Thirties*. The review, which appeared in the *New English Weekly* on 25 April 1940, two weeks before Hitler attacked Belgium, Holland and France, encapsulates Orwell's emerging conception of patriotism. He believed that beneath Muggeridge's fashionable sense of despair 'there lies the unconfessed fact that he does after all believe in something-England'. Orwell understood what Muggeridge was talking about. 'It is the emotion of the middle-class man, brought up in the military tradition, who finds in the moment of crisis that he is a patriot after all. It is all very well to be "advanced" and "enlightened", to snigger at Colonel Blimp and proclaim your emancipation from all traditional loyalties, but a time comes when the sand of the desert is sodden red and what have I done for thee, England, my England?' Orwell contrasts Muggeridge's patriotism with what he calls 'the shallow self-righteous of the leftwing intelligentsia'.[13] Orwell might have been writing about himself not Muggeridge.

Even at this early point in the war, the role that patriotism would play in the future was on Orwell's mind. In his book *Inside the Whale* published in March 1940, a collection of literary and political essays, Orwell found time to focus on the importance of patriotism. One of the reasons left wing political parties had been unable to formulate a coherent response to Nazism and Fascism, he wrote in 'Boys Weeklies', was their 'failure to understand the patriotism of the ordinary person'.

II A Revolutionary Patriot

The Second World War changed everything for Orwell. After the war broke out on 3 September 1939 he left the Independent Labour Party, which remained committed to pacifism. He attempted to join the military in some capacity but was rejected for health reasons. The tone of his writing now took on a clear political direction as his patriotism was stirred by the events of the early months of the war.

The reaffirmation of his patriotism may also have been influenced by the fact that the Nazi-Soviet Pact had placed the Communists and their left wing allies in a bind. After years of bitter denunciation of Nazism now they suddenly were forced by Moscow's party line to denounce the war and demand English neutrality. Orwell enjoyed the left's embarrassment. He took some well-aimed pot shots at them in *Inside the Whale*. In a phrase designed to wound and outrage the left, he described Communism as nothing more than 'the patriotism of the deracinated'.[14]

Other than scattered remarks Orwell's first serious analysis of the renewed importance of patriotism appeared in 'My Country, Right or Left' which he wrote in the midst of the greatest crisis in English history since the Spanish Armada.

By June 1940 England stood alone facing a German blitzkrieg that had swept through Western Europe in a matter of weeks. Invasion seemed likely and early in July the Germans began a bombing campaign designed to weaken England's resolve and force a negotiated peace. During this dangerous summer of 1940 Orwell formulated his thoughts on patriotism. In June he joined the Local Defence Volunteers, later called the Home Guard but continued his literary work, often writing for eight to ten hours a day. He enjoyed his time in the Home Guard although he remained frustrated that his health barred him from the military. He believed that the Home Guard was important because it could become the germ of a People's Militia.

'My Country, Right or Left', written during the summer of 1940, appeared in John Lehmann's *Folios of New Writing* in the fall of the year. The title borrowed from the American naval officer, Stephen Decatur's toast to the United States, 'My Country, Right or Wrong', is actually an expression of the nationalism that Orwell despised, not patriotism as he defined it.

The essay had a number of purposes. It was Orwell's justification for his reversal of stance since 1938 when he believed that a war would lead to the eventual triumph of an English form of Fascism. He began by comparing his attitude toward the outbreak of war in 1914 with his current situation – in neither case did he want to see England defeated. While he knew that there was much wrong with England, its rotten class system in particular, Orwell argued that the nation was worth preserving. He argued that the long tradition of patriotism had entered his bones and that when his country faced an enemy he would fight to defend her. He bitterly rejected the pacifism that he had flirted with, saying that the pacifists had not found a substitute for 'patriotism and the military virtues' – toy pacifists would not do for inspiration.

In one of his most important observations Orwell noted that the patriotism he was talking about had nothing to do with traditional conservatism. He wanted to make this distinction clear as patriotism had traditionally been associated with the political right. Patriotism, he argued, is a living concept, the 'devotion to something that is changing but is felt to be mystically the same'. Therefore, difficult as it might seem, one could simultaneously 'be loyal to Chamberlain's England and the England of tomorrow'.

Orwell wanted patriotism to be a force for political and social change and he believed the present crisis afforded such an opportunity. His fellow socialists, he argued, had to understand that if they wanted to see a trans-formed England they had to tap the resurgent patriotism that swept through the nation during the summer and fall of 1940.

'My Country, Right or Left' began the process of co-opting the concept of patriotism for socialism and trying to sever its association with political conservatism. This reconfiguration would be at the heart of much of his writing over the next two years – using patriotism as a vehicle to bring about a social revolution.

The period between Dunkirk in early June and the Blitz, the German nighttime raids on England, beginning in October, constitute one of the most dramatic moments in English history. Fears of an invasion were rampant throughout the summer. The Battle of Britain (usually dated July–October) was unprecedented – the first time a decisive military engagement was fought in the air as well as a conflict the people could watch unfold before their eyes. The night raids that followed the victory in the Battle of Britain brought the war home to the English public.

In a strange way Orwell thoroughly enjoyed the war with its deprivations and shortages. It meant the end of one England – fat, corrupt and blind to reality – and the possible beginning of a new better one. To Orwell, the conditions that prevailed resembled Barcelona in 1937, when the people were in charge and class distinctions and titles were abolished. He believed that England had entered a potential revolutionary phase, one when for the first time it was realistic to believe that the English people were ready to embrace socialism.

At this time Orwell, the writer Tosco Fyvel, and the publisher Fredric Warburg planned a series of small pamphlets or booklets, called 'Searchlight Books' to discuss the main issues of the war. They would be cheap, just two shillings and targeted to reach a broad audience. Orwell undertook to write the first volume of the series and he served as editor for some of the others that appeared, a distinguished list that included works by Joyce Cary, Ritchie Calder and Stephen Spender.

Orwell's contribution, *The Lion and the Unicorn: Socialism and The English Genius* was written between August and October 1940, toward the climactic phase of the Battle of Britain. The 20,000 word monograph was published on 19 February 1941 and contains Orwell's mature thinking about the role that patriotism could play in the present crisis. Unlike so many of his socialist contemporaries, Orwell recognised the potential force of patriotism not only at this moment but also as a historical phenomenon in English history. Repeating and refining some of the arguments he made in 'My Country, Right or Left', Orwell sought to link the patriotism of the English middle and working classes with the need for socialism. In effect, he argued that patriotism could be a revolutionary force as it had been during the French Revolution and for a time in Spain.

The Lion and the Unicorn is divided into three parts: 'England Your England', 'Shopkeepers at War', and 'The English Revolution'. Part one was published separately in December 1940 in a new journal, *Horizon*, edited by Orwell's close friend Cyril Connolly. It would later appear in a highly successful *Collection of Essays* published in the United States three years after Orwell's death.

'England Your England' contains the key to Orwell's argument about patriotism and socialism. It begins with one of those unforgettable openings Orwell was the master of. 'As I write, highly civilized human beings are flying over head, trying to kill me'. They are only doing their duty, he wrote, and are motivated by the powerful force of patriotism. Orwell argued that

one could not understand 'the modern world as it is unless one recognizes the overwhelming strength of patriotism, national loyalty . . . as a positive force. Christianity and international Socialism are as weak as straw in comparison with it'.

Orwell believed that patriotism was the defining element in the English character. Patriotism is something palpable and real, not a useless sentiment. This Englishness is distinctive, not a romantic figment of someone's imagination. Then Orwell provides a brilliant word picture of what makes England unique: 'It is a culture as individual as that of Spain. It is somehow bound up with solid breakfasts and gloomy Sundays, smoky towns and winding roads, green fields and red pillar-boxes. It has a flavour of its own. Moreover, it is continuous, it stretches into the future and the past, there is something in it that persists, as in a living creature. What can the England of 1940 have in common with the England of 1840? But then, what have you in common with the child of five whose photograph your mother keeps on the mantelpiece? Nothing, except that you happen to be the same person'.[15]

Orwell believed the left underestimated the significance of these unique English qualities because they were trained to think in broad Marxist categories and because they rejected the concept of national character. As a result the left wing intelligentsia were caught off guard by the patriotism the war engendered in the working classes.

Throughout his career Orwell seemed to take special pleasure in attacking those he agreed with. Nowhere is this more apparent than his bitter attacks on Socialists intellectuals in *The Lion and the Unicorn*. He argued that they had to share blame with Baldwin and Chamberlain for leaving England unprepared for war. This contradicted the argument put forth in the hugely popular book *Guilty Men* published in July 1940 by socialists like Michael Foot which argued only the English left wanted to stand up to Fascism and Nazism in the 1930s and that appeasement was a purely Conservative policy. The book was a blatantly dishonest attempt to obfuscate the left's support for disarmament in the face of the threat from Fascism and Nazism throughout the 1930s. Orwell noted that in fact the pacifism of the left, in particular their adamant rejection of rearmament, led Hitler and Mussolini to believe that English democracy was decadent and would not fight for its survival. 'England is perhaps the only country', he wrote, 'whose intellectuals are ashamed of their own nationality . . . Patriotism and intelligence will again have to come together' united around the two groups of English society instinctively loyal, the middle classes and working classes.[16]

Orwell argued that, contrary to what the left wing intelligentsia believed, patriotism was not a conservative concept. It should be used to rally the different social classes behind the idea of creating a new England – in Orwell's words 'to build a Socialist on the bones of a Blimp'. The left had to grasp that a Nazi victory would not just be a defeat of the appeasers but it would also be a defeat for the idea of revolution. The left failed to understand what was being fought for now wasn't bourgeois democracy but socialism.

For Socialists, Orwell's argument in *The Lion and the Unicorn* was heresy and confirmed their view dating back to *The Road to Wigan Pier* that he could not be trusted. As good Marxists they believed that the working class had no country and had nothing in common with the middle class. Orwell was saying that because of the unique history of English society these two classes could cooperate in saving their nation. Class hatred had to be over-come and the patriotism of the English was the way to do it. But the Socialist intellectuals should understand that because of the special revolutionary sit-uation that prevailed at this point in the war there was potential for radical change. The resurgent patriotism that unites the middle and working classes provides the lever to bring about profound economic, political and social transformation in England. If the left doesn't act quickly the opportunity will pass.

England is changing in the face of the war, Orwell believed. It is still class-ridden, 'a land of snobbery and privilege, ruled largely by the old and the silly'. But it is a society in which all the classes share certain traits. In one of his most famous metaphors, Orwell described England as resembling nothing less than a family: 'a rather stuffy Victorian family . . . in which the young are generally thwarted and most of the power is in the hands of irresponsible uncles and bedridden aunts. Still it is a family. It has its private language and its common memories . . . A family with the wrong members in control – that perhaps, is as near as one can come to describing England in a phrase'.[17]

Those who will save England in this crisis and begin the creation of a fairer society, Orwell argued, are not the ruling class. They are finished. It will be the heirs of Cromwell and Nelson who 'are in the fields and the streets, in the factories and the armed forces, in the four ale bars and suburban back gardens'. But the glue that binds these disparate groups together is the abiding appeal of patriotism. The last sentence of *The Lion and the Unicorn* begins 'I believe in England', a sentiment that few of his fellow Socialists would have written at that time and one that set Orwell apart from many on the intellectual left.

There is evidence that by the time *The Lion and the Unicorn* appeared in February 1941 Orwell feared that the moment for his revolutionary brand of patriotic socialism was passing. Around this time he was asked by Victor Gollancz who had published *The Road to Wigan Pier* to contribute to a volume entitled, *The Betrayal of the Left: An Examination and Refutation of Communist Policy*. Gollancz and the former Communist John Strachey wrote most of the book, which was a sustained attack on the behaviour of the Communists since the Nazi-Soviet Pact, especially their neutralism in the face of the Nazi triumph in the West.

Orwell contributed two short chapters to *The Betrayal of the Left*. 'Fascism and Democracy' reprised an idea that Orwell had floated early in the war – that the sheer materialism of the left led them to underestimate the appeal of Fascism. He first made this argument in March 1940 when he reviewed Hitler's *Mein Kampf* for the *New English Weekly*. Among his observations, Orwell argued that Hitler grasped a profound truth that the left wing intelligentsia did not understand: 'the falsity of the hedonistic attitude to life'. All progressives believed that people desire nothing more than 'ease, security and avoidance of pain'. Hitler saw through that. While Western democracy promises the good life Orwell noted, Hitler said, 'I offer you struggle, danger and death, and as a result a whole nation flings itself at his feet'.[18] Who else on the left would have made that point? Interestingly Orwell's phrasing of Hitler's sentiments is reminiscent of Churchill's words to the nation when he first became Prime Minister: 'I have nothing to offer but blood, toil, tears and sweat'.

Orwell's second contribution 'Patriots and Revolutionaries' repeated the arguments in *The Lion and the Unicorn*, showing that Orwell, like most writers, wasn't above repeating himself. He hints that the revolutionary moment was missed. It came right after Dunkirk, when the disillusioned troops returned from France, bitter and ready to wipe away the corrupt system that had led an unprepared England into the war. Capitalism was dead or dying but the left in their intellectual blindness and confusion failed to grasp this fact. Now the confidence of the ruling class was returning, boosted by the failure of the Germans to invade, the resilience of the British public in the face of the Blitz and the first British victory of the war, the defeat of the Italians in Libya in December 1940.

Orwell continued to believe that there is a slim chance that socialism could be brought about. But it has to come through the union of socialism and patriotism. 'Socialists may laugh at the patriotism of the middle class', he writes, 'but let no one imagine that it is a sham. Nothing that makes men willing to die in battle – and relative to numbers more of the middle class than of the working class are killed in war – is a sham'. We socialists have to understand 'the fact that at this moment of time a revolutionary has to be a patriot, and a patriot has to be a revolutionary'.[19]

A month after the publication of *The Betrayal of the Left*, Orwell noted in his diary that he was pessimistic that a revolutionary opportunity comparable to the summer of 1940 would appear again. He thought that genuine radical change was taking place 'but in slow motion'. The tone of much of his writing for the rest of the year was focused, especially after the German attack on the Soviet Union in June, on the theme of totalitarianism and its role in England's future.

By early 1942 the importance of patriotism in bringing about the kind of revolutionary society that Orwell sought had faded. His attention had shifted to the growing popularity of Communism as the Soviet Union fought valiantly against Nazi Germany. He was fearful that just as the intelligentsia had misjudged Fascism they would fail to grasp the dangers of Communism. Shortly after the German attack on the Soviet Union Orwell observed in his diary: 'One could not have a better example of the moral and emotional shallowness of our time, than the fact that we are now all more or less pro-Stalin. This disgusting murderer is temporarily on our side, and so the purges etc are suddenly forgotten'.[20] The left fell at Stalin's feet, Orwell wrote, because they had lost their patriotism and sense of religious belief while continuing to need a god and a fatherland.[21] It is difficult to imagine anyone else on the left developing these insights at this stage in the war.

Orwell's focus on the slavish admiration for Communism and Stalin was the beginning of a new phase in his life – exposing the totalitarian dangers inherent in Communism. His analysis of Soviet totalitarianism would carry him to his greatest fame with the publication of *Animal Farm* and *Nineteen Eighty-Four*. In spite of this new interest Orwell never lost sight of the critical role that patriotism had played in shaping England's political, cultural and social life. After 1942 patriotism lost its centrality for Orwell but it remained a recurring theme in his writing. Of the generation of left wing writers who flourished in England during the years between the First World War and the onset of the Cold War, Orwell was unique in the impact that it had on him. In essence, he remained what he always was: a patriotic Englishman to the core.

NOTES

1. Malcolm Muggeridge, 'Knight of the Woeful Countenance', in Miriam Gross (ed.), *The World of George Orwell*. London, 1971, pp. 166–75.
2. John Newsinger, *Orwell's Politics*. New York, 1999, p. 91.
3. George Orwell, *Down and Out in Paris and London*. New York, 1971, pp. 112–13.
4. George Orwell, *The Road to Wigan Pier*. New York, 1958, p. 187.
5. Ibid, p. 214.
6. G. K. Chesterton, 'Paying For Patriotism', in Katherine Feldberg (ed.), *Of Men and Manners: The Englishman and His World*. Coral Gables, Florida, 1970, p. 22.

7. George Orwell, *The Lion and the Unicorn: Socialism and the English Genius* in Sonia Orwell and Ian Angus (eds.), *The Collected Essays, Journalism and Letters of George Orwell*, New York, 1968, II, p. 74, hereafter cited as *CEJL*.
8. 'Notes on Nationalism', *CEJL*, III, p. 362.
9. Orwell to Gorer, 9/15/1937, *CEJL*, I, p. 284.
10. Review of *Workers' Front* by Fenner Brockway, in *New English Weekly*, 2/17/1938, *CEJL*, I, p. 305.
11. 'London Letter', *Partisan Review*, March–April 1941, *CEJL*, II, p. 54.
12. 'My Country Right or Left', *CEJL*, I, p. 539.
13. 'The Limits of Pessimism', a review of Malcolm Muggeridge, *The Thirties*, *CEJL*, I, p. 535.
14. 'Inside the Whale', *CEJL*, I, p. 515.
15. 'England Your England', in *The Lion and the Unicorn*, *CEJL*, II, pp. 57–59.
16. Ibid, p. 75.
17. Ibid, pp. 67–68.
18. Review of Adolf Hitler, *Mein Kampf* in *New English Weekly*, 3/21/1940, *CEJL*, I, pp. 12–14.
19. George Orwell, 'Patriots and Revolutionaries', in Victor Gollancz and John Strachey, *The Betrayal of the Left: An Examination and Refutation of Communist Policy*, London, 1941, pp. 234–45.
20. Diary, 6/30/1942, *CEJL*, II, p. 407.
21. 'London Letter', *Partisan Review*, July–August, 1943, *CEJL*, II, p. 286.

8

IAN WILLIAMS

Orwell and the British Left

According to his own last words on the subject, just before his death, Orwell was a supporter of Socialism and of the British Labour Party which had swept to power in 1945.[1] Before then, for most of his writing career, certainly from *The Road to Wigan Pier* in 1937 onwards, George Orwell was an avowed proponent of socialism, although his conceptions of what that meant certainly changed over the years.

Despite his own unequivocal and often expressed views, the popularity of the Orwell 'brand' has led many people to misrepresent his views since his death, and to appropriate his prestige for their own political projects. That was typified by the introduction to the most popular edition of *Nineteen Eighty-Four* in the US, which quotes him accurately as saying that all his work 'was against totalitarianism', while in a somewhat Orwellian manner cutting out his important following phrase 'and for democratic socialism'. Since his death of course, other people's ideas of socialism have also changed, and even geography has an effect. Socialism will have entirely different connotations, for example, for West Europeans, East Europeans and for Americans, as the truncated Orwell quote would suggest.

This chapter briefly traces Orwell's political development in the context of the British socialist politics of his era and shows how at an early stage he defined himself specifically as a 'democratic socialist', thus intending to distance himself, and indeed socialism itself, from the various totalitarian tendencies that claimed, spuriously in his view, to be socialist.

Just as Orwell in some ways tried to define his socialism by exclusion, of communism for example, this chapter will rebut some of the posthumous claims about his political thought that have been made in clear disregard for his own stated words. In doing so, it relies mostly on Orwell's own writings, substantiated as they are by many contemporary accounts of colleagues and correspondents. However, if we are to rely upon Orwell's own works they do need to be put in context for modern readers. The changes in the British Labour Party and society since he died, not to mention the clear difference between British and American domestic politics, despite recent signs of convergence, demand some explanations.

Striking Back at the Empire: Orwell and Class

Any reference point for Orwell's politics has to be British, indeed, even more precisely, English, since that is where, despite his internationalism, he drew his political inspirations. Although it sometimes evokes comment, it was not at all anomalous that Orwell, an old Etonian scion of a family of imperial civil servants should have become a socialist. Many leaders of the Labour Party, Clement Attlee, or Hugh Gaitskell for example, came from similar and even loftier social positions. What is more surprising is the gradualness of his transition to socialism, and it may be that which kept him more firmly attached to the politics he eventually chose, as opposed to the instant conversions to Communism, and often equally instantaneous apostasy, that sometimes characterised others of his milieu.

Orwell's political metamorphosis from his imperialist chrysalis began with his experience in the British imperial police in Burma which gave him a profound distaste for the British Empire at work, although the later literary manifestation of that dislike in *Burmese Days* in 1934 certainly seems to have come as a surprise to his colleagues in the force.

Not long after his return from the outposts of empire, he described himself as a 'Tory Anarchist', to the editor of the *Adelphi* magazine and repeated this designation several times over the years.[2] This was not the same as being a conservative: Samuel Johnson, William Cobbett, Jonathan Swift and others have provided a respectable precedent for writers by calling themselves Tories while defending what they saw as ancient liberties.

Apart from his distaste for the effect of imperialism on subject peoples, his Burmese experience doubtless accentuated his sensitivity to the caste system at home in Britain. Although the minute gradations of the hierarchy of rank in the Raj were notorious, it was simply a more codified and explicit version of the informal but still rigidly delimited social system in Britain, as reflected in Orwell's very precise calibration of his own origins in the 'lower upper middle-class'.

That sensitivity to the caste order of the British social hierarchy was reinforced by his excursions into the lower orders for *Down and Out in Paris and London* (1933) and *The Road to Wigan Pier*. His excursions not only moved him to concern for how society treated its poorer sections, the *plongeurs* of Paris, the tramps of England and the miners of Wigan but emphasised how the British, or rather the English, caste system was not necessarily reducible to crude Marxist economic class analysis.

In the famous repartee between Ernest Hemingway and Scott Fitzgerald, the latter declared 'The rich are different from you and me', to be robustly and famously countered by Hemingway. 'Yes, they have more money'. But Orwell discovered the obverse, that the poor really *were* different from the middle classes and that the difference between a British working class person and their upper middle class compatriots, even a 'lower' upper middle class Orwell, was more deep-rooted than any mere quantitative difference in salary.

Indeed, Orwell went beyond accepting that the poor are different. He decided that they were *better*, in their ethics, their social cohesion and even their patriotism. The latter concept was, of course, anathema to orthodox Marxists who held that the working class has no country. Unfortunately for dogma, twentieth century history seems to have settled this question in Orwell's favour. But then one of the qualities of the working class in Britain, according *The Road To Wigan Pier* was that he had yet to meet 'a working miner, steel-worker, cotton weaver, docker, navvy or what not, who was "ideologically sound".'

Most of Orwell's contemporaries and subsequent critics see *The Road to Wigan Pier* as his personal road to a socialist Damascus. It was there that he discovered that poverty and squalor were the fate, not only of the tramps and what Marx had once unkindly called the lumpenproletariat, who had fallen through the gaps in the floor of society. He found that the miners of Wigan and the dockers of Liverpool, workers whose toil kept the whole British economic enterprise going, were trapped in hopelessness if unemployed, and dire insecurity even if they had a breadwinner working.

His research came as a revelation to him and to many of his readers. Before the Second World War and the social reforms in its wake, British society was much more stratified even than now. Workers and their children were rarely likely to get beyond elementary school, and even the autodidacts among them rarely had the leisure or opportunity to develop the literary skills that would allow the middle class reader a glimpse through the class curtain. Orwell had gone beyond the event horizon for most of the middle class of Britain. With an outsider's senses, for example, of smell, he had gone to a different social planet – and discovered intelligent life there.

His experience completed his conversion from 'Tory anarchist' to convinced socialist, but it should be remembered that within the broad church of British Labour, there has always been room for Tory anarchists and similar eccentrics, and he clearly did not rid himself of all his prejudices and idiosyncrasies.

For example, he gratuitously added a Blimpish growl against other middle class socialists to *The Road to Wigan Pier*, 'vegetarians with wilting beards, Bolshevik commissars (half gangster half gramophone), of earnest ladies in sandals.., escaped Quakers, birth-control fanatics . . .).[3] There is an element of exorcism in the exercise, since his own chosen life-style, keeping goats, running small holdings, fervent chain-smoking and ritualistic tea making, made him eminently parodiable in his own terms.

For example, it is difficult to believe, looking at the perennial scruffiness of his attire in all his contemporary photographs, that he ordered his clothes custom-made from his tailor! He may have been affecting an insouciance to distance himself from his origins. Even at the end of his life, in the hospitals, he was comparing, unfavourably, the middle class accents of visitors with the regional dialects of the staff.

There was also a Dickensian element in his outlook, which is not surprising in view of his own deep appreciation for the novelist. Just as Dickens actually made the trade union officials in *Hard Times* almost as culpable as Gradgrind the capitalist, Orwell's phobias included the labour leaders who had come up in the world, and he did not seem to relate strongly to the trade unions, the cooperative movement, and the other genuinely working class bodies that made up much of the Labour Party's base in Britain.

Indeed, the class struggle, in its more mundane form, of strikes and go-slows, do not enter Orwell's works, whether essays or novels, in any significant way. While in *Nineteen Eighty-Four* Winston Smith thought the only hope lay with the Proles, it is noticeable that they were not joining unions or striking! Even allowing for the fact that strikes were relatively rare and unions relatively weak after the defeat of the General Strike in 1926, one suspects that for Orwell, the English Proles were almost an equivalent of the Russian peasantry for Tolstoy, a moral force more than the socio-political unit of traditional Marxism.

The Independent Labour Party

When he did get involved in politics, Orwell chose to join a distinctively British body, the Independent Labour Party, which was towards the left and indeed the revolutionary flank of the British Labour movement, but which had many distinctive approaches that Orwell shared. He was not as lonely a figure as an American socialist with similar ideas may have been, not least since socialism was in the mainstream in Britain.

The ILP had left the Labour Party earlier in 1932, but still had a wide, albeit shrinking base, members of parliament, and indeed still had many close connections and sympathisers inside the Labour Party itself and the unions. Although the ILP considered itself revolutionary, it was by no means Leninist and was open and non-dogmatic in its beliefs, with a mixture of pragmatic belief in improving the lot of people now and a firm belief that things could and should get much better – without being too specific about the form that future society would take.

It held what it called a 'Third Way' position between Leninism and the Labour Party right's reformism, which is, of course, not to be confused with Tony Blair's and Bill Clinton's later appropriation of that title.

The ILP believed that socialism could be brought about by an elected Labour Party, which could suppress counter-revolution 'by ordinary legal power backed by a Labour organization, and could thus effect the revolutionary change to socialism'.[4] Indeed the ILP's identification of a distinctively 'British Road to Socialism', backed by the power of mass organisations, was later usurped by the Communist Party of Great Britain itself, even down to the name, after the Second World War.

The ILP's indigenous, non-dogmatic but robust politics is clearly one of the sources that Orwell was drawing on, when he declared, 'England is the only European country where internal politics are conducted in a more or less humane and decent manner'. He claimed, along with the ILP, that it 'would be possible to abolish poverty without destroying liberty', and its people were 'more capable than most people of making revolutionary changes without bloodshed'.[5] The emphasis of the ILP was just this, the abolition of poverty in the course of a makeover of society made possible by mass support.

While some commentators have inferred that Orwell was repudiating the Labour Party by suggesting that it was converging with the Conservatives, if read in context, Orwell was actually *celebrating* such convergence as a distinctively British and implicitly better way of doing things. He elaborated 'Thus, no Conservative government will ever revert to what would have been called conservatism in the nineteenth century. No Socialist government will massacre the propertied class, nor even expropriate them without compensation'.[6]

It was ILP leaders like Fenner Brockway who introduced him to Secker and Warburg for publication of *Homage to Catalonia* in 1938, and later *Animal Farm* in 1945 when the more communist-inclined Victor Gollancz demurred at Orwell's political direction. Showing the same humanistic approach that Orwell certainly shared, and in a way anticipating the theme of *Nineteen Eighty-Four*, the ILP's leader, James Maxton MP, in his last major speech in 1945, repudiated statist versions of socialism, declaring, 'We must not allow ourselves to become ants in an anthill'.[7] For that he could draw upon the support of a vociferous cooperative movement whose political representatives in the inter war years had also warned of the dangers to workers of state control.

Orwell's ILP connection explains how he could consider himself to be a revolutionary, while strongly spurning 'foreign' ideologies such as the various forms of Leninism.

The Spanish Disconnection

Orwell had initially alienated the Communists and many others of the more rigid left with his excoriation of them in *The Road to Wigan Pier*, but what undoubtedly sundered any vestigial comradely feelings with them was the publication of *Homage to Catalonia* in 1938, and its exposure of the behaviour of the Soviets, their agents and supporters in Spain during the Civil War.

While he joined the militia of the Spanish sister party of the ILP, the POUM, in Catalonia at the end of 1936, it would appear that he was initially somewhat innocent of the sectarianism of the left and would at one point have happily joined the Communist-dominated International Brigades, because they were on a more active front near Madrid. However, he was already on the Communist Party's blacklist, with Comintern agents tracking him, as he became aware when the Communist-dominated Spanish Republican forces moved against the POUM and Anarchists in Barcelona. The Soviet line was that the POUM was Trotskyist, and commentators have often accepted that at its face value, although its leader, Andreas Nin had had strong disagreements with Trotsky. Regardless of whether or not it was Trotskyist, it certainly was not, despite what the Communist press declared, in league with the Fascists.

Orwell's shock at the blatant lies of pro-Soviet writers was compounded by the perils of his own flight across the frontier, just ahead of the KGB, and the fate of several of his colleagues who did not make it. The vegetarians and escaped Quakers against who he had inveighed in *The Road to Wigan Pier* may have seemed an impediment to the onward march of socialism, but his Spanish experience persuaded him that the Soviet Union and its supporters were outright enemies. The experience exposed Orwell to the concepts for which he later coined the memorable phrases 'doublethink' and 'duckspeak'.

Critics debate whether Orwell was actually well versed in Marxism, but several very close to him say that he had read Marx extensively. What may fool people is that like those around the ILP or Tribune, Orwell would have instinctively revolted against the idea of using the specific Marxist dialect, which sounded so foreign to native English speakers.

The Second World War and Orwell's Politics

After Catalonia, the Soviet Pact with Nazi Germany in 1939 would not have surprised him as much as it did more trusting souls on the Left, but both the Pact, and the way that some intellectuals in Britain turned on a sixpence to match Moscow's new love affair with the former Nazi enemy provided rich material for both *Animal Farm* and *Nineteen Eighty-Four*, not to mention a steady stream of wartime commentaries. As a result Orwell invited many on the Left to the ultimate in thoughtcrime. As befits one who fought against both, he came to 'the old, true and unpalatable conclusion that a Communist and a Fascist are somewhat nearer to one another than either is to a democrat'.[8] Although this essential identity of totalitarianism despite its rhetorical colours was the constant theme of Orwell's well-argued work for the last decade of his life, it was still a shocking concept to many who had adopted the slogan 'No enemies on the Left!' during the late 1930s. That was when Moscow had decided that democratic socialists were no longer the 'Social-Fascists' of 1933, but essential partners in the Popular Front period. Many of them kept up kept up that belief even as Stalin decided he had no enemies in Berlin.

The mainstream Labour Party was broadly in favour of the war effort, despite a large pacifist element. Some ILP leaders, such as Maxton, continued to oppose the 'imperialist' war with Germany without, however, ever subscribing to the Soviet embrace of their new Nazi ally – which caused a rapid realignment of the far left. The British Communist Party had promptly followed Moscow's lead and declared it to be an imperialist war, a position held more consistently by people like Maxton and the tiny Trotskyist movement who remained antiwar even after the Soviet Union had involuntarily joined the war when Hitler attacked it.

While the ILP's position of revolutionary opposition to the war was also initially reflected by Orwell, he and many others soon moved to strong, albeit highly conditional support for the British war effort. He rapidly lost his earlier pessimistic fear that it would bring about a form of fascism in Britain, deciding instead that the social changes and pressures of total war on the home front presented, not so much the opportunity, but more the indispensability of revolution. He had joined the Home Guard, the equivalent of the old militia, and the possibilities of an armed and trained populace excited him. In the course of the Second World War, the British government would seize control of the economy and direct it towards the war effort to an extent far beyond anything that even Nazi Germany managed. Of course, it was all done in the name of victory, but when the scaremongers warned that socialism would mean draconian rationing and taxation, wartime Britain already had them both, unchallenged by the rich. The war brought about a large element of social and economic levelling, indicating what was possible in peacetime.

At the same time, with Orwell's customary tendency to see the skull beneath the skin, his experience of wartime Britain, the shortages, the rationing, the bureaucratic regulation also provided the backdrop for *Nineteen Eighty-Four*. He had already detected this in the siege mentality of the Soviets and the bellicosity of the Nazis, but the direct experience in Britain was a chilling evocation of the possibilities inherent in war hysteria and the numbing effect of war's deprivations. It could happen here after all.

His time at the BBC, where he produced programmes for India in 1941, tempered any tendency to euphoria. His not always successful attempts to get radical and nationalist Indian guests on the programme showed that the old imperialist establishment was far from dead and his direct experience of ideological control of the content, much magnified, became a crucial component of *Nineteen Eighty-Four*.

Then as the war went on, the social unity, and the enforced egalitarianism that it entailed brought him to explicit support for the Labour Party or at least its left wing, where many had drifted from the ILP.

The Labour left mostly organised around *Tribune*, the independent weekly newspaper which Orwell joined as literary editor after leaving the BBC in 1943. He wrote some of his most memorable essays, including the *As I Please* columns, for it. It was an accurate title. His colleagues did not always share all his views, but it is a reflection of the eclectic nature of the Labour Party that, unlike in the more Leninist sectarian milieu, there was no hint of censorship. Orwell had found an appropriate journalistic home at last.

He retained his old school and class connections and their contacts with decision makers and his new Labour party connections added more as people connected with *Tribune* or the ILP joined both the wartime coalition cabinet and the postwar Labour government. His editor, Aneurin Bevan, not only joined the cabinet, he was instrumental in setting up the National Health Service.

Although we are unsure whether or not Orwell actually joined the Labour Party, he certainly canvassed for it in the May 1945 election that returned the self-declared socialist party to power with a massive majority. As we have seen, right up to his death, as we know from his attempts to correct American misapprehensions about the purpose of *Nineteen Eighty-Four*, he described himself a supporter of the Party and the government.

Socialist Anti-Soviet

In the heat of the war and even after, many on the Left were prepared to overlook the Soviet German pact, not least as the Red Army for several years rolled back the Axis forces in a way that the western allies did not.

Orwell's incisively unforgiving attitude to the Soviet Union made him an uncomfortable partner for some of the Labour left, who while deploring Communism as it was practiced in Eastern Europe were equally, or more, concerned about the growing tendency for London and Washington to realign against their former Soviet ally. For example, Michael Foot, a collea-gue and subsequent editor of *Tribune* and leader of the Labour Party, while speaking admiringly of Orwell, still mischaracterises him as a Trotskyist because of his firm anti-Soviet attitudes compared with the more ambivalent attitude that others had to the Soviet ally. The real Trotskyists, as Orwell was discovering from his correspondence with *Partisan Review* in the USA, where they were relatively much stronger than in Britain, consistently opposed the war.

Even before the 1945 election he had warned, 'There is the impending showdown with Russia which people at the top of the Labour Party no doubt realize to be unavoidable'.[9] He left no doubt which side he would put himself on. 'In case of war breaking out, if one were compelled to choose between Russia and America, I would always choose America', he told his former publisher Victor Gollancz warning that 'In international politics . . . you must be prepared to practice appeasement indefinitely, or at some point you must be ready to fight'.[10] However, he kept a sense of proportion, for example, curbing Bertrand Russell's initial enthusiasm for a pre-emptive nuclear strike against Russia.

The publication of *Animal Farm*, in 1945 'that anti-Soviet Farrago' as it was described in the communist *Daily Worker*, compounded his many sins with the Moscow-inclined left, whose vitriol level rose along with its phe-nomenal sales. What disgruntled Orwell more than their predictable attacks were the people on both the left and the right who agreed with the fable's core message of a revolution gone bad, but felt it inexpedient to publish it during a war in which the USSR was an ally. Their determined efforts to thwart the satire's publication provided yet more inspiration for the world of tightly controlled information in *Nineteen Eighty-Four*.

The List

In recent years, the release of government documents showed that Orwell had provided a list to the British government of people that he thought the government's 'Information Research Department' should not employ. For many people on both sides of the Atlantic, this has conjured up House Un-American Activities Committee hearings and McCarthyite purges and dismissals, and some saw it as a vindication of their long-time questioning of Orwell's socialism.

However, that begs far too many questions. The Labour government elected in 1945 had set up the IRD specifically to subsidise publications that championed 'social-democracy as a successful alternative to Communism'.[11]

Not one of those on Orwell's 'List' lost their jobs, were imprisoned, or can be proven to have had any resulting impediments to their chosen careers, except possibly missing freelance assignments from a government department that they presumably disagreed with anyway!

Indeed, in 1948, just a little before, Orwell had written to his anarchist friend George Woodcock suggesting that their organisation, the Freedom Defence Association, consider action against blacklisting. He explained, 'It's not easy to have a clear position, because, if one admits the right of governments to govern, one must admit their right to choose suitable agents, & I think *any* organization has the right to protect itself against infiltration methods. But at the same time, the *way* in which the government seems to be going to work is vaguely disquieting'.[12]

Indeed, he went on to point out that the communists were victims of the type of measures that they had themselves been calling for against fascists, while he himself more consistently lamented a general public indifference to freedom of speech. Despite his uncomfortable anti-Sovietism, he never forgot that 'one defeats the fanatic by not being fanatic oneself, but on the contrary by using one's intelligence',[13] and did not apply double standards. He opposed the blacklisting and repressive action against individual fascists and communists alike, hewing to a higher, inexpedient, standard of civil liberties.

Orwell's socialism

Orwell's memorable final books ensured that he is remembered more for what he was against, totalitarianism, than what he was for, which as he often asserted, was democratic socialism. *Animal Farm* and *Nineteen Eighty-Four*, as the Cold War chilled down all over the world, led to Orwell's adoption by many conservatives in Europe and America, thus confirming for many of the communist-influenced left the dark suspicions they already had about Orwell's political positions.

His death in 1950 not long after the publication of *Nineteen Eighty-Four* froze Orwell's political development in the coldest days of the Cold War and presented a stationary target for those of his opponents whose Manichaean worldview considered any criticisms of the Soviet Union, especially those as trenchant as Orwell's, as giving aid and comfort to the 'real' enemy – 'Western Imperialism'.

While his vision of socialism definitely excluded the Bolshevik model, it was an empirical and pragmatic version. He wrote during the war 'Socialists don't claim to be able to make the world perfect: they claim to be able to make it better',[14] – a view that would have been entirely in harmony with the broad church that the Labour Party represented.

'Better' could apply ethically as much as financially. For example, in 1941, as he wrestled with the reality of a capitalist British government that had more controls on industry, labour and even food, clothes and furniture, than any other Western nation had ever tolerated – and still basically retained a free society, he warned, 'I think we ought to guard against assuming that as a system to live under, socialism will be greatly preferable to democratic capitalism'.[15]

He was not suggesting that socialism was less ethical, or even less efficient, than capitalism, but he consistently maintained that relative British prosperity under capitalism depended on the unsustainable and unethical exploitation of the subject peoples of the Empire. It typified his political approach, which combined a strong empirical and pragmatic streak with what a later Labour Foreign Secretary, Robin Cook, was to say about his approach to foreign policy, that it should have 'an ethical dimension'. There is no doubt that his experience of working for *Tribune*, and with people like Michael Foot and Aneurin Bevan helped consolidate his support for the Labour Party. Along with the left around *Tribune*, he cavilled at the Labour leadership's occasionally overcautious attitude to social change – even as he agreed with its staunch anti-Sovietism. However the postwar social democratic consensus in Britain ensured that Orwell and his works became not only part of the popular consciousness, but also a generally accepted part of political discourse. For democratic socialists, Orwell has become an icon, someone who could reconcile a concern for social justice with a concern for civil rights, and indeed who saw that there was no possibility of one without the other. When conservative Prime Minister John Major quoted Orwell in an election speech, there were guffaws from those, mostly Labour supporters who compared the writer's socialism with the prime ministers recidivist conservatism, but the quotation bespeaks a popularity. The fact that Orwell is so often misappropriated is a tribute to his popular stature, but also to the failure of his misappropriators to read what he wrote so clearly and eloquently about his beliefs. Despite the posthumous claims by conservatives and communists alike that Orwell had abandoned socialism by the end of his life, none of his colleagues at *Tribune* or in the Labour Party and ILP, has ever disagreed with the continuing force of Orwell's self-assessment, 'Every line of serious work that I have written since 1936 has been written, directly or indirectly, *against* totalitarianism and *for* democratic Socialism, as I understand it'.[16]

NOTES

1. Sonia Orwell and Ian Angus, *The Collected Essays, Journalism and Letters of George Orwell*, (CEJL) Volume IV Harmondsworth: Penguin, 1970), p. 564.
2. Bernard Crick, *George Orwell, A Life*, (London: Secker & Warburg, 1980), p. 102.
3. George Orwell, *The Road To Wigan Pier* in Orwell (London: Secker & Warburg, 1980), p. 223.
4. Gordon Brown, *Maxton* (Edinburgh and London: Mainstream Publishing, 2002), p. 182.
5. Orwell and Angus, *CEJL* Vol. III *The English People*.
6. Op. cit, p. 29.
7. Brown, *Maxton*, p. 302.
8. *CEJL IV*, p. 192.
9. *CEJL III*, p. 432.
10. *CEJL IV*, p. 355.
11. John Rodden, *George Orwell, An After Life* (Wilmington: ISI Books, 2003), p. 175.
12. *CEJL IV*, p. 471.
13. *CEJL IV*, p. 539.
14. *CEJL II*, p. 265.
15. George Orwell, 'Will Freedom Die With Capitalism?' *The Left News* (April 1941), p. 1683.
16. *CEJL III*, 'Why I Write', p. 28.

9

JOHN NEWSINGER

Orwell, anti-Semitism and the Holocaust

In May 1949, the American journal, *Partisan Review*, carried a contribution by George Orwell to the controversy surrounding the award of the Bollingen Prize for Poetry to Ezra Pound earlier that year. Pound's fascist sympathies, his violent anti-Semitism and his wartime collaboration inevitably called into question the judges' decision so soon after the war. In his contribution, Orwell argued that as far as he was concerned if Pound's poetry was judged deserving of the prize then it should be awarded to him regardless of his politics. Nevertheless, he went on to insist that 'one ought to keep Pound's career in memory and not feel that his ideas are made respectable by the mere fact of winning a literary prize'. Pound, he pointed out, was 'an ardent follower of Mussolini . . . and never concealed it'. His embrace of fascism was quite open and unashamed, although Orwell believed that his underlying motivation was, in fact, hatred of Britain and the United States, and more particularly, of 'the Jews'. Pound's wartime broadcasts for fascist Italy 'were disgusting' and Orwell remembered 'at least one in which he approved the massacre of the East European Jews and "warned" the American Jews that their turn was coming presently'. If the murder of the Jews 'in the gas vans' had still been going on, then the decision to award Pound the prize would have been 'undesirable', but this was no longer the case. If the judges believed Pound's poetry worthy of the prize then he should receive it, but, Orwell went on, they should have stated 'more firmly' that Pound's political opinions were 'evil'. The very deliberate use of the word 'evil' here is quite unusual in Orwell's writings. He made the point in an aside that he personally thought Pound's poetry 'entirely spurious'.[1]

This was one of the last pieces for publication that Orwell ever wrote (the *Complete Works* includes only two subsequent book reviews). What it makes clear is both his quite uncompromising hostility towards anti-Semitism and, it will be argued here, his failure to comprehend the enormity, the significance, of the Holocaust. If he had grasped its full meaning, his attitude to Pound's prize would have been considerably more robust and the attempt (largely successful) to rehabilitate the fascist poet would have been more forcefully condemned. How did he arrive at this paradoxical position?

The young Eric Blair grew up in an environment where anti-Semitism was very much an accepted cultural attitude. This anti-Semitism consisted, in the main, of the adoption and use of vicious stereotypes and did not necessarily involve support for discrimination, let alone persecution. Indeed, it was not incompatible with having Jewish friends who did not, of course, fit the supposed stereotype, or even with being opposed to discrimination and persecution. Nevertheless, it is still legitimate to describe it as anti-Semitism, even if only of a mild kind, and its ability to wound and offend has to be acknowledged. The emergence of political anti-Semitism in the shape of Fascism in Britain and in Europe in the 1930s, together with his own commitment to the left, led George Orwell, as the young Eric Blair had become, to question the anti-Semitic prejudices that he had earlier embraced. The outbreak of war in September 1939 led to a more full-blooded confrontation with anti-Semitism in Britain and also to an encounter with the Nazis' mass murder of European Jews. While Orwell's engagement with anti-Semitism on the Home Front has to be seen as a commendable attempt at understanding, his encounter with the Holocaust was more problematic. Although he was, as we shall see, more aware than most people in Britain of the scale of Nazi crimes against the Jews, nevertheless a good case can be made that he never understood their significance. He was certainly not alone in this. What is striking in Orwell's case, however, is the contrast between the considerable and to a large extent successful effort he put into understanding the Stalin regime's crimes and his failure to make a similar effort with regard to the Hitler regime's crimes.[2]

More controversial perhaps is his opposition to Zionism which inevitably brought accusations, even from friends, that he remained tainted by his earlier anti-Semitism. This was not the case. His hostility to Zionism derived from his anti-Imperialism and cannot be seriously considered as evidence that he remained in any way an anti-Semite. On one occasion he was to criticise some Zionists for being anti-Semites turned upside down for their claim that there was no place for Jews in European countries. The other side of his opposition to Zionism was that Jewish refugees should be welcomed in Britain.[3]

What a consideration of Orwell provides us with is a useful case study of a middle-class socialist grappling with the problem of anti-Semitism in the 1930s and 1940s, a case study that reveals both strengths and weaknesses. This is a somewhat neglected area in the otherwise crowded area of Orwell Studies. Melvyn New's 'Orwell and Antisemitism: Toward 1984' that appeared in *Modern Fiction* in 1975, David Walton's essay 'George

Orwell and Antisemitism' that appeared in the journal *Patterns of Prejudice* in 1982, and most recently Kristen Bluemel's 'St George and the Holocaust' that appeared in *Literature Interpretation Theory* in 2003 standing virtually alone. The discussion here is a complement to these contributions.[4]

Orwell's most graphic and offensive use of anti-Semitic stereotypes occurs in *Down and Out in Paris and London*, published in January 1933, at a time when the Nazis were in the process of taking power in Germany. Here, Orwell reports his White Russian friend Boris's anti-Semitism with a certain relish, in particular his tale of the old Jew who tried to sell his own daughter. This, according to Boris, was 'the Jewish national character for you' and he boasted about how in the Tsarist Army before the Revolution, 'we thought the Russian officer's spittle was too precious to be wasted on a Jew'. The uncritical reporting of such sentiments would have been unthinkable in Orwell's later writings, informed as they were by the rise of Nazism. A good case can be made, however, that they should have been unthinkable at the time he wrote them. It is inconceivable that he was not aware of Tsarist persecution of the Jews, of the pogroms of the 1880s and 1900s, of the wholesale massacre of Russian Jews carried out by the White Armies during the Russian Civil War. Such an awareness would surely have given pause to someone who did not share some of Boris's prejudices. This is certainly not to say that Orwell condoned in any way Tsarist atrocities, but rather that he did not connect them with his own attitudes. One suspects a Jewish reader would not have found a White Russian's anti-Semitism so colourful, so amusing. The point as far as Orwell is concerned is that if he had made the connection, he would have taken a completely different attitude towards Boris's anti-Semitism. This is not to condone Orwell's own anti-Semitism, but rather to understand how he was able to go beyond it. Elsewhere he uncritically endorses the force of the proverb: 'Trust a snake before a Jew and a Jew before a Greek, but don't trust an Armenian'. Immature politics and literary inexperience combined in his recourse to offensive stereotypes.

Also helpful in this respect is the episode, recounted in *Down and Out*, of a personal encounter with a Jewish shopkeeper. It would, he remarks, 'have been a pleasure to flatten the Jew's nose, if only one could have afforded it'. Of course, this is not the only occasion where Orwell considers the merits of assaulting someone. Indeed, in *Down and Out*, he actually writes of having to use his fists to get 'common civility' from waiters when he was working as a *plongeur*. Nevertheless, taken out of context, the sentiments expressed here would have fitted quite comfortably in the publications of the British Union of Fascists (BUF).[5] Indeed, one cannot help feeling that it was, at least in part, an awareness of this (the BUF was established in 1932) that led Orwell to abandon the use of anti-Semitic stereotypes and to begin an examination of the nature of anti-Semitism. Orwell came close to acknowledging as much himself in a letter to Julian Symons, written after the War. Here he discusses T. S. Eliot's 'antisemitic remarks' of the 1920s, playing down their significance. If they had been made 'after the persecutions began they would have meant something different'. This was surely meant to apply to his own early anti-Semitic failings in this respect as well. His argument is not particularly convincing and amounts to little more than special pleading. Indeed he accompanies it with a quite outrageous attempt to equate prejudice against the British or the Americans with anti-Semitism, arguing that unless they were accompanied by persecution they were not important. He made the point that if six million Englishmen had 'recently been killed in gas vans', then anti-English jokes would take on a completely different complexion. What made the difference was the act of persecution. Prejudices of this kind were, Orwell argued, 'ridiculous', but they were not really important if people were 'not being persecuted'. The trouble with this commonsense argument is that it ignored the history of persecution, discrimination and massacre that Jews have endured, a history that even before the Holocaust made anti-Semitism something very different from dislike of Americans or the British. Orwell did not recognise the extent to which anti-Semitism had made the Holocaust possible. He displayed a similar blindspot in his discussion of another 'block' of people, insisting that dislike of 'Negroes' while obviously ridiculous in itself was similarly of no importance without persecution. Once again this apparent commonsense argument only worked by ignoring the history of slavery, racism and Imperialism. And this from someone who was both an anti-racist and an anti-Imperialist.[6] What we see in the course of the 1930s is Orwell abandoning the use of anti-Semitic stereotypes in his writing, in response to the coming to power of the Nazis in Germany and to a lesser extent, to the activities of the BUF in Britain. What we do not see, however, is any serious attempt to understand the phenomenon. Arguably, this is part of a larger lacuna in Orwell's thinking: his failure to engage intellectually with Fascism. This is not to suggest that Orwell was in any way half-hearted in his opposition to Fascism or had any secret sympathy for that cause. Indeed, such a contention would be ridiculous in view of his journey to Catalonia to fight against Fascism, gun in hand. From this point of view, he is very much what in the United States would have been described as a 'premature anti-fascist'. His experiences in Spain, however, convinced him that the more urgent task was to 'spill the Spanish beans' with regard to the role of the Communists. He came back from Spain determined to expose Comintern activities during the Civil War and as a corollary to this to come to some sort of understanding as to why, very much against his expectations, the Communists had behaved as they had. For Orwell, 'the Russian Question' was to become the dominant political concern. He invested considerable effort in developing an understanding of what had gone wrong with the Russian Revolution, what sort of society the Soviet Union had become, and what expectations one could have about that country and its admirers. To a considerable extent, Orwell took hostility to Fascism for granted and consequently felt under no pressing obligation to find out more about it. People on the left did not have any illusions about Hitler, but they did have considerable illusions about Stalin. This was his starting point. To some extent, this neglect of Fascism on his part was made easier by the belief that he came to share towards the end of the 1930s that the Soviet Union and Nazi Germany were beginning to converge, that they were becoming similar kinds of society, some sort of bureaucratic collectivism. This is, of course, the notion that informs *Nineteen Eighty-Four*.

What was pressing in the late 1930s as far as Orwell was concerned was the debate about how best to fight Fascism. On his return from Spain, he made clear on numerous occasions his opposition to the Popular Front strategy. This was, he believed, mistaken for a number of reasons. Firstly, while the Communists might have been opposed to Fascism, once in positions of influence and power they would themselves proceed to establish a police state with all the paraphernalia of torture chambers, concentration camps and secret executions. They would suppress without any discrimination their opponents on both the left and the right. As far as he was concerned, this was the 'real' lesson of Spain. The Communists were not unreliable allies, as many on the left believed, they were not allies at all. And second, he believed that while Fascism might be a real danger in Britain, the threat did not come from the BUF (on one occasion he described Mosley as 'a red herring in a black shirt'), but from some sort of 'slimy Anglicized form of Fascism' which would be introduced incrementally with Communist support in the event of war with Germany. This particular aspect of his thinking was, of course, to collapse with the conclusion of the Hitler-Stalin pact and the actual outbreak of war in 1939.[7]

No more dramatic demonstration of both the strengths and weaknesses of Orwell's understanding of Fascism need be provided than the review of Hitler's *Mein Kampf* that he contributed to the *New English Weekly* during the so-called 'Phoney War' in March 1940. First of all, he noted that when the edition under review first appeared Hitler was still 'respectable' and that consequently the book had been edited from a 'pro-Hitler angle' with its 'ferocity' toned down and its author presented 'in as kindly a light as possible'. This was when he was still seen as the man who had smashed the German labour movement rather than as the man who threatened the British Empire. Times had changed. He went on to acknowledge that the Nazis had been 'financed by the heavy industrialists' in Germany, but made the important point that Hitler had already 'talked a great movement into existence'. He put this down to 'the attraction of his own personality' in conditions of mass unemployment. Orwell confessed that personally he had 'never been able to dislike Hitler'. He would certainly be prepared to kill him if the opportunity arose but not from any personal animosity. Indeed, he regarded Hitler as some sort of victim wreaking vengeance. One of his great political strengths was that he had realised that people did not *only* want comfort, but also wanted 'at least intermittently . . . struggle and self-sacrifice, not to mention drums, flags and loyalty parades'. As for Hitler's ambitions, judging from *Mein Kampf*, they amounted to establishing 'a horrible brainless empire, in which, essentially, nothing ever happens except the training of young men for war and the breeding of endless cannon-fodder'. What is missing from this mixture of insight and obfuscation is any mention of Hitler's anti-Semitism or of the Nazis' persecution of the Jews. The Nuremburg Laws, the Crystal Night pogrom, the expulsion of tens of thousands of Jews from Germany, all go unmentioned. This is really quite extraordinary at the time, let alone in the light of subsequent events.[8]

One possible reason for this reticence was the fear that to dwell on the Nazis' persecution of the Jews would strengthen the hand of those who argued that the war was a Jews' war. This seems most unlike Orwell, who certainly never displayed such sensitivity when tackling 'the Soviet myth'. His review of John MacMurray's book, *The Clue of History*, that appeared in *The Adelphi* in February 1939, suggests that this might have been a concern, however. Here, Orwell challenged MacMurray's contention that there was a 'Jewish consciousness' that had persisted since Biblical times. How much, he asked, did a modern Jew, say a New York lawyer, really have in common with a Bronze Age nomad. The idea was highly suspect. But more than that, MacMurray identified this 'Jewish consciousness' as the source of progress in western societies, of progress that would inevitably culminate in the triumph of Communism. Orwell dismissed this as so much mysticism. While there had always been Jews in the Socialist movement, socialism could not be characterised as a Jewish movement. More particularly, he argued, Russian Communism was certainly not Jewish, as was shown by the considerable reluctance of Jewish refugees to actually go there. More to the point, the logic of MacMurray's argument was that Hitler's belief in a Jewish threat to society that had come down the ages was actually true. Hitler had stumbled on one of the great motive forces of history, 'the Jewish consciousness', but whereas he considered it to be evil, MacMurray proclaimed it to be good. This was very dangerous territory, Orwell wrote. You could not fight Hitler by turning his arguments on their head. Indeed, to say with whatever caveats that Hitler was right about the Jewish threat was 'simply to encourage anti-Semitism'. He went on: 'This is the worst possible moment for airing theories about "the Jews" as a mysterious and from a western point of view, sinister entity'. The way to fight anti-Semitism was to continually 'remind people that Jews are human beings before they are Jews'. This, in itself, is a suspect formulation that can almost be read as 'they might be Jews but they are still human'. Nevertheless, this was Orwell striving to find a way to oppose anti-Semitism. He made clear that the 'evil results' of theories such as MacMurray's, however well-meaning, were such that even if there were any possibility of their being true, which he thought unlikely, they should still not be put forward. They would only strengthen the Nazis. Orwell put his own undeveloped thoughts on the origin of anti-Semitism, on 'the truth about the Jews', in the same review: 'because in the past they have been persecuted and have followed the oriental practice of not intermarrying with foreigners, they were just different enough from their neighbours to be unpopular and to make useful scapegoats'. Orwell was certainly opposed to anti-Semitism, but not even his greatest and most uncritical admirer could seriously claim he understood it.[9]

What focused Orwell's attention more directly on the problem of anti-Semitism was the danger that it posed on the Home Front and the terrible fate of the European Jews at the hands of the Nazis. The best source for the development of his thinking during the war is provided by the 'London Letters' that he wrote for the American journal, *Partisan Review*. He despatched no less than 15 of these across the Atlantic between the start of 1941 and the summer of 1946. They were written for a journal that he felt close to politically and that incidentally had a large readership among New York's Jewish intelligentsia. His contributions to *Partisan Review* are of particular importance.[10]

In his January 1942 'Letter', he considered whether or not British xenophobia was in decline. Although he acknowledged that many people might disagree with him, he thought it was. Whereas before the War, the trade unions had been hostile to and instrumental in preventing any 'big influx of human Jewish refugees', now he thought the situation had improved. There was not the same 'scramble for jobs' there had been in the inter-war years and there was more 'personal contact'. Nevertheless, Orwell still recognised that there was 'a certain amount of anti-Semitism . . . pockets of it, not violent but pronounced enough to be disquieting'. He went on:

> The Jews are supposed to dodge military service, to be the worst offenders on the Black Market, etc., etc. I have heard this kind of talk even from country people who had probably never seen a Jew in their lives. But no one actually

wants to do anything to the Jews, and the idea that the Jews are responsible for the war never seems to have caught on with the big public, in spite of the efforts of the German radio.[11]

A year later in a 'Letter' that reluctantly acknowledged that 'the forces of reaction have won hands down' in British domestic politics, Orwell still argued that while anti-Semitism certainly persisted, there was 'no sign that it is growing'.[12]

By the time his 'London Letter' appeared in the July–August 1943 issue of *Partisan Review*, Orwell had changed his mind on this last point. Anti-Semitism, he now believed, was becoming a 'problem': 'I said in my last letter that it was not increasing, but now I think it is'. The good thing was that 'everyone is very conscious of it and it is discussed interminably in the press'. According to Orwell, in England before the War, the middle class would 'laugh at Jews and discriminate against them to some extent', but it was only among the working class that you would 'find the full-blown belief in the Jews as a cunning and sinister race who live by exploiting Gentiles'. It was, he went on, a 'fearful thing' to still hear a working man, after all that had happened in the last ten years, say 'Well I reckon 'itler done a good job when 'e turned 'em all out'. What he thought was happening now was that this particular kind of anti-Semitism was spreading to the middle class. Anti-Semitic comments were always prefaced with 'Of course I don't want you to think I'm anti-Semitic, but. . . '. This would be followed by accusations that Jews evaded military service, were active in the Black Market or even pushed to the front of queues. 'People', he wrote, 'dislike the Jews so much that they do not want to remember their suffering'. The problem was not that there was going to be some sort of anti-Semitic outbreak in Britain: 'no one wants to have pogroms and throw elderly Jewish professors into cesspools'. Instead he described British anti-Semitism as 'milder' but still

> cruel in an indirect way, because it causes people to avert their eyes from the whole refugee problem and remain uninterested in the fate of the surviving Jews of Europe. Because two days ago a fat Jewess grabbed your place on the bus, you switch off the wireless when the announcer begins talking about the ghettoes of Warsaw; that is how people's minds work nowadays.[13]

There is much to recommend Orwell's discussion of anti-Semitism in his 'London Letters', remembering, of course, that they were not academic treatises, but political journalism written by a seriously overworked individual in wartime. He was worried by the persistence of the phenomenon and by what he believed by the summer of 1943 to be its expansion. The apparent lack of sympathy with the plight of the European Jews clearly disturbed him, although it has to be questioned whether the 'fat Jewess' on the bus is an adequate explanation. Because his understanding of anti-Semitism was inadequate, even though he was completely opposed to it, he inevitably came back to the belief that somehow the conduct of some Jews was helping to sustain it.

What did Orwell know of the persecution and massacre of European Jews at this time? Between August 1941 and November 1943 he worked for the BBC, writing, among other things, news commentaries that were broadcast to the Far East (India, Malaya and Indonesia). On 12 December 1942, Orwell read a commentary written by himself that dealt mainly with news from North Africa and the Pacific but ended with a rehearsal of the Nazi persecution of the Jews that is worth quoting at length:

> The Polish Government has just published the evil facts about the systematic massacre of the Jews in German-occupied Poland. The Polish Government's statement is not propaganda. It is verified from many sources, including the pronouncements of the Nazi leaders themselves. For instance, in March of this year Himmler, the head of the Gestapo, issued a decree calling for the 'liquidation' – remember that in totalitarian language liquidation is a polite name for murder – of 50 per cent of the surviving Polish Jews. It seems as if his programme is being carried out successfully. The Polish Government's figures show that of something over 3 million Jews living in Poland before the war, well over a third – that is well over one million human beings – have been killed in cold blood or died of starvation and general misery. Many thousands of them, men, women and children, have been deported to Russian territory, sealed up in cattle trucks without food or water for journeys that may take weeks, so that when the trucks were opened sometimes half the people inside were dead. This policy, which Hitler himself has proclaimed over and over again as his chosen one in speeches both before and after the war, is carried out wherever the Nazis are in control.[14]

In his broadcast the following week, he returned to this theme, noting the way Nazi crimes had 'caused the most profound horror all over the world'. The British government, he went on, had promised 'that after the war those responsible for these cold-blooded massacres will be punished'. He reported the possibility that Jewish children might be evacuated from occupied Europe and hoped that they would be welcomed in Britain. This would show 'that the people of this country have not forgotten what cause they are fighting for'.[15] He was not too confident of this because that same day he wrote to R. R. Desai urging that the evacuation of a large number of Jewish children from Europe should not be represented 'as a sort of Jewish invasion of other countries'. They had to make clear 'what sort of persecution of the Jews has been going on during recent weeks in Poland and other places'. Even so far as broadcasting to the Far East was concerned, 'the subject of Jews is full of thorns'.[16]

Orwell returned to this subject in his broadcast of 27 February 1943. He discussed Hitler's speech on the anniversary of the foundation of the Nazi Party that year, a speech that consisted in the main of 'ravings against the Jews'. The Fuhrer made quite clear 'that he intended to kill off every Jew in Europe – he said this quite plainly'. The point was not explored further.[17]

What is clear from this is that as early as December 1942 Orwell knew that a terrible massacre was being carried out by the Nazis in Poland and the Soviet Union, a massacre on an unprecedented scale. Even so, he had no idea of the full horror of what was underway or, of course, of what was still to come. He was aware though that even in broadcasts to the Far East, focusing on Nazi crimes against the Jews, involved difficulties. More importantly, it is the contention here that although he 'knew' that the Nazis were attempting to exterminate Europe's Jews, he along with most others at the time (including many British Jews) did not have the conceptual apparatus to comprehend the nature of the crime. He never got beyond regarding it as a particularly large-scale pogrom. We shall return to this.

Orwell's most sustained discussion of anti-Semitism is contained in an article that he published in the *Contemporary Jewish Record* in April 1945 that was entitled appropriately enough, 'Anti-Semitism in Britain'. This piece is obviously the result of considerable thought. He starts out by insisting that there is no 'real Jewish problem' in Britain. There are only some 400,000 Jews in Britain and their wealth and influence were not such as to distinguish them from the rest of the population. Despite this, there was a pervasive anti-Semitism that, he insisted, had got worse during the War. This anti-Semitism was 'irrational', a 'neurosis' and consequently not amenable to reason. He makes the important point, a point absent from his earlier discussions, that when people accuse Jews of specific offences, for example, 'bad behaviour in food queues', in fact 'it is obvious that these accusations merely rationalize some deep-rooted prejudice'. Moreover, it was absolutely useless and often counter-productive to try to counter this prejudice 'with facts and statistics'. One consequence of the War was that anti-Semitism was not respectable, but all this meant was that it went disguised. He described an intercession service on behalf of Polish Jews that was held in a synagogue in St John's Wood in 1943. He knew for a fact that 'some of the men sitting around me in the synagogue were tinged' with anti-Semitism, indeed, one of them was a former BUF member. More to the point perhaps, this showed that even people 'tinged' with prejudice could be appalled by persecution and murder. Of course, 'antisemitism as a fully thought-out racial or religious doctrine has never flourished in England' so that there was never any serious danger of anti-Semitic pogroms or legislation. Nevertheless, the prejudice persisted and he believed it important to investigate and understand it.

What of the origins of anti-Semitism? Orwell considered the 'two current explanations', first 'that it is due to economic causes' and second that 'it is a legacy of the middle ages'. He regarded neither as satisfactory, 'although I admit that if one combines them they can be made to cover the facts'. For his part he considered anti-Semitism to be part of 'the larger problem of nationalism which has not yet been fully examined'. One last point is worth making here: Orwell insisted that if anti-Semitism was to be really understood, then it had to be investigated 'by people who know that they are not immune to that kind of emotion'. The investigator had to begin his investigation 'in the one place where he could get hold of some reliable evidence – that is, in his own mind'. The point was important enough to be reiterated: 'it would probably be best to start not by debunking anti-Semitism, but by marshalling all the justifications for it that can be found in one's own mind or anybody else's'. One can safely assume that Orwell considered himself to be one of those who knew they had not been 'immune to that kind of emotion'.[18]

Orwell's own 'Notes on Nationalism' that appeared in the journal *Polemic* in October 1945 did not really carry the argument forward. Part of the problem was his eccentric definition of nationalism which seemed to encompass just about any system of strongly held beliefs. Trotskyism, anti-Semitism, Communism and Pacifism were, for example, all classed as nationalisms. As for his actual discussion of anti-Semitism, it was included under the heading of NEGATIVE NATIONALISMS and really amounted to little more than the observation that there was a 'general conspiracy of silence' concerning the problem that 'probably helps exacerbate it'. Even people on the Left were not immune to anti-Semitism, he observed, probably because Trotskyists and Anarchists 'tend to be Jews'.[19]

Orwell briefly returned to the problems involved in conducting a serious investigation into anti-Semitism in late 1948. In a letter to Julian Symons, he complained of people who went 'round smelling after antisemitism all the time'. Any attempt to understand anti-Semitism was taken as showing sympathy with it. He was sure that his friend, Tosco Fyvel, thought that he was anti-Semitic which, he insisted, was not true. There was, he observed, more rubbish written on the subject than anything else he could think of. A good example of this, he told Symons, was Jean Paul Sartre's new book, *Portrait of the Anti-Semite*. He did not think it would be possible 'to push more nonsense into so short a space'. His review of Sartre's book appeared in the *Observer* newspaper on 7 November 1948. He dismissed it as an exercise 'in casting motes out of other people's eyes', ridiculed Sartre's claim that the working class was immune to anti-Semitism, and concluded that books like this were likely to make anti-Semitism 'slightly more prevalent than before' if anything. As far as Orwell was concerned Sartre was more concerned with condemning anti-Semitism as 'aberrant', as a 'crime', than with understanding it. The book was a product of what he described as 'the uneasy, self-justifying, quisling-hunting period that followed on the Liberation'. While his comment that the book has 'much cerebration' but 'little real discussion of the subject, and no factual evidence worth mentioning' is largely justified, his review is remarkably short on context. Sartre was after all writing from the point of view of experiences very different from Orwell's. France had been occupied, a collaborationist government had introduced anti-Semitic legislation, French Jews had been rounded up by a collaborationist police force, and thousands of them had been brutally murdered by the Nazis. To review Sartre's book without any mention of this was seriously misleading to say the least.[20]

In his article, 'Orwell and Antisemitism: Toward 1984', Melvyn New argued that *Nineteen Eighty-Four* derived 'directly from Orwell's response to, and attempt to explain, what happened to the Jews under Hitler'. Orwell, he went on, produced 'not a fantasy of the future, but a nightmare of his own time, not another anti-Utopia, but a dreadful warning of what human life could become if the meaning of Buchenwald were not comprehended'.[21] This proposition, it will be argued, is completely wrong. Indeed, the contention here is that although Orwell knew the 'facts' of the Holocaust, that six million Jews had been murdered by the Nazis, he never actually understood either the enormity or the significance of the crime. Evidence for this is provided by the fact that Orwell never actually wrote anything specifically about the greatest crime of the twentieth century. If it had been as central as New suggests then there would have been some grappling with the subject in his political journalism. In fact, there is no mention of Auschwitz, Belsen, Buchenwald, no specific discussion of the concentration camps and the gas chambers, no investigation of the genocidal anti-Semitism that informed the Holocaust in his writings. All of his discussion of anti-Semitism was concerned with its 'milder' British form. While he certainly knew about and wholeheartedly condemned the mass murder of European Jews perpetrated by the Nazis, there is just no evidence to show that this was in any way central to his thinking. This is certainly disappointing. What is important to note, however, is that he was not unusual in this at the time. For most people, the murder of the Jews was subsumed into a general awareness of the horrors of Nazi rule in Europe. The Jews were one among numerous groups of victims and this understanding prevailed over any awareness of the Holocaust as something distinct, as something unique. This attitude was shared by many British Jews at the time.[22]

This is not to say that *Nineteen Eighty-Four* was not influenced by Orwell's knowledge of the Nazi regime and its crimes. It clearly was, but this was a subordinate influence. The dominant influence was Orwell's understanding of Stalinism. This was absolutely central to his thinking. Stalinism was Orwell's most important concern from 1936 onwards and there is a striking contrast between the effort that he devoted to understanding the nature of Stalin's tyranny compared with the effort he devoted to Nazism. What is more surprising is that Orwell seems to have been unaffected by the writings of those such as Dwight Macdonald and Hannah Arendt who argued for a different response. He must have read Macdonald's 'The Responsibility of the Peoples' that appeared in the journal *Politics* in March 1945. Macdonald was a friend. Orwell admired *Politics* and on a number of occasions published in it. Similarly it is difficult to believe that he never read Arendt's 'The Concentration Camp' that appeared in *Partisan Review* in July 1948.[23] Once again Orwell wrote for the journal on a regular basis. Nevertheless, there is no evidence that he was affected by their arguments. Disappointing though it might be, the evidence is that Orwell, who was so clear-sighted on so many other issues of the time, never succeeded in comprehending the Holocaust.

NOTES

All references to Orwell's essays, journalism and letters are to Peter Davison's magnificent edition of *The Complete Works of George Orwell*. They are identified by their individual titles.

1. Peter Davison, ed., *Our Job is to Make Life Worth Living 1949–1950*, London 1998, pp. 100–102.
2. For a discussion of the development of Orwell's thinking concerning the Soviet Union see my *Orwell's Politics*, Basingstoke 1999, pp. 110–35.
3. Peter Davison, ed., *It Is What I Think 1947–1948*, London 1998, p. 24.
4. David Walton, 'George Orwell and Antisemitism', *Patterns of Prejudice* 16, 1, 1982, Melvyn New, 'Orwell and Antisemitism: Toward 1984', *Modern Fiction* 21, 1, 1975 and Kristen Bluemel, 'St George and the Holocaust', *Literature Interpretation Theory* 14, 2003.
5. George Orwell, *Down and Out in Paris and London*, London 1984, pp. 18, 33, 65.
6. *It Is What I Think*, op. cit, pp. 460–62.
7. George Orwell, *The Road to Wigan Pier*, London 1986, p. 202.
8. Peter Davison, ed., *A Patriot After All 1940–1941*, 1998, pp. 116–18.

9. Peter Davison, ed., *Facing Unpleasant Facts 1937–39*, London 1998, pp. 327–29. John MacMurray is, of course, often cited as one of the formative intellectual influences on the other Blair, the New Labour Prime Minister.

10. See my *Orwell's Politics*, op. cit, pp. 90–100.

11. Peter Davison, ed., *All Propaganda is Lies 1941–42*, London 1998, p. 109.

12. Peter Davison, ed., *Keeping our Little Corner Clean 1942–43*, London 1998, pp. 292, 296.

13. Peter Davison, ed., *Two Wasted Years 1943*, London 1998, pp. 110–11.

14. *Keeping Our Little Corner Clean*, op. cit, p. 234.

15. Ibid, pp. 244–45.

16. Ibid, pp. 245–46.

17. Ibid, p. 361.

18. Peter Davison, ed., *I Belong to the Left 1945*, London 1998, pp. 64–70.

19. Ibid, pp. 151–52.

20. *It Is What I Think*, op. cit, p. 461.

21. Ibid, pp. 464–65.

22. New, op. cit, pp. 84–85.

23. For Dwight Macdonald see Robert B. Westbrook, 'The Responsibility of Peoples: Dwight Macdonald and the Holocaust', *Holocaust Studies Annual 1*, Greenwood, Florida 1983 and for Hannah Arendt see New, op. cit.

IO

ROBERT CONQUEST

Orwell, Socialism and the Cold War

I

As an observer (and satirist) of realities, Orwell was – reliable. Yet that is too weak a word (though he changed his views on some points, and in any case never posed as an ex cathedra pundit). A man of the Left, our champion in the Cold War, he, better than most of his contemporaries, could take in the phenomena, the actualities.

But theory, or abstraction, was – as Clive James has pointed out – not his forte. What he saw of the injustices of colonial rule was, at a more second-hand level, attributed to imperialist exploitation and the source of comparative Western prosperity – refuted as James points out, by the existence of Sweden, but anyhow untenable on various grounds.

More central to Orwell's work was his view that the poverty and distress he saw in England was attributable to capitalism, and would be cured by the socialist state. So he was indeed a keen advocate of Socialism – though definable (as he put it) as justice and liberty.

But at the same time he had little use for some socialists. His reason was that the idea of justice and liberty had been 'buried beneath layer after layer of doctrinaire priggishness, party squabbles and half-baked "progressivism" until it is like a diamond hidden under a mountain of dung'.[1]

Even worse, 'The underlying motive of many Socialists, I believe, is simply a hypertrophied sense of order. The present state of affairs offends them not because it causes misery, still less because it makes freedom impossible, but because it is untidy . . .'[2]

Again, Orwell comments that this sort of socialist sought

> a set of reforms which 'we', the clever ones, are going to impose upon 'them', the Lower Orders. On the other hand, it would be a mistake to regard the book-trained Socialist as a bloodless creature entirely incapable of emotion. Though seldom giving much evidence of affection for the exploited, he is perfectly capable of displaying hatred – a sort of queer, theoretical, in vacuo

hatred – against the exploiters. Hence the grand old Socialist sport of denouncing the bourgeoisie. It is strange how easily almost any Socialist writer can lash himself into frenzies of rage against the class to which, by birth or by adoption, he himself invariably belongs'.[3]

He added that,

'And this type is drawn, to begin with, entirely from the middle class, and from a rootless town-bred section of the middle class at that'.[4]

And again that

'there is the horrible jargon that nearly all Socialists think it necessary to employ. . . . When an ordinary person hears phrases like 'bourgeois ideology' and 'proletarian solidarity' and 'expropriators' he is not inspired by them, he is merely disgusted. Even the single word 'Comrade' has done its dirty little bit towards discrediting the Socialist movement. How many a waverer has halted on the brink, gone perhaps to some public meeting and watched self-conscious Socialists dutifully addressing one another as 'Comrade,' and then slid away, disillusioned, into the nearest four-ale bar!'[5]

Orwell in fact seems to have wanted socialism on condition that it would not be run by socialists. (We might suggest, if it comes to that, that many citizens, after Enron, would favour capitalism so long as not run by capitalists. Or bureaucracy not run by bureaucrats).

Now, of course, it must be said that no one was as unlike the socialists Orwell had run into than Atlee, Bevin and Morrison. Indeed he – if not uncritically – supported the Labour governments. And the quasi-intelligentsia which he so reviled had fairly little input into their regime.

II

It will be clear, again, that – like Engels! – Orwell was strongly against what he called cranks, though not so much cranks as activist militant cranks.

I will quote briefly from his dramatic description of what he took to be two typical elderly specimens seen on a bus in Letchworth:

'They were dressed in pistachio-coloured shirts and khaki shorts into which their huge bottoms were crammed so tightly that you could study every dimple. Their appearance created a mild-stir of horror on top of the bus. The man next to me, a commercial traveler I should say, glanced at me, at them, and back again at me, and murmured, 'Socialists. . . .' He was probably right – the I.L.P. were holding their summer school at Letchworth. But the point is that to him, as an ordinary man, a crank meant as Socialist and a Socialist meant a crank'.[6]

But to confine ourselves to the generalities of socialism, or of one variety of socialist, would be a simplification. When Orwell saw immediate realities, he had no blockage against them – as with his description of pre-Second World War Liverpool, with the Conservative city council 'ruthless' towards private home ownership and in effect putting through the 'socialist legislation' of 'rehousing from public funds'. Thus, he says 'Beyond a certain point therefore Socialism and capitalism are not easy to distinguish', and in support he notes a fine quarter the other side of the river, built by the Leverhulme soap works.[7]

He thus saw, empirically, (and – as so often with Orwell – against his preconceived generalisations), a tendency: and one whose positive side conflicted with what he came to see (partly under James Burnham's influence) as the possible future development of an anti-popular merger into corporatism, to which it may be said, we are notably vulnerable today.[8]

And if he sometimes saw the emerging, or impending, post-capitalist society as at least probably and potentially benign and socialist in the best sense, he retained his commonsense attitude even to fine-sounding and well-meaning projected Utopias.

Here he is (in his essay on Swift):

> In a Society in which there is no law, and in theory no compulsion, the only arbiter of behaviour is public opinion. But public opinion, because of the tremendous urge to conformity in gregarious animals, is less tolerant than any system of law. When human beings are governed by 'thou shalt not', the individual can 'practise a certain amount of eccentricity: when they are supposedly governed by 'love' or 'reason', he is under continuous pressure to make him behave and think in exactly the same way as everyone else'.[9]

III

Apart from their implicit appeal to reality and commonsense we find Orwell, in his essays on literature, and other themes, seeking humanity and clarity. His output in those fields is hard to categorise. The word 'critic' doesn't seem quite right. 'Humaniser' or 'clarificator' perhaps. And if he has a non-literary point, he does not disguise it. Kipling, for example, is understandably rebuked for his imperialism – but more for the odd outbursts of gutter chauvinism than for the imperialism as such, which, indeed, Orwell notes to be concerned, unlike his critics, with real problems. Anthony Powell wrote that what was often missing in writing on Kipling was his extraordinary 'originality', a claim traditionally confined to a different category of writers, but one which Orwell could see. And in a more political context Orwell's open-mindedness can be seen in his remarks about Churchill, a political enemy – that though the British people rejected his policies, they 'liked' him, and one had to admire in him 'a certain largeness and geniality'.[10]

IV

On Stalinism, though, the really extraordinary thing was not that Orwell was essentially right but that so many Westerners were so spectacularly wrong. Of course there were other voices of sanity – Koestler (though not exactly a Western intellectual), Humphrey Slater, the senior British officer in Republican Spain and editor of *Polemic*. (The British CP had a special meeting devoted to how to handle the problem of Orwell, Koestler and *Polemic*.)

Orwell's main concern was the gullibility of the intelligentsia. How could so many educated minds believe all that fantasy and falsification? The head of the Austrian CP, Ernst Fischer, tells of his later wife asking him how he could have believed that all the leading Old Bolsheviks were Nazi agents. Wasn't it more likely that the lone survivor had faked all that? Fischer found that he couldn't answer.

Orwell's worldwide fame rests of course mainly in this context on his two works of what I suppose should be called political science fiction, *Animal Farm* and *Nineteen Eighty-Four*.

We are often told that Russians and East Europeans could not believe that Orwell had not lived in the Soviet Union. I read *Animal Farm* soon after its publication, and I made a minor contribution to its effect. In Sofia in 1946 or 1947, when I was Press Attaché at the British Legation, I got to know Georgi Andreichin. He had been imprisoned in the USA soon after the First World War, had gone to Moscow a Communist devotee – his name is mentioned in the Kaganovich correspondence recently published by Yale. He was attached to Averell Harriman in the late 1920s when the latter was in Moscow on some commercial project. When Harriman was back in 1941 for the US government he asked after Andreichin. He was by now in a labour camp and it took some time to find him. But he was released, and later joined his friend, the Comintern veteran Vasil Kolarov who, returning to become President of Bulgaria, took Andreichin with him as a chief aide, with the rank of cabinet minister.

He had heard of, and I lent him, *Animal Farm* – which enthralled him. He told me that in his long revolutionary career, all he had been able to accomplish was to nominate his native village as the rural-show place for foreigners – thus giving them a prosperity denied to the rest of the peasantry.

An Orwellian perspective, I agreed. After I left Bulgaria he seems to have disappeared in the Stalinist purge of the local Communist leaders and others – Orwell, alas, again.

It is occasionally denied that *Nineteen Eighty-Four* targeted the Soviet Union. Bernard Williams, editing Orwell, complained about the tendency. But others spoke, even speak, of it as a general satire on tyranny everywhere.

In fact the Stalin regime is identifiable in great specificity. The Unperson was a common Moscow unphenomenon. The 'Spies' are based on the heroic denouncers of parents in the USSR, where the 'sacred and dear' Pavlik Morozov museum rose in the site where this young Stalinist hero had 'unmasked his father' – a recalcitrant peasant who had been shot.

As to Facecrime, an authoritative instruction issued in Moscow runs:

> One must not content oneself with merely paying attention to what is being said for that may well be in complete harmony with the Party programme. One must pay attention also to the manner – to the sincerity, for example, with which a school-mistress recites a poem the authorities regard as doubtful, or the pleasure revealed by a critic who goes into detail about a play he professes to condemn.[11]

The sudden switch of international alliances in the middle of a party orator's speech is modeled on the circumstances of the Nazi-Soviet pact, when some editions of Communist newspapers on the same day accused the Germans of war-mongering in the afternoon, and celebrated them as friends in the evening.

Doublethink is virtually a translation of the Russian 'dvoeverye'. Of dozens of examples which might be given, the most obvious is Soviet elections. Vybor (election) in Russian as in English means 'choice'. The ballot forms contained elaborate instructions on crossing out all but one name. But there never was more than one name . . . or again, 'concentration camp' was changed in Stalin's time, as the camps got more deadly, to 'corrective labour camp': 'joycamp' takes the process further still.

As to the origins of the party, Orwell tells us that lngsoc (like communism) 'grew out of the earlier Socialist movement and inherited its phraseology'; and, while rejecting all that Orwell understands by socialism, 'chooses to do it in the name of Socialism'.[12]

Walter Cronkite, in his preface to *Nineteen Eighty-Four* (1983), suggests (quite contrary to the novel's economic lessons) that 'greater efficiency, ease and security may come at a substantial price in freedom', whereas, of course, Orwell saw that totalitarianism destroys efficiency, ease and security together with liberty, and because of the destruction of liberty.

When Orwell wrote, his main concern, as he makes clear time and again, was less to attack the Stalin regime as such than to combat a whole herd of intellectual quislings at home; to expose the delusions of intellectuals. He remarks, in his 1947 Introduction to the Ukrainian edition of *Animal Farm*, 'I would not have condemned Stalin, and his associates merely for their barbaric and undemocratic methods . . . But on the other hand it was of the utmost importance that people in Western Europe should see the Soviet regime for what it really was', his aim being 'the destruction of the Soviet myth' in Western minds.[13]

When it comes to the future, Orwell predicts the eventual collapse of the Soviet regime. He was strong not only on the lethal falsifications of Stalinism, but also on a phenomenon to be found, and partly out of Sovietophilia, in the British intelligentsia – anti-Americanism, seen not only as political foolishness, but as yet another example of a mulish conditioned reflex. 'To be anti-American nowadays is to shout with the mob. Of course it is only a minor mob, but it is a vocal one . . . But politico-literary intellectuals are not usually frightened of mass opinion. What they are frightened of is the prevailing opinion within their own group. At any given moment there is always an orthodoxy, a parrot-cry which must be repeated, and in the more active section of the Left the orthodoxy of the moment is anti-Americanism'.[14]

Only the intelligentsia could be wrong in the ways Orwell indicts – and this was at a time when universities processed those who had already received a reasonable education. The present decline of the universities has exacerbated a problem that Orwell was also much concerned with – the projection of unreal verbalisations and complexities. Long since validated on communism, Orwell needs to be vigorously promoted in his capacity as a supreme critic, not only politically, of the misuse of language. Some of his targets – J. B. Bernal (the Communist physicist), for example, were consciously lying; they knew what they were doing. Orwell writes of the crypto-Communist M. P. Konni Zilliacus that he was not honest, but he was sincere (though later denounced as a British spy in a Stalinist show trial). Orwell's emphasis was not against them so much as their actions against clarity and reality. He often complained not merely of conscious or unconscious obfuscation, but also of the mere abuse met with in those circles where, as he put it, words like 'red baiter' and 'rabid', were used instead of argument, so that 'if from time to time you express a mild distaste for slave-labour camps or one-candidate elections, you are either insane or actuated by the worst motives'.[15]

Orwell would not have stooped to 'yank-baiters'. Still, he rated 1776 *et seq* higher than 1917/1984.

NOTES

1. Orwell, George. *The Road to Wigan Pier*. Harmondsworth, Middlesex: Penguin Books Ltd. 1974, p. 248.
2. Ibid, p. 211.
3. Ibid, p. 212.
4. Ibid, p. 214.
5. Ibid, p. 255.
6. Ibid, p. 206.
7. Ibid, p. 189.
8. Orwell, George, 'Burnham's View of the Contemporary World Struggle', *New Leader* (New York), 29 March 1947 (in *Collected Essays*, Vol. 4, pp. 313–26).
9. Orwell, George, 'Politics vs Literature – an Examination of *Gulliver's Travels*', *Polemic*, No. 5, September 1946, in *Collected Essays*, Vol. 4, pp. 215–16.
10. Orwell, George, 'Review: *Their Finest Hour*, by Winston S. Churchill', *New Leader* (New York), 14 May 1949, in *Collected Essays*, Vol. 4, p. 494.
11. *Oktyabr*, No. 2, 1949.
12. Orwell, George, *1984*, Chapter 1 of 'The Theory and Practice of Oligarchical Collectivism', passim.
13. Orwell, George, *Collected Essays*, Vol. 3, pp. 404–405.
14. Orwell, George, 'In Defence of Comrade Zilliacus', *Collected Essays*, Vol. 4, pp. 397–98.
15. Ibid, p. 399.

II

MORRIS DICKSTEIN

Animal Farm: history as fable

George Orwell considered *Animal Farm* (1945) his breakthrough, the book which brought together his gifts as a novelist with his commitment as a political writer. '*Animal Farm* was the first book in which I tried, with full consciousness of what I was doing, to fuse political purpose and artistic purpose into one whole', he wrote in his 1946 essay 'Why I Write'.[1] The Spanish Civil War, which began in 1936, turned the storyteller and journalist into a political writer, and the experience of fighting in that war alongside idealistic young Trotskyists and anarchists made him deeply hostile to the Soviet Union. He felt that Stalin had damaged the Republican cause in Spain in his effort to control it, just as he had betrayed the revolution at home. As Orwell saw it, the Soviet Union had become a brutal dictatorship built around a cult of personality and enforced by a reign of terror. He was especially incensed by the apologetics of its Western sympathisers, who felt that the cause of building socialism in a backward country excused many abuses. As he saw it, the rise of totalitarianism in Russia and Germany in the 1930s made his own political commitments inescapable. 'Every line of serious work that I have written since 1936 has been written, directly or indirectly, *against* totalitarianism and *for* democratic socialism, as I understand it'. Above all, he adds, 'what I have most wanted to do throughout the past ten years is to make political writing into an art' (*CEJL*, 1:28).

If *Animal Farm* was a major step forward as political art, it also introduced Orwell to a far wider audience. Before *Animal Farm* his work, published in small radical journals, was largely directed at the left-wing intelligentsia in London and New York. He thrashed the Communists and their liberal allies for failing to acknowledge the simplest truths about Stalin's Russia. Both in his essays, which today are the most respected part of his literary legacy, and in nonfiction books like *Homage to Catalonia* and *The Road to Wigan Pier*, Orwell had carved out a role as the critic of the left from within. Using his own experience as fieldwork for a new kind of participatory journalism, he defended the fundamental ideals of socialism from the misdeeds of those who claimed to speak in its name. This was the context for *Animal Farm*, where he would take on the Russian Revolution and its aftermath in the deceptively simple form of a barnyard fable and satirical allegory.

Partly because it was written at the height of the wartime alliance with the Soviet Union in 1943 and 1944, the book was turned down by a number of British and American publishers, among them Orwell's own publisher, Victor Gollancz. By some editors, including T. S. Eliot at Faber, it was rejected for political reasons: Eliot distrusted Orwell's socialist politics but also thought it was a bad moment to attack the Russians. Other publishers simply failed to get the point. (The Dial Press in New York complained that 'it was impossible to sell animal stories' in the United States. [*CEJL*, 4:138]) Though its publication was seriously delayed in both countries, it became a huge commercial success when it finally appeared, in part because the Cold War followed so quickly on the heels of the Second World War. Thus a book that at first spoke for an anti-Stalinist splinter of the left, a minority within a minority, was quickly projected onto the front lines of the new East-West conflict.

Animal Farm went on to become one of the most widely read books of the twentieth century, selling upwards of twenty million copies. Because it was cast as a fable – brief, effortless to read, and seemingly easy to interpret – it became a favourite text for secondary school, the one literary work that adolescents are almost certain to have studied. But the book's bright clarity and accessibility worked to undermine critical respect. Today Orwell is rightly admired as a superb essayist. There's also a vastly greater critical literature on *Nineteen Eighty-Four* than on *Animal Farm*, though they pursue the same critique of Stalinist totalitarianism by different means. *Nineteen Eighty-Four*, with its terrifying Kafkaesque atmosphere of entrapment, surveillance and extreme psychological pressure, as well as its thrilling account of small pockets of personal resistance in love, language and memory, in the pleasures of everyday life and the residues of intellectual conscience, is seen as a book for grownups, a serious human drama. *Animal Farm*, on the other hand, has been typed as a primer for the uninitiated, a beautifully crafted tale only a few cuts above propaganda. Even Lionel Trilling, whose influential 1952 essay helped define Orwell's image as a postwar cultural figure, described *Animal Farm* as 'overrated'.[2]

It isn't hard to understand why *Animal Farm* has been seen as Orwell Lite, a kind of Totalitarianism for Beginners. The very ingenuity that enabled Orwell to telescope Russian history from 1917 to 1943 into an animal story ensured that it could be seen as a simplified version of a merely topical subject. Orwell's inspiration came as much from the vogue of animated cartoons in the previous decade, featuring Mickey Mouse, Porky Pig and

Donald Duck, as from any literary source. The fables of Aesop or La Fontaine were brief parables attached to pointed morals, timeless and conservative in their wisdom. Only the third and fourth books of *Gulliver's Travels*, a special favourite of Orwell's, provided him with a model for an extended narrative on larger questions of human society. Swift's brilliant reversal of the role of horses and human beings in the fourth book licensed Orwell's transformation of the loutish farmer Jones into the decadent old Czarist regime, with his farm animals as the repressed and finally rebellious common people. Often neglecting to feed his charges, who are truly reduced to beasts of burden, the drunken Mr. Jones is as mean and coarse as one of Swift's Yahoos. Orwell brought to the novel not only a pleasure in nature and a fine feeling for animals and farm life but also a dose of Swiftian misanthropy, looking ahead to a time 'when the human race had been finally overthrown'.[3] When the ruling pigs slip into human ways – walking on two legs, taking up drink, living in houses, sleeping in beds – we genuinely feel they are degrading themselves, falling away from the simpler community of the animal world. Orwell's political allegory is so effective on the literal level that it could be read as a story for children or a polemic on behalf of animal rights.

As tracts against totalitarianism, *Animal Farm* and *Nineteen Eighty-Four* complement one another. Where Orwell's final novel, written when he was already gravely ill, describes a closed world, seemingly immutable, an ice age in which personal freedom is barely a memory, *Animal Farm*, its light-handed predecessor, showed how the initial idealism of the revolution decayed by steps into inequality, hierarchy and finally dictatorship. But cast into the tricky form of a fable, *Animal Farm* manages to raise its readers' consciousness without really moving them at the deepest level. It is complex enough to evoke the rivalry between Stalin and Trotsky and the conflict between 'socialism in one country' and worldwide revolution. It brilliantly mocks many features of the Soviet system but makes little show of explaining how or why they came about.

Modern totalitarian systems make extraordinary use of purges, confessions and show trials, as Stalin's henchmen did in the late 1930s. Along with the Soviets' duplicitous role in Spain, this was one of the turns that convinced Orwell, along with other anti-Stalinists, that the Bolshevik Revolution had been perverted and the Soviet system was rotten. But when the animals rush forward hysterically to confess their nonexistent crimes, and are slain on the spot, Orwell initially does scant justice to that horrendous moment in Soviet history – the purge trials that Arthur Koestler had explored so keenly in 1940 in *Darkness at Noon*. Only at the end of this orgy of violence does the impact tell for animals and readers alike:

And so the tale of confessions and executions went on, until there was a pile of corpses lying before Napoleon's feet and heavy with the smell of blood, which had been unknown there since the expulsion of Jones. . . . These scenes of terror and slaughter were not what they had looked forward to on that night when old Major first stirred them to rebellion.   (74–75)

What moves Orwell here is less the horror itself – which, like everything else in *Animal Farm*, is understated, purified into fable – than the shock of recognition in the minds of simple creatures: the contrast between their bright hopes and the grim realities. But when Clover, the nurturing mare who often serves as the conscience of the book, looks at the scene before her, the old ideals reawaken:

If she herself had had any picture of the future, it had been of a society of animals set free from hunger and the whip, all equal, each working according to his capacity, the strong protecting the weak.

This recollection pushes Orwell outside the frame of his tale, to write almost discursively.

Instead – she did not know why – they had come to a time when no one dared speak his mind, when fierce, growling dogs roamed everywhere, and when you had to watch your comrades torn to pieces after confessing to shocking crimes.

Clover remains faithful even in her incomprehension.

There was no thought of rebellion or disobedience in her mind. She knew that, even as things were, they were far better off than they had been in the days of Jones. . . . But still, it was not for this that she and all the other animals had hoped and toiled. . . . Such were her thoughts, though she lacked the words to express them.   (75–76)

This note of puzzled pride and mute disappointment echoes through the book, reflecting the novel's plebeian viewpoint, as well as the decay of high ideals into the sordid realities of power and betrayal.

But if we ask ourselves *why* these things happened in Russia, if we wonder whether Orwell is saying that *all* revolutions inevitably deteriorate from their egalitarian beginnings, falling under the control of power-hungry elites, the novel ventures no answer. T. S. Eliot, who believed that society required a competent ruling class, complained in a letter to Orwell that since 'your pigs are far more intelligent than the other animals, and therefore the best qualified to run the farm . . . what was needed (someone might argue), was not more communism but more public-spirited pigs'.[4] This is not an issue the book itself could handle. It tells us only how the pigs accumulated power and shows that we remain wilfully obtuse or dishonest if we fail to see it. The very simplicity of the tale, like the bracing directness of Orwell's essays, bolsters his brief against subtle thinking and tortuous rationalisation. The elemental character of the story makes its own case for plain decency and the need to face up to simple truths.

To Orwell, undue subtlety and rationalisation were the occupational hazards of intellectuals, especially political intellectuals. If he were pressed to give us one reason why the Russian Revolution failed, he would undoubtedly have stressed that it was the work of intellectuals, whose theoretical minds, fervently committed to higher goals yet often blinded by self-interest, allowed for behaviour from which most people would instinctively shrink. Writing to the Dickens scholar Humphrey House in 1940, Orwell argued that because Dickens's '*moral* sense was sound he would have been able to find his bearing in any political or economic milieu. The thing that frightens me about the modern intelligentsia is their inability to see that human society must be based on common decency, whatever the political and economic forms may be'. Turning to the situation in Russia, he adds that 'Dickens, without the slightest understanding of Socialism etc., would have seen at a glance that there is something wrong with a régime that needs a pyramid of corpses every few years. . . . All people who are morally sound have known since about 1931 that the Russian régime stinks' (*CEJL*, 1:582–3).

Everywhere in Orwell's letters and essays we find similar gibes at the intelligentsia combined with forceful appeals to decency and truth, the evidence of one's senses. It takes no fancy footwork to know that if something looks bad, if it smells bad, it *is* bad. Most of his remarks dealing with Russia are far harsher than anything in *Animal Farm*, which is not only *about* a society of animals but maintains a naive, wide-eyed tone that reflects their point of view. Though Stalin himself was scarcely an intellectual, the pigs are the 'brain-workers' of this commonwealth, the cadre of intellectuals and bureaucrats who gradually separate themselves from the others and by the end claim full title to the farm. But we never see the farm from the pigs' own viewpoint, only that of the animal community they've come to dominate. In the final scene, the animals peer in through the windows of the farmhouse on a scene in which pigs and men have become indistinguishable, the leaders negotiating (and drinking) with capitalist powers on an equal footing – the last stage of the Revolution in decline.

In his essays Orwell has no difficulty explaining why the influence of intellectuals distorts the ideals with which the revolutionary movement began. 'It was only *after* the Soviet régime became unmistakably totalitarian that English intellectuals, in large numbers, began to show an interest in it', he says, for it came to express 'their secret wish: the wish to destroy the old, equalitarian version of Socialism and usher in a hierarchical society where the intellectual can at last get his hands on the whip' (*CEJL*, 4:212). This is almost a précis of *Animal Farm*, which traces the stages by which equality gives way to hierarchy and concludes, in one of Orwell's inspired touches, with the pigs walking on their hind legs, holding whips in their trotters. But the novel itself, keeping within the bounds of the fable, contains no such fierce accounting of why this comes to pass. Compared to *Nineteen Eighty-Four* or to Orwell's essays, this is a work of wonderfully controlled under-statement – 'A Fairy Story', as its subtitle proposes – in which such factors as the relentless pursuit of power or the motives and behaviour of intellec-tuals are merely implied, never underlined. This mask of naiveté, moulded to the shape of Orwell's plain-man politics, is at once the book's strength and limitation. *Animal Farm* expresses Orwell's sense that the simplest way of looking at things may also be the most honest and accurate. But as the animals are gradually subdued, their hopes betrayed and their common-wealth taken over, the book shows how the simple view can prove altogether ineffective.

Orwell manages to include an astonishing range of political history and an exceptional number of viewpoints within his fable. *Animal Farm* begins with the revolutionary vision of Karl Marx as refined into a speech by the venera-ble old Major, a prize-winning boar nearing the end of his life. He describes his dream that all the animals will someday be free of human oppression, running their own farm on a basis of nonviolent equality. (Once it's been pointed out, we're struck by the resemblance between the patriarchal Marx and a bewhiskered old boar.) Before passing on, he even leaves them with an anthem of their movement, a stirring song called 'Beasts of England' which feeds their revolutionary excitement and helps bind them into a community.

There may be few better socialist primers than this opening chapter. Orwell goes on to dramatise the haphazard way the revolution unfolds, the war that ensues when the neighbours invade, and the exhilarating state of free-dom and comradeship that follows. This was the sense of liberation that excited Wordsworth when he first arrived in revolutionary France in 1790 and Orwell himself in December 1936 when he landed in a part of Spain temporarily controlled by anarchists defending the Spanish Republic. In Barcelona, Orwell wrote, 'it was the first time that I had ever been in a town where the working class was in the saddle'.

> Waiters and shop-walkers looked you in the face and treated you as an equal. Servile and even ceremonial forms of speech had temporarily disappeared. . . . In outward appearance it was a town in which the wealthy classes had

practically ceased to exist. Except for a small number of women and foreigners there were no 'well-dressed' people at all. . . . Above all, there was a belief in the revolution and the future, a feeling of having suddenly emerged into an era of equality and freedom. Human beings were trying to behave as human beings and not as cogs in the capitalist machine.[5]

This is the euphoric atmosphere we encounter in the third chapter of *Animal Farm*:

> The animals were happy as they had never conceived it possible to be. Every mouthful of food was an acute positive pleasure, now that it was truly their own food, produced by themselves and for themselves, not doled out to them by a grudging master. . . . [E]veryone worked according to his capacity. . . . Nobody stole, nobody grumbled over his rations, the quarrelling and biting and jealousy which had been normal features of life in the old days had almost disappeared. (26–27)

Even at the height of his campaign against totalitarianism, Orwell never gave up his belief in the egalitarian socialism outlined by the old Major and briefly achieved at Animal Farm. He saw his attacks on Russia as a way of saving socialism from the travesty of its dark double. In his preface to the Ukrainian edition of *Animal Farm*, he complained of 'the negative influence of the Soviet myth upon the Western Socialist movement'. 'In my opinion', he concluded, 'nothing has contributed so much to the corruption of the original idea of Socialism as the belief that Russia is a Socialist country. . . . And so for the past ten years I have been convinced that the destruction of the Soviet myth was essential if we wanted a revival of the Socialist movement' (*CEJL*, 3:457–58). *Animal Farm* strikes not at the original ideals of the Revolution but at the ways they were taken over and distorted. This has always made it a problematic text for the political right, widely misread during the Cold War as a sweeping anti-Communist polemic. At the conclusion of his 1940 letter to Humphrey House, Orwell wrote that 'my chief hope for the future is that the common people have never parted company with their moral code. . . . I have never had the slightest fear of a dictatorship of the proletariat, *if it could happen*, and certain things I saw in Spain confirmed me in this. But I admit to having a perfect horror of a dictatorship of theorists, as in Russia and Germany' (*CEJL*, 1:583) (emphasis mine).

How and why is the revolution in *Animal Farm* betrayed? Even before Orwell develops the conflict between Napoleon and Snowball, who represent Stalin and Trotsky, he shows us the beginnings of inequality as the serpent within this animal paradise. When the pigs stealthily take first the milk and then the apples for their own mash, they are already emerging as a ruling class, accumulating special prerogatives as if by right. From the beginning, deceit is their weapon of choice. When they send Squealer, their propagandist, to justify what they've taken, it propels them down the road in which small lies lead to big lies, in which early ideals can be revised, even upended, without the admission of any change, and history can be rewritten in the presence of living witnesses. Orwell wisely makes no effort to mimic the rhetoric of the Party or of *Pravda* in Squealer's speeches, but as the front man he epitomises everything dishonest about the new order. When the animals invariably grow confused and go along with each twist and turn of the official line, questioning their own memories, the reader may wonder how much Orwell blames this emerging dictatorship on the threat of force, the amoral cleverness of those who manipulate public opinion, or the innocent stupidity of the masses, who are so easily cowed.

The Marxist critic Raymond Williams, who tried to struggle free of his early debt to Orwell, argued that his very use of animals showed how the book's allegory condescended to the common people in whose name the writer spoke. But as the economic and managerial planning of Snowball gives way to the thuggish violence, coarseness, and sheer animal cunning of Napoleon, the pigs rely more on force and intimidation to secure their position. From its egalitarian beginnings, Animal Farm becomes a state in which, in Orwell's memorable phrase, 'ALL ANIMALS ARE EQUAL BUT SOME ANIMALS ARE MORE EQUAL THAN OTHERS' (114). Gradually the proud communal spirit gives way to a ritual deference to the ossified symbols of the Revolution, such as the skull of the old Major, and blind obedience to the will of the Leader, whose minions continue to speak in the name of the old revolutionary ideals.

There is no single tipping point in the inexorable shift from the genuine equality that marked the early days after the Revolution. Gradually, the privileges and abuses of the old regime are restored in a systematic, tyrannical form – this is what Orwell means by totalitarianism. Each step, beginning with the milk and apples and continuing with the expulsion of Snowball, his demonisation as the source of all trouble, and the harsh response to the hens' protest (loosely based on Trotsky's suppression of the Kronstadt rebellion of young Soviet mariners in 1921), violates some revolutionary principle enshrined in the Seven Commandments. As this shift continues, each commandment is secretly rewritten, confounding the animals who either cannot read or cannot recall precisely what they once said. 'No animal shall drink alcohol' becomes 'No animal shall drink alcohol *to excess*'. 'No animal shall kill any other animal' becomes 'No animal shall kill any other animal *without cause*' (78). The last commandment, 'All animals are equal', is transformed into the memorable phrase quoted above, which foreshadows Newspeak and other linguistic innovations in *Nineteen Eighty-Four*.

At each stage the machinery of propaganda goes hand in hand with the threat of force. The first is personified by the mouthpiece of the system, Squealer, who 'could turn black into white' (16), the second by the blood-thirsty dogs – the secret police – whom Napoleon has secretly trained as instruments of a new reign of terror. Bolstering this oppression is the habit of obedience represented by the sheep, who drown out dissenters as they bleat in unison whatever the current official slogans happen to be. Here Orwell does show how the stupid and the gullible help dictators stage-manage the political system. This is a flaw that may, in Orwell's view, be built into the DNA of mass movements, since it can be traced back to the preaching of the old Major and the already simplified message of the original commandments. The bleating of the sheep, 'Four legs good, two legs bad' (30), has been conceived by Snowball as a rote version of the ideals of the Revolution, boiled down for mass indoctrination. When separated from actual thinking, turned into a mindless chant, the plain style shows its dark side.

Though Orwell may be ambivalent toward the common people, one of the triumphs of *Animal Farm* is the variety of viewpoints he gives them, which correspond beautifully to each family of the animal kingdom. If the sheep represent blind conformity and the high-strung hens are easily agitated, then Boxer the horse stands for the hard work, endurance and patriotic loyalty of the working class, just as Benjamin the donkey, though equally tenacious, remains stoically apart from all utopian ideas. There is perhaps a touch of Orwell himself in this creature's timeless scepticism. What he had said from the beginning he maintains to the end, that 'things never had been, nor ever could be much better or much worse – hunger, hardship, and disappointment being, so he said, the unalterable law of life' (111). It adds immeasurably to the novel for Orwell to include a stubborn nay-sayer like Benjamin or a vain creature like the mare Mollie, who flees the farm and accepts servitude to human masters in return for their care and attention. But *Animal Farm* is written in a form that can also be reductive, as Angus Fletcher showed in his seminal book *Allegory: The Theory of a Symbolic Mode* (1964). Orwell's animals, he says, 'are "types" of human behavior, but by their restriction of character they become so *narrowly* human that they do not have what we usually call "character"'.[6]

Orwell remains conventionally socialist in portraying religion as the black raven of priestcraft, embodied in figures doing no useful work, promising pie in the sky when you die, and faithfully serving whoever happens to be in power. The raven, named after the Hebrew lawgiver, Moses, 'was Mr. Jones's especial pet, was a spy and a tale-bearer, but he was also a clever talker' (17). When the Revolution turns conservative and nationalistic, Napoleon brings the raven back, as Stalin brought back the Russian Orthodox Church. What damns the raven and damns the pigs, for Orwell, is what also damned the farm's human overseers before them: they don't produce anything. Productive labour remains the ultimate test of social value. Reflecting Marx's theory of surplus-value, the old Major says that 'man is the only creature that consumes without producing' (9). Orwell admired the stolid and dull-witted Boxer, the farm's most prodigious worker, despite his unswerving loyalty to Napoleon, for Orwell sees 'brainwork' as almost a contradiction in terms. In place of useful work, it becomes a vehicle for clever people to amass power, exploit others, and play fast and loose with truth and language. There is a strain of classically English anti-intellectualism in Orwell's treatment of those who work with their minds.

By the time he wrote *Nineteen Eighty-Four*, Orwell's critique of the abuses of truth and language would be worked up into his most original blow against totalitarianism. But it was already a rich theme in his best essays and in *Animal Farm*. He saw propaganda as a feature of all modern governments but especially brazen in totalitarian systems, which wholly depended on it. In 'The Prevention of Literature' (1946), he portrays 'organized lying' as a crucial element of totalitarian states, 'not, as is sometimes claimed, a temporary expedient of the same nature as military deception'.

> From the totalitarian point of view history is something to be created rather than learned. A totalitarian state is in effect a theocracy, and its ruling caste, in order to keep its position, has to be thought of as infallible. . . . Totalitarianism demands, in fact, the continuous alteration of the past, and in the long run probably demands a disbelief in the very existence of objective truth.

Orwell treats totalitarianism as the forerunner of what we today think of as postmodern relativism. 'The friends of totalitarianism in this country tend to argue that since absolute truth is not obtainable, a big lie is no worse than a little lie'. He anticipates the distinction that developed in the Soviet Union between the physical sciences and history or the social sciences. 'Already there are countless people who would think it scandalous to falsify a scientific text-book, but see nothing wrong in falsifying a historical fact' (*CEJL*, 4:85–86).

In *Animal Farm* this reliance on deceit is accompanied by reminders that though life under the new system may be hard, though some of the promises of the Revolution may remain unfulfilled, things remain better than they were under Jones. The animals at least have a commonwealth they can call their own, achievements in which they can take collective pride, and a dignity long denied to them. At the frequent celebrations of the Revolution, 'they found it comforting to be reminded that, after all, they were truly their own masters and that the work they did was for their own benefit'. Thus 'they were able to forget that their bellies were empty, at least part of the time' (98). At times Orwell seems to agree with this positive note. He uses the building and rebuilding of the windmill to convey the rapid industrialisation of the Soviet Union even as he mocks Napoleon for taking full credit for it, since it was Snowball's idea to begin with. With Boxer as the tireless engine of industrial growth, Orwell pays tribute to the achievements of the Russian working class even under conditions of totalitarian domination and horrendous errors of leadership.

But gradually, Orwell's position evolves. Boxer has two maxims. The first, 'I will work harder', which he says whenever things go badly, is taken over from Upton Sinclair's socialist novel *The Jungle* (1906). In that book, working harder does the hero no good at all, since the system is fixed against him; his almost superhuman determination keeps him going but also ensures that he'll break down sooner, only to be discarded. And Boxer's second maxim, 'Comrade Napoleon is always right', belongs to the mind-set of obedience to authority that sustains the maximum leader's cult and his dictatorial power. The animals have all been promised a humane retirement; they've been told that after a lifetime of labour and privation, they would be taken care of in their final years. But when Boxer falters and can no longer work, the pigs, behind the usual smokescreen of disinformation, ship him off to the knackers to be boiled down for glue, just as the old Major once warned that Jones would do. This is not only the most poignant scene in the novel; it is the ultimate betrayal that shows up the regime of pigs as no better than the old system. The pathos of the scene is not only for Boxer, whose innocent faith in the new order enables it to use him up and throw him away, but for the working class everywhere, whose hopes for a better world, enshrined in the early chapters, have so often come to naught.

In the last part of the novel, everything comes full circle. Each of the original commandments is systematically violated, then recast in the dead of night to conform to the violation. The pigs move into the farmhouse, sleep in beds, start drinking and wearing clothes, begin negotiating trade agreements with their human adversaries, and walk on their hind legs – all accompanied by ritual professions of faith in the Revolution. In one of Orwell's many brilliant yet understated touches, the pigs drink up the proceeds of Boxer's demise after weeping crocodile tears over his sad fate and adding him to the pantheon of revolutionary saints. Squealer outdoes himself in his tearful account of Boxer's last days and Napoleon himself pays tribute to him. All the genuinely popular expressions of revolution have now been eliminated. The pigs have banned the singing of 'Beasts of England', since the aims of the Rebellion have been accomplished, and finally they restore the farm's feudal title, Manor Farm, ratifying the return to the old system. They reassure their neighbours that the animal republic is no threat to anyone. At times Orwell seems to be looking ahead not only to 1943, when Russia and the West were meeting in Tehran as he was writing, but to 1991, when the Soviet Union was dissolved, predatory capitalism introduced, and cities like Leningrad reverted to their pre-Revolutionary names.

Another drinking scene drives the point home. While Napoleon and his henchmen toast their capitalist neighbours, denying that they ever had any revolutionary designs upon them, 'no one noticed the wondering faces of the animals that gazed in at the window' (116). Napoleon's British counterpart, congratulating the pigs on keeping the lower orders in check, makes the following toast: 'If you have your lower animals to contend with', he says, 'we have our lower classes!' (117–18). Not only have inequality and hierarchy been restored to Animal Farm, but it is exactly the same hierarchy that socialists had challenged in the capitalist states. 'Was not the labour problem the same everywhere?' (117). The Revolution proved to be only a changing of the guard; the animals won the right to be oppressed by their own kind. As an earlier radical, William Blake, put it in his poem 'The Grey Monk': 'The hand of Vengeance found the bed/ To which the Purple Tyrant fled;/ The iron hand crush'd the Tyrant's head/ And became a Tyrant in his stead'.

Though he wrote *Animal Farm* at a time when criticism of our Soviet ally was strongly discouraged in the West, when even Hollywood produced a handful of pro-Soviet films such as *The North Star* and *Mission to Moscow*, Orwell recognised that by the time the book appeared the allies might already have fallen out. He saw this happening already in Tehran. The West's illusions about Stalin could soon be dispelled. But he could hardly have imagined how his book might be pressed into service in the Cold War. By the early 1950s, the CIA even helped to fund a full-length animated version of *Animal Farm*, which eliminated several characters and gave Orwell's fable a happy ending – the animals rebel against their new masters.

The weakness of Orwell's tale was not that it could so easily be distorted but that it was written in the mode of allegory, which, as William Empson reminded Orwell, was a form that, if effectively done, was prone to quite different interpretations and could take on meanings of its own. In the light of Orwell's emphasis on straight talking, it's ironic that his two most influential works should be built on elaborate metaphors – futuristic exaggeration in one case, childlike allegory in the other. Empson told Orwell that his young son Julian, 'the child Tory', was delighted with the book; he had gleefully read it as 'very strong Tory propaganda', which was not exactly what the writer had intended. 'It is a form that inherently means more than the author means, when it is handled sufficiently well'.[7] Like *Nineteen Eighty-Four*, *Animal Farm* is a thesis-novel whose thesis has been claimed by different schools of thought, yet its basic message is clear. If part of Orwell's case against totalitarianism rests on its reliance on propaganda, *Animal Farm* could be seen as counter-propaganda, pursued in the name of decency and truth rather than power. It shows how an initial idealism can turn into exploitation and how ordinary people can lose their freedom in small incremental steps. The Soviet Union may be history but its techniques for amassing power and channelling the popular will have only been refined. *Animal Farm* belongs to a literature of argument, a committed literature that means to make a difference in the world, yet it still resonates long after the system that occasioned it has passed from the scene.

NOTES

1. *The Collected Essays, Journalism and Letters of George Orwell*, 4 vols., eds. Sonia Orwell and Ian Angus (1968; Harmondsworth: Penguin, 1970), 1:29. [Hereafter cited in text as *CEJL* by volume and page number.]
2. Lionel Trilling, 'George Orwell and the Politics of Truth' (1952), *The Opposing Self* (New York: Viking Press, 1955), p. 157.
3. George Orwell, *Animal Farm: A Fairy Story* (1945; Harmondsworth: Penguin, 1951), p. 28. [Hereafter cited by page number in parenthesis.]
4. Quoted in *Understanding Animal Farm*, ed. John Rodden (Westport, CT: Greenwood Press, 1999), p. 126. See also Bernard Crick, *Orwell: A Life* (1980; Harmondsworth: Penguin, 1982), pp. 456–59.
5. George Orwell, *Homage to Catalonia* (1938; Boston: Beacon Press, 1955), pp. 4–6.
6. Angus Fletcher, *Allegory: The Theory of a Symbolic Mode* (Ithaca: Cornell University Press, 1964), pp. 339–40.
7. Quoted in Crick, *Orwell: A Life*, pp. 491–92.

12

Nineteen Eighty-Four: context and controversy

Nineteen Eighty-Four is misread if not read in the context of its time –
around 1948: a postwar world brutally and arbitrarily divided into spheres
of influence by the great powers; the atom bomb exploded; and the fictive
London of Winston Smith a recognisable caricature of the actual postwar
London that Orwell had walked, and that this author can vividly remember.
And three common misreadings can be challenged on biographical evidence.
Firstly, *Nineteen Eighty-Four* was not his last will and testament: it was
simply the last book he wrote before he happened to die. Secondly, it was not
a work of unnatural intensity dashed off hastily by a man choked with a sub-
conscious death-wish and regressing while writing the novel to childhood
memories of his preparatory school (as some claim is demonstrated by his
essay on school days, 'Such, Such Were the Joys' – as if the world of Stalin
and Hitler did not exist). Thirdly, the book does not represent a repudiation
of his democratic socialism as so many American reviewers assumed; for he
continued to write for the *Tribune* and American left wing journals right up
to his final illness, during the time of the composition of *Nineteen Eighty-
Four*.[1]

   Yet for someone who consciously sought to become the master of the plain
style, and is famous for it, it is astonishing how many varied interpretations
have been put upon *Nineteen Eighty-Four* – the most famous of his works,
although I think not his best. It has been read as deterministic prophecy,
as a kind of science fiction or a dystopia, as a conditional projection of the
future, as a humanistic satire on contemporary events, as a total rejection of
socialism of any kind, and as a libertarian socialist – almost an anarchist –
protest against totalitarian tendencies and abuses of power both in his own
and in other possible societies. Most bad or partial readings occur through
not grasping the context of the time – the immediate postwar period.

   It may help if we write it out, as it was first published in London, as indeed
a title, 'Nineteen Eighty-Four', and not as a date – 1984 – as it is too often
rendered. For it is not a prophecy, it is plainly a satire and a satire of a

particular, even a peculiar kind – a Swiftian satire. Reading it when it first appeared, or now, we should no more expect the future to be quite like that than when reading Swift's *Gulliver* we should expect to find the islands of Lilliput or Brobdingnag – although when we look around us we see on every side little men and women pretending to be great and all powerful; and big men and women regardlessly or carelessly treading on smaller folk.

Satiric Rage

So much for generality and genre, but if we look at the time it was written we find some specific objects of satire, targets for his Swift-like rage, as well as enduring matters. He wrote to his publisher criticising a first draft of a blurb:

> It makes the book sound as though it were a thriller mixed up with a love story, and I didn't intend it to be primarily that. What it is really meant to do is to discuss the implications of dividing the world up into 'Zones of influence' (I thought of it in 1944 as a result of the Tehran Conference), and in addition by parodying them the intellectual implications of totalitarianism.[2]

This is very specific. But it is not, of course, a full statement of his intentions or targets of 'parody' or satire. A close reading of the text suggests seven broad satiric themes.

(i) The division of the world at Tehran by Stalin, Roosevelt and Churchill.

(ii) The mass media and proletarisation (what we now call dumbing-down).

(iii) Power-hunger and totalitarianism – those who believe in 'power for the sake of power' are not just condemned morally by the satirist but, in the portrayal of O'Brien, shown to be driven mad by power-hunger.

(iv) The betrayal of the intellectuals: all those portrayed in the Outer Party who prostitute their talents for propaganda and are too fearful for their lives (or in reality, their jobs) to challenge the Inner Party (the boss).

(v) The debauching of language in the drive towards Newspeak so that criticism of the party would become linguistically impossible (but note from the last sentence of the Appendix on Newspeak that the project has had to be delayed until 2050: the satirist implies that demotic language and literature cannot be controlled).

(vi) The destruction by the Ministry of Truth of any objective history and truth – again a satiric exaggeration of how historical figures like Trotsky and Bukharin had simply vanished both from the Soviet historical and even photographic archives.

(vii) James Burnham's once well-known thesis of convergence between communism and capitalism via managerialism – that neither capitalism nor
communism would win out but that their managers would develop a
common culture.[3]

Perhaps there were too many different themes to be easily contained in
one narrative, which helps to account for so many varying interpretations. A
multi-layered satire can stir some profound but none-the-less myopic reactions. Czeslaw Milosz, the Polish poet and writer, wrote in 1953 in his *Captive
Mind*, having only recently defected from the Communist Party:

> Because [*Nineteen Eighty-Four*] is both difficult to obtain and dangerous to
> possess, it is known only to certain members of the Inner Party. Orwell fas-
> cinates them through his insight into details they know well, and through his
> use of Swiftian satire. Such a form of writing is forbidden by the New Faith
> because allegory, by nature manifold in meaning, would trespass beyond the
> prescriptions of socialist realism and the demands of the censor. Those who
> know Orwell only by hearsay are amazed that a writer who never lived in
> Russia should have understood the functioning of the unusually constructed
> machine of which they are themselves a part. Orwell's grasp of their world
> astounds them and argues against the 'stupidity' of the West.[4]

Few of the above viewpoints can be rejected completely, rather like those
famous many causes of the French or American Revolutions over which
students are invited in essays to exercise their judgement: it is a question
of proportion and relative weight. There is no single message in *Nineteen
Eighty-Four*: it contains multiple messages. It is, after all, a *novel* not a
monograph, albeit of a peculiar kind and the most complex Orwell ever
attempted; and more complex in its *variety* of themes than most readers and
critics appreciate. If he had wanted to write a straight or even a more or less
non-fiction book, he would have done so as he had done before. But a general
difficulty with satires is that they depend greatly on contemporary references
which time can erode or misconceive, and warnings depend on plausibility in
the circumstances of the day (now often misunderstood, underestimated or
re-imagined).[5] And there is the special difficulty that satire and warning are a
difficult mixture to bring off: it is difficult to judge how specific and precise
the author is being. H. G. Wells wrote novels of both these kinds, but on the
whole he kept them well apart. Orwell attempted something artistically very
difficult. That is why in my *George Orwell: A Life* I called this extraordinarily
powerful, complex and disturbing book 'a flawed masterpiece'.

As well as a satire on aspirations of totalitarianism, *Nineteen Eighty-Four*
is plainly a satire on hierarchical societies in general. This has created a

foolish misunderstanding. If Orwell was still a democratic socialist, it is said, where in the text does he assert his libertarian and egalitarian values? Some ask this question rhetorically and assume that somehow, because he does not mention these things explicitly, he has abandoned them, certainly that he has abandoned his egalitarianism. This view is strengthened if one 'locates', as has become a routine academic exercise, *Nineteen Eighty-Four* in the tradition of Huxley's *Brave New World*, Zamyatin's *We*, Jack London's *Iron Heel*, and H. G. Wells's *The Sleeper Awakes*. The issue is a complex one. Certainly there are borrowings from and echoes of all these books – and many more – in *Nineteen Eighty-Four*. But finally it is arbitrary and foolish to read the text in the mental straight-jacket of a course on utopian and anti-utopian literature. *Nineteen Eighty-Four* owes as much to Swift's *Gulliver* as to any of them, and, in any case, also needs locating both in the political events of the 1930s and 1940s and in Orwell's reading of non-fiction such as James Burnham's *Managerial Revolution*. However, let us play this curricular game for a moment. Compare *Nineteen Eighty-Four* to *Brave New World*. Even in the broadest features of their plots they are as chalk to cheese. Aldous Huxley was satirising equality, he disliked and feared egalitarianism, therefore a parodied equality is an explicit theme in his satire, which shows equality through enforced happiness carried rather too far. Orwell also disliked 'happiness', or rather he often railed against hedonism both as a proper motive for life and as a sufficient explanation of human conduct, although, doubtless to Huxley's horror, he professed to find a true happiness in the ordinary, decent life of a working-man in employment – the idealised 'common man' of Kant, Jefferson and William Morris, and not in the hyped-up higher moments of the literary intelligentsia. Orwell is far from satirising equality, he is satirising the pretensions of hier-archy. Good satire is neither cynical nor utterly pessimistic (which is why so much so-called satire today is simply, at best, frivolous, or, at worst, nihilistic – denying that any alternative positions are better). If mankind can never be perfect, says the satirist, he always has the capacity to be better.

Hierarchy destroys fraternity. Orwell's satire is so consistent that the dic-tator is actually called 'Big Brother'. 'Big Brother is watching you', but not watching over you as a brother should. Satires turn moral truths upside down. This configuration of the friendly into the threatening is a perfect piece of *double-think*. It has a touch of the Stalinist perversion of early Com-munism, but also has a touch of the *Volksgemeinschaft* and *Bruderschaft* of the Nazis, their false fraternity and contempt for individual liberty. In satire the positive values of a writer emerge as the contrary of what he or she is attacking, or of the fanatical and usually disgusting world portrayed.

Mutual Trust

Consider for a moment *Nineteen Eighty-Four* simply as a story of a man, Winston Smith, trying to struggle against a new despotism. The story makes clear right from the beginning that effective resistance is impossible – if things are ever allowed to come to such a pass. On one level Winston attempts to resist by activism, by rebellion, seeking out the enemies of the regime; but on another level he simply struggles to maintain his individuality (the original title was to have been *The Last Man in Europe*). In this struggle – which this unhealthy and unheroic man pursues with surprising courage and tenacity right up to the final torture – *memory* and *mutual trust* become positive themes. That he is finally defeated is inevitable in this satire of total power. A happy ending would be a satirical deflating of the pretensions of a grim satire. But Orwell believes that individuality can only be destroyed when we are utterly alone. While we have someone to trust, our individuality cannot be destroyed. For man is a social animal, our identity arising from interaction, not autonomy. 'Do thyself no harm for we are all here'.

'Mutual trust' is that virtue praised by Aristotle, asserted to be necessary to true citizens and the very thing that a tyrant must smash (he tells us in Book V of *The Politics*) if he is to perpetuate his rule successfully. Mutual trust is a component of that overworked word in Orwell, that essential concept, 'decency' (Orwell's equivalent of 'fairness' in John Rawls' moral philosophy or 'mutual respect' in Kant's). Decency is mutual trust, toleration, behaving responsibly toward other people, acting with empathy – all of these. Mutual trust is of supreme importance to a civic culture, for political action is impossible without it. Again the author is no more explicit about 'mutual trust' than he is about 'equality'. In a satire only the contrary or the negation is explicit, but then perfectly explicit. O'Brien, the interrogator, torturer of the Inner Party, tells Winston Smith: 'Already we are breaking down the habits of thought which have survived from before the Revolution. We have cut the links between child and parent, between man and man, and between man and woman. No one dares trust a wife or a child or a friend any longer'.[6]

> And a wretched old man, grieving in an air-raid shelter for someone dead, kept repeating, 'We didn't ought to 'ave trusted 'em. I said so, Ma, didn't I? That's what comes of trusting 'em. I said so all along. We didn't ought to have trusted the buggers'.[7]

And when Winston and Julia meet again after their torture, defeat and release, she says:

'You *want* it to happen to the other person. You don't give a damn what they suffer. All you care about is yourself'.

'All you care about is yourself,' he echoed.

'And after that you don't feel the same towards the other person any longer.'

'No,' he said, 'you don't feel the same'.[8]

'Mutual trust' is thus a minimum demand on us if we want to stay human, but it is also a maximum demand: there is no need to treat all one's fellow citizens with more than mutual trust, respect and decency. Certainly there is no need to love everybody equally, which is either impossible or a debasement of 'love'; but there is a categorical imperative to treat people equally, as if everyone were an end in themselves and not a means toward some other's ends. Some critics have argued that 'love' is asserted as a positive value in *Nineteen Eighty-Four* and is necessary for a good society, as shown by the love affair between Winston and Julia. They then say, not surprisingly, that the portrayal of love is clumsy and shallow. But it begins simply as sexual desire, a 'love affair'; anything like real love only grows on them toward the end – their betrayal by one they trusted, and then of each other. Indeed that Julia really loves him is shown in the story to have been a mistake on Winston's part. She falls asleep when he reads Goldstein's testimony and she is bored by his tale of the photograph; and for her part promiscuity is a gesture of contempt for the regime (she boasts that she has had it off with Party members many times before, and that turns Winston on again). She is closer in her behaviour to the proles than is Winston, because she has come from the proles, but not in sympathies – she wants to get away from them. She is no intellectual, but she is shrewd, tough and courageous. But Winston is more the middle-class intellectual who is determined to find hope amid the common people. If the affair is not a love affair in a genuine sense, it is, however, exemplary of 'mutual trust' right up to the end when they are tortured. Mutual trust, fellowship, fraternity and decency are recurrent themes in all of Orwell's writings after *The Road to Wigan Pier* and *Homage to Catalonia*. These themes qualify his earlier individualism.

Memory and History

The second positive and major theme, *memory*, is explicit in the satire, and links *Nineteen Eighty-Four* with *Coming Up for Air* and with Orwell's general view of morality. He held (rightly or wrongly, but so he did) that a good and decent way of life already existed in tradition: an egalitarian or genuine post-revolutionary society would not transfigure values or expect them to be different (his anti-Marxism comes out here) but would simply end exploitation and draw on the best of the past. Quite simply, Orwell did not believe that poverty and class oppression (which he fiercely believed were real forces in the history of the West) had dehumanised people completely. Rather these forces had created a genuine fellowship and fraternity in the common people that the middle classes, wracked by competitive individualism, lacked. Hence the importance of the proles in the story, much more positively characterised (if perhaps too briefly for emphasis) than is always noticed. Winston Smith observed when he walked among the proles:

> What mattered were individual relationships, and the completely helpless gesture, an embrace, a tear, a word spoken to a dying man, could have value in itself. [The proles] . . . it suddenly occurred to him, had remained in this condition. They were not loyal to a party or to a country or to an idea, they were loyal to one another. For the first time in his life he did not despise the proles or think of them as merely an inert force which would one day spring to life and regenerate the world. The proles had stayed human. They had not become hardened inside. They had held on to the primitive emotions which he himself had to relearn by conscious effort.[9]

This is a crucial passage in the book, completely consistent with Orwell's moral and social perspectives elsewhere. Thus the authenticity of memory, thus the diary: the attempt to write the diary begins the main thread of the plot in which private memory is defended against the official attempts to rewrite history; and these become parallel themes.

My suggestion is that the themes of the importance of memory, of mutual trust and of plain language work together as a satire on modern mass-produced writing. Orwell sees even the nominally nonpolitical writings of prolefeed and prolecult as having a political, deadening, perverting, and pacifying effect generally. If we read them primarily as part of a future totalitarian society, then we actually distance the thrust at ourselves. Consider this passage from his essay of 1946, 'The Prevention of Literature':

> It would probably not be beyond human ingenuity to write books by machinery. But a sort of mechanising process can already be seen at work in film and radio, in publicity and propaganda, and in the lower reaches of journalism. The Disney films, for instance, are produced by what is essentially a factory process, the work being done partly mechanically and partly by means of artists who have to subordinate their individual style. Radio features are commonly written by tired hacks to whom the subject and the manner of treatment are dictated beforehand. Even so, what they write is merely a kind of raw material to be chopped into shape by producers and censors. So also with the innumerable books and pamphlets commissioned by government departments.[10]

One of the satiric rages that moved Orwell was plainly a result of bitter disappointment that almost a hundred years of the democratic franchise and of compulsory secondary education had not realised the liberal dream of an educated, active and politically literate citizenry, but that industrial society had turned people into proles: '. . . films, football, beer and, above all, gambling filled the horizon of their minds. To keep them in control was not difficult'. Several of his essays bristle with contempt for what he still called 'the yellow press' and, as a working journalist, he had obviously believed that through writing plain English one could, if not prevented or edited out, reach ordinary people with important issues. He implied that most intellectuals now lived off the backs of a debased populace by supplying prolefeed, no longer trying to 'educate and agitate' – that fine old British radical slogan.

He only erred in his satire on two-way television by seeing its development primarily as a device of surveillance; but, even so, these other things had so debased the proles that 'the great majority of the proles did not even have telescreens in their homes'. They did not need watching, they were so debased as to be no political threat. The actual development of mass television today would have been added grist to Orwell's satiric mill, prolefeed indeed.

Seen as a projective model of actual or would-be 'totalitarian' societies, the narrative text of *Nineteen Eighty-Four* works badly. The proles are left passive, they are not mobilised systematically as nearly every social scientist or contemporary historian who used the term *totalitarian* thought was the essence of the concept – including Orwell himself in a whole group of wartime and postwar essays. *Nineteen Eighty-Four* is not a precise model of actual totalitarian society, as he was well aware, simply because the demands of the specific satiric targets in his own society make the proles debased by the state rather than fit human material for political mobilisation towards revolutionary transformation. Of course, the details of the Ingsoc regime cannot be viewed as a precise model but only as parts of a satiric story. It is almost as absurd to object to Orwell that the class structure in Oceania is obscure or contradictory as to tell Swift that the babies of the Irish poor would have been too emaciated to serve as food for the starving.

If Not Prophecy Yet Warning

However, both the intensity of the writing and his immediate reactions to reviewers must convince us that, even if it is not a prophecy of totalitarianism (still less neither timetable nor precise model), the book is certainly in part a warning that 'something like this could happen even here'. Orwell was disturbed when a first wave of American reviewers (notably from the

Time-Life Corporation's journals) hailed *Nineteen Eighty-Four* as, first and last, an explicit attack on socialism. Not unexpectedly, Communists took exactly the same line. So Orwell dictated two sets of notes for a press release:

> It has been suggested by some of the reviewers of *Nineteen Eighty-Four* that it is the author's view that this, or something like this, is what will happen inside the next forty years in the Western World. This is not correct. I think that, allowing for the book being after all a parody, something like *Nineteen Eighty-Four could* happen. This is the direction in which the world is going at the present time, and the trend lies deep in the political, social and economic foundations of the contemporary world situation.
>
> Specifically the danger lies in the structure imposed on Socialist and on Liberal capitalist communities by the necessity to prepare for total war with the USSR and the new weapons, of which of course the atomic bomb is the most powerful and the most publicised. But danger lies also in the acceptance of a totalitarian outlook by intellectuals of all colours.
>
> The moral to be drawn from this dangerous nightmare situation is a simple one: *Don't let it happen. It depends on you.*[11]
>
> George Orwell assumes that if such societies as he describes in *Nineteen Eighty-Four* come into being there will be several super-states. This is fully dealt with in the relevant chapters of *Nineteen Eighty-Four*. It is also discussed from a different angle by James Burnham in *The Managerial Revolution*. These super states will naturally be in opposition to each other or (a novel point) will pretend to be much more in opposition than in fact they are. Two of the principal super states will obviously be the Anglo-American world and Eurasia. If these two great blocs line up as mortal enemies it is obvious that the Anglo-Americans will not take the name of their opponents and will not dramatise themselves on the scene of history as Communists. Thus they will have to find a new name for themselves. The name suggested in *Nineteen Eighty-Four* is of course Ingsoc, but in practice a wide range of choices is open. In the USA the phrase 'Americanism' or 'hundred percent Americanism' is suitable and the qualifying adjective is as totalitarian as anyone could wish.
>
> If there is a failure of nerve and the Labour Party breaks down in its attempt to deal with the hard problems with which it will be faced, tougher types than the present Labour leaders will inevitably take over, drawn probably from the ranks of the Left, but not sharing the liberal aspirations of those now in power. Members of the present British government, from Mr. Attlee and Sir Stafford Cripps down to Aneurin Bevan, will *never* willingly sell the pass to the enemy, and in general the older men, nurtured in a liberal tradition, are safe, but the younger generation is suspect and the seeds of totalitarian thought are probably widespread among them.[12]

So Orwell thought that something like it *could* happen, but notice how contemporary (the division of the world between the great powers and his fears for the Labour Party) the specific elements of the satire become, and notice his use of the phrase that it was 'after all a parody'. The problem still remains, a parody of what? Here the book as a plain text perhaps ceases to speak directly to the modern reader without some editorial note. For a major theme is a parody of James Burnham's thesis in particular and of the power-hunger of intellectuals (an old Orwell theme) in general. 'Who was James Burnham?' many readers of *Nineteen Eighty-Four* may well ask.

Burnham had a double thesis: that the two great ideologies of the super-powers would one day converge, neither the commissars nor the congress-men winning; and that the state would be taken over not by politicians or party men (of whatever ideology) but by technocrats. They were develop-ing a common culture and common interests. Orwell was fascinated by both views. He wrote two major essays on Burnham, as if to think it out; although in the end he rejected both views. Nonetheless, if one saw intellectuals as a sub-class of managers, as Orwell seems to do, he had considerable ambiva-lence about them. While he defends intellectual liberties, he seems to distrust intellectuals as a class and suspect most of them as coming to be more inter-ested in power and place than in free thought. He fears, impressed by his wartime experience in the BBC, that intellectuals sell out to the machine all too easily: 'the motives of those English intellectuals who support the Russian dictatorship are, I think, different from what they publicly admit, but it is logical to condone tyranny and massacre if one assumes that progress is inevitable'.[13] Orwell packed a lot into that cheery little aside, not merely his continual polemic against the Fellow Travellers of Communism, but a Karl Popper-like philosophical position: that belief in theories of historical inevitability or prophecy inevitably become excuses for the tyranny needed to try to make them come true. 'The fallacy is to believe that under a dicta-torial government you can be free inside. Quite a number of people console themselves with this thought now that totalitarianism in one form or another is visibly on the upgrade in every part of the world'.[14]

Controlling past and future?

Certainly in *Nineteen Eighty-Four* the Ministry of Truth is doing more than debasing the masses, it is rewriting history: he who controls the present controls the past and the future. On one level, the satire is fairly obvious: anyone at the time who cared to know would have followed the gallows-humour of successive editions of *The Soviet Encyclopaedia* which first had Trotsky as a hero of the Civil War, then condemned him as an agent of the Mensheviks and British Intelligence, then dealt with him in the sim-plest and sweetest way by removing him entirely from historical record, making him an un-person. That is Winston Smith's daily work in the ministry.

However, Orwell on a deeper level tries to wrestle with the epistemological problem as to whether it is *possible* so to control the past, to destroy or distort both record and memory. Although Winston strives to authenticate vague memories, what he finds among the proles is extremely disturbing: their memories are short, random, wandering and often ridiculous; it needs a trained mind to have a trained memory in oppressive circumstances. It emerges from some of Orwell's earlier essays that (a) he fears that totalitarian regimes believe their own propaganda and can create a coherent and viable false reality, and (b) a contradictory theme, that totalitarian regimes could not possibly function if some of their leaders or functionaries, scientists or bureaucrats, did not know what was really happening. Orwell never resolved this profound and difficult epistemological dilemma.

Nor did he fully resolve whether he was satirising Burnham's view of the primacy of pure power as an impossibility: 'It is curious that in all his talk about the struggle for power, Burnham never stops to ask *why* people want power' ('Second Thoughts on James Burnham', 1946); or whether he thinks it all too possible that party leaders and civil servants who begin as civilised men end up simply as a regime of office-holders, brutally interested in nothing but power for the sake of power. O'Brien gives the nihilistic reply to Winston Smith when he allows Winston to ask him what it is all for: 'If you want a picture of the future, imagine a boot stamping on a human face forever'.

Could there be such a thing as power devoid of ideology? Can history be completely rewritten? Consider these two rather different reflections on the possibility of total thought control in the same long paragraph of his essay, 'The Prevention of Literature' (1946).

> The organised lying practised by totalitarian states is not, as is sometimes claimed, a temporary expedient of the same nature as military deception. It is something integral to totalitarianism. Among intelligent Communists there is an underground legend to the effect that although the Russian government is obliged now to deal in lying propaganda, frame-up trials, and so forth, it is secretly recording the true facts and will publish them at some future time. We can, I believe, be quite certain that this is not the case, because the mentality implied by such action is that of a liberal historian who believes that the past cannot be altered and that a correct knowledge of history is valuable as a matter of course. From the totalitarian point of view, history is something to be created rather than learned. A totalitarian state is in effect a theocracy, and its ruling caste, in order to keep its position, has to be thought of as infallible. But since, in practice, no one is infallible, it is frequently necessary

to rearrange events in order to show that this or that mistake was not made, or that this or that imaginary triumph actually happened . . . Then, again, every major change in policy demands a corresponding change of doctrine and a revaluation of prominent historical figures. *This kind of thing happens everywhere*, but is clearly likelier to lead to outright falsification in societies where only one opinion is permissible at any given moment. Totalitarianism demands, in fact, the continuous alteration of the past, and in the long run probably demands a disbelief in the very existence objective of truth.[15]

But then, in the same paragraph, he asserts a contradictory opinion.

The friends of totalitarianism in this country usually tend to argue that since absolute truth is not attainable, a big lie is no worse than a little lie. It is pointed out to us that all historical records are biased and inaccurate or, on the other hand, that modern physics has proved that what seems to us the real world is an illusion, so that to believe in the evidence of ones senses is simply vulgar philistinism. A totalitarian society which succeeds in perpetuating itself would probably set up a schizophrenic system of thought, in which laws of commonsense held good in everyday life and in certain exact sciences, but could be disregarded by the politician, the historian and the sociologist. Already there are countless people who would think it scandalous to falsify a scientific text-book, but would see nothing wrong in falsifying an historical fact. It is at the point where literature and politics cross that totalitarianism exerts its greatest pressure on the intellectual.[16]

He appears to – or does – contradict himself because now he assumes not a total system of false thought but a schizophrenic one. The speculative essayist sees the plausibility of both points of view. The schizophrenic or two-truth theory is perhaps the most plausible and the mildly less nightmarish. Orwell simply was not sure on both these big issues: could there be a total divorce of power from morality and of history and ideology from truth? Few people were sure at the time he wrote, when Soviet power, if containable, seemed impregnable, and Nazi power was a very recent memory and many feared its recurrence. Now we have only North Korea that raises this dilemma. Orwell felt the dilemma acutely. Perhaps he had not got the philosophical ability to resolve the question of whether or not all truths are socially conditioned, but he had the literary genius to go right to the heart of the problem. Because they were open-ended dilemmas, he chose to write a novel, not a tract, even though so many people now read it out of context as if it were a tract for all times, to be judged as literally true or not in every detail, rather than a grim satirical caricature of the conditions of his time.

But the essay 'The Prevention of Literature' does reach out in some respects to chasten and worry us, as all great satire can.

Let me repeat what I said at the beginning of this essay: that in England the immediate enemies of truthfulness, and hence of freedom of thought, are the Press lords, the film magnates and the bureaucrats, but that on a long view the weakening of the desire for liberty among the intellectuals themselves is the most serious symptom of all.[17]

Orwell radiates mistrust for the debasing effect of the press and he feared that intellectuals were betraying their principles. These two satiric thrusts are the enduringly topical relevance of *Nineteen Eighty-Four*. But after all the dark pessimism of the narrative, the book ends on an optimistic note – not Winston loving Big Brother under which it says 'The End', but the end paragraph of the Appendix, 'The Principles of Newspeak'. That is the real end of the text. And it tells us that translations into Newspeak of 'Various writers, such as Shakespeare, Milton, Swift, Byron, Dickens . . '. (Orwell's pantheon) was an unexpectedly 'slow and difficult business'; and therefore the 'final adoption of Newspeak had been fixed for late a date as 2050. If we read *Nineteen Eighty-Four* as Swiftian satire, this is as good as to say 'this year, next year, sometimes, never'. Colloquial language, the common people and common-sense will survive the most resolute attempts at total control.

NOTES

1. See Crick, B. (ed.), *George Orwell: Nineteen Eighty-Four, with a critical introduction and annotations*, (Oxford: Clarendon Press, 1984), and Crick. B., *George Orwell: A Life*, rev. ed., (London: Secker & Warburg, 1981); and 'Reading *Nineteen Eighty-Four* as Satire' in Crick, B., *Essays on Politics and Literature* (Edinburgh: Edinburgh University Press, 1989), from which some passages in this chapter are drawn. So I disagree with William Steinhoff, in his otherwise masterly book, when he sees *Nineteen Eighty-Four* 'as a culminating work which expresses, almost epitomizes, a lifetime's ideas, attitudes, events, and reading'. *George Orwell and the Origins of 1984* (Ann Arbor, Michigan: University of Michigan Press, 1975).
2. Davison P. (ed.), *The Complete Works of George Orwell, Nineteen* (London, Secker & Warburg, 1998), p. 487.
3. Crick, *Nineteen Eighty-Four*, 55–84.
4. Milosz, C., *The Captive Mind*, trans. Zielonko (New York: Knopf, 1953), p. 40.
5. When the poet William Empson wrote to thank Orwell for *Animal Farm*, he pointed out that his precocious son of ten had read it as 'Tory propaganda', whereas Empson knew that Orwell *intended* it as a socialist lament for revolution betrayed by the power-hungry. (Letter of 24 August 1945, quoted in Crick, *Orwell*, 340.)
6. Davison, *Nine*, 280.
7. Davison, *Nine*, 36.
8. Davison, *Nine*, 305–6.
9. Davison, *Nine*, 172.

10. 'The Prevention of Literature', Davison, *Seventeen*, 378.
11. Crick, *Orwell*, 395.
12. Davison, *Twenty*, 134–5.
13. Davison, *Seventeen*, 343.
14. Davison, *Sixteen*, 172.
15. Davison, *Seventeen*, 373–4.
16. Davison, *Seventeen*, 374.
17. Davison, *Seventeen*, 374.

13

NEIL McLAUGHLIN

Orwell, the academy and the intellectuals

George Orwell is a central figure in recent debates about the relationship between contemporary academics and their publics. Since the late 1980s, the notion of the public intellectual has spread through bestselling books, the use of the term by journalists, various 'top public intellectual' contests, academic research and even a PhD programme in the 'Public Intellectual'. Long before the currently popular term 'public intellectual' was ever used, Orwell helped create and then exemplified the role of the independent 'gadfly' intellectual who writes clearly and with conviction to a general educated audience. Recent commentators on the public intellectual have not emphasised two of the most important and interesting aspects of the reception of Orwell. Orwell was not an academic, but his ideas *have* entered into university debates and discussion in a very substantial way without there being an Orwell 'school of thought' or a formal canonisation of him as an academic 'founder' of a discipline. Second, Orwell is at the very centre of debates about the politics of the literary critic as an 'amateur' non-professionalised vocation in this age dominated by the influence of the university professor. Each of these two questions will be discussed below, before ending on some brief thoughts on how Orwell can help us think about the possibilities of what might be called the 'global public literary intellectual'.

Orwell and the academics

How much influence does Orwell have within the contemporary university? One useful place to start discussing Orwell's influence is American judge and writer Richard Posner's *The Public Intellectuals* (2001). Posner attempts to trace the influence of selected public intellectual figures using three distinct measures. Posner's analysis of coverage in the media, 'hits' on the internet and counts of citations in academic journals highlights three different ways in which modern social and political debates are shaped by complex and overlapping spheres of institutions and professional knowledge producers.

Orwell, in particular, retains an important place in our popular and intellectual culture, and this can be explored by Posner's examination of his influence in both the media and the internet, although Orwell's academic reputation is not discussed in *The Public Intellectuals* (2001).

Orwell's cultural influence

Posner gathered a list of the top 100 most-mentioned intellectuals in the media – Orwell ranks 11th overall, an extraordinary ranking given the fact that he has been dead for more than half a century.[1] Most of the intellectuals ranked ahead of Orwell are directly associated with elite journalism (George Will, William Safire, William Bennett and Sydney Blumenthal) or were involved in wielding political power (Henry Kissinger, Daniel Patrick Moynihan, Robert Reich and Lawrence Summers). It makes sense, of course, that mainstream media sources would give extensive attention to journalists linked to the elite media themselves, as well as to powerful political figures. Orwell's continuing presence in the media far beyond the media frenzy in the countdown to the year 1984 is truly remarkable for a literary intellectual of the left without powerful allies in the state.

The only literary intellectuals above Orwell in media influence were Arthur Miller and Salman Rushdie. Arthur Miller, of course, is clearly one of America's most well-known literary figures. And Rushdie's presence on the list is due, one can speculate, to both his literary talent *and* the controversy involving his book *The Satanic Verses* (1988) where his life was threatened by Iranian clerics angry at his representation of Islam. Literary figures below Orwell on Posner's list include Nobel-prize winning author Toni Morrison, Tom Wolfe, Norman Mailer and Kurt Vonnegut. The literary figures that reside in the upper tier of Posner's list are divided into two groups: contemporary writers (mostly Americans) and canonical writers (mostly British). Other than Rushdie, Orwell is the only non-American among the top 15. Orwell's posthumous reputation is remarkable; no other literary intellectual from the last 100 years has maintained such a hold on our broader popular and intellectual culture (with the possible exception of Shaw).

Orwell on the Net

The list of media citations is clearly influenced by the power and dominance of mainstream elite newspapers in the formation of popular opinion, as we discussed above. What about the potentially democratising influence of the internet? What kind of visibility does Orwell have in our culture when visibility measured by the internet? According to Posner's data, Orwell has 48,874 internet 'hits'. When viewed against others on the list, we once again witness the continued attention to Orwell's work. Among the names with a comparable number of hits are some fairly influential, and controversial, intellectuals: Ayn Rand, Jean-Paul Sartre, William James and Michel Foucault. Among literary figures, Orwell ranks among the most popular on the internet. Only C. S. Lewis and William Butler Yeats rank higher. Orwell garnered more internet 'hits' than Toni Morrison, George Bernard Shaw, Arthur Miller, Aldous Huxley, Umberto Eco and H. G. Wells.

Posner did not gather data on Orwell's influence in the university sphere, however, thinking that since Orwell was not an academic this would be 'not applicable'. This is a shame because what is striking about the reception of Orwell is *precisely* how much influence he has had within contemporary university life as measured by citations, despite the fact that he did not even have a university degree, was not a trained academic and did not publish in scholarly journals or book presses. I have collected[2] some data that documents that scholars in the academy continue to show interest in Orwell and his works, as measured by their willingness to cite his work in peer reviewed journal articles. I selected a number of Orwell's most famous novels, collections of essays and books including *Coming Up for Air, Shooting An Elephant and Other Essays, Road to Wigan Pier, England Your England, Lion and the Unicorn, The Clergyman's Daughter, Homage to Catalonia, Keep the Aspidistra Flying* and, of course, *Nineteen Eighty-Four* and *Animal Farm*. Relying on the citations indices widely used in the sciences, social sciences and humanities I produced the following results broken down first into ten-year periods between 1976–85 and 1985–95 as well as the seven-year period from 1996–2003.[3]

This number of citations, 656 between 1976–85, 519 between 1986–95 and 358 between 1996–2003 is a large amount of academic citations given the fact that we know that the vast majority of academic books and articles receive only one or two citations, if they are cited at all (Collins, 1998). This data suggests the need to modify the argument made in John Rodden's writings on 'Orwell in the Classroom' where he claims that '[w]ith the exception of the use of selected essays such as 'Politics and the English Language'or 'Shooting An Elephant' in introductory college rhetoric and expository writing courses, Orwell's essays are rarely encountered in most universities' (Rodden, 2003:210). Rodden is correct, of course, that few students will actually read Orwell in their university courses, since he is not part of the literary canon nor is he widely assigned in upper level or graduate classes. But it is clear, however, that academics themselves are reading and citing Orwell and thus he does have a presence in the academy. Orwell's work is clearly part of the learning experience of contemporary

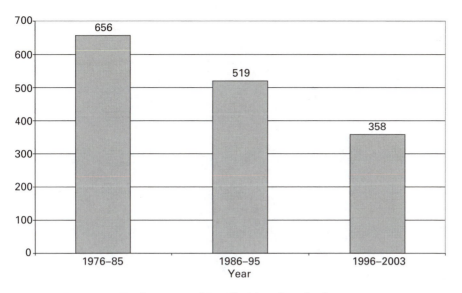

Figure 13.1 Total Citations of Orwell's Selected Works, from 1976–2003

undergraduate students if the writings of their professors can be relied on to give us a sense of what is talked about in classrooms. It is useful, further-more, to break citations to Orwell down by disciplines, as we can see in the chart below.

These citation patterns raise some important questions: where in the academy is Orwell more likely to be discussed?[4] What kind of scholars cite Orwell? And, how does this help us understand Orwell's position in the contemporary academy? It is clear that literary studies shows the great-est interest in Orwell. It makes sense, of course, that Orwell would be cited most often in literary studies, the humanities and general interdisci-plinary journals, as suggested by the figures of 43 per cent, 10 per cent and 12 per cent respectively. This is to be expected since Orwell is best known for his literature and his non-fiction essays on the English language. Orwell's influence, however, is not limited to literary studies – historians, anthropologists, sociologist, philosophers, psychologists and political scien-tists find Orwell's work useful in their research. History is the discipline that is next likely to cite Orwell with 9 per cent followed by, perhaps surprisingly, psychology at 6 per cent and sociology and political science tied at 5 per cent. Philosophers follow closely behind with 4 per cent of the total citations to Orwell followed by anthropology and economics, the major disciplines that seem to exhibit the least interest in Orwell by this measure. Not only does this underscore Orwell's continued relevance to

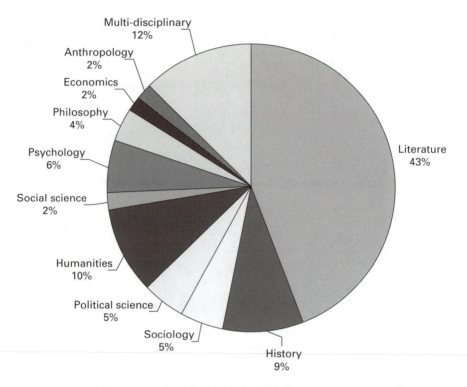

Figure 13.2 Orwell Citations by Discipline, 1976–2003

academics, but the dispersion of these citations highlights the versatility of his works. Breaking down the citations further by specific Orwell book adds a further angle on the question, since his academic reception is uneven and varied.

The data in figure 13.3 shows us that *Nineteen Eighty-Four* is by far the most cited of Orwell's books, followed by *Animal Farm* with a good deal less than half of the citations and *Road to Wigan Peer* with a third of *Nineteen Eighty-Four*'s influence in the academy. *Homage to Catalonia, Burmese Days, Lion and the Unicorn, Down and Out in London and Paris, Coming up for Air* and *Shooting an Elephant and other Essays* follow in that order. The least cited books are *Keep the Aspidistra Flying, England your England* and *The Clergyman's Daughter* (Orwell's weakest novel, by his own admission). We will discuss the citation patterns of each, in this order of influence.

Nineteen Eighty-Four, Orwell's most famous work, has left an indelible mark on English language and literature. His cautionary tale highlighting the dangers of Stalinism brought new words and phrases into the language: 'War

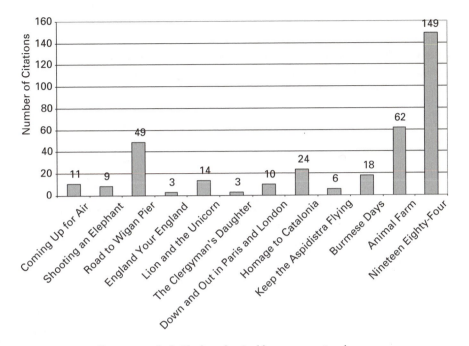

Figure 13.3 Individual works cited between 1996 and 2003

is Peace'; 'Big Brother is Watching You'; and 'Doublethink'. Not surpris-ingly, academics are more likely to cite *Nineteen Eighty-Four* than anything else. Over the course of six years, the book was cited 149 times. Consider-ing the relatively small number of Orwell specialists and the lack of a cen-tralised 'invisible college' of institutionally powerful Orwell scholars, this is an impressive feat for a non-academic writer. Once again, the majority of the citations can be found in literary studies, but the citations are evenly spread among other types of journals. With *Animal Farm*, Orwell's appeal to multi-disciplinary journals is also demonstrated – more than one-third of the cita-tions to Orwell's anti-Stalinist allegory are from non-specialised and multi-disciplinary journals. Surprisingly, *Animal Farm* is cited more frequently in psychology than in political science, history and economics journals. This is quite remarkable, given the tendency of psychology journals towards highly scientific even scientistic research programmes, and this phenomenon would thus be worth further examination. If one were to posit an explanation of Orwell's appeal in psychology without further research, then one might spec-ulate that the themes of rebellion, authority and, social change in the fable and novel tap into the concerns about the 'authoritarian personality' and the like in psychological literature. Both *Nineteen Eighty-Four* and *Animal*

Farm, it seems, raise issues of psycho-politics particularly with regards to the psychology of power in the context of totalitarianism, domination, and so on.

Next in influence is *Road to Wigan Pier*, Orwell's sociological study of the living conditions in the north of England that was commissioned by the Left Book club in 1936. A product of his long fascination with the working class, the book has wide appeal to scholars and is the most discussed of Orwell's writings aside from his two most famous novels. The book is cited among the general humanities and multi-disciplinary journals, something that suggests its broad appeal. Not surprisingly, Orwell's study of the working class is cited often by historians and sociologists. Given the criticism often expressed about this book from the political left, one might speculate that at least some of these citations are criticisms from the left academy while many others are likely to be citations to the ethnographic approach taken in the book and the early findings on the lives of the poor before modern social science had studied the issues extensively.

Chronicling one of the most monumental chapters of both his life and the broader history of the twentieth century, Orwell's first-person account of the Spanish Civil War in *Homage to Catalonia* is the fourth most cited book in this period. Continuing the trend previously seen, the majority of the references also occur in the field of literary studies. Sociologists and political scientists have taken an interest in *Homage* – despite the autobiographical approach of the work.

Most of the citations *Burmese Days* garnered can be found in literary studies. Furthermore, it has been of interest to historians and more generalised humanities studies. Very few political scientists or anthropologists take up the work, despite its dealing with issues of imperialism and representation.

England Your England, his essay addressing the country's changing political, social and economic conditions, has a distinct appeal to political science. While this is to be expected, the remaining citations are divided among literary studies, general humanities and multi-disciplinary journals. Orwell celebrated the non-specialist intellectual, and his citation in numerous non-specialised journals reflects this fact.

Coming up for Air is Orwell's 1939 tale of social and political change set in pre-war England, and it continues to be discussed not only by literary specialists, but also in the fields of history and sociology. This can be attributed to the book's prescience: many see the book as not only anticipating the coming war, but also the massive social and political upheaval that it would inflict on England. While the implications of this analysis of a particular moment in European life for historians are clear, that sociologists would find the book worthy of citations is intriguing.

Exemplifying Orwell's broad appeal, *Down and Out* is also cited through-out various disciplines. While it is not surprising that sociologists interested in ethnographic methods (17 per cent of the citations to this book are in soci-ology journals) and historians find this work valuable, the most intriguing pattern is the book's appeal to psychologists despite Orwell's lack of formal training in psychology. When compared to anthropology, history and politi-cal science – disciplines that explicitly take up the issues raised by the book – *Down and Out* garnered more citations by psychologists. Perhaps the issue of the social psychology of poverty helps explain this pattern, but we would need to look at the issue more closely in order to say more.

'Shooting an Elephant', Orwell's celebrated essay on British imperialism in Burma, has a wide appeal.[5] We know this book is heavily used in English-language composition manuals as an example of the expository essay. Other disciplines have clearly taken an interest in the book, as evidenced by the citation patterns. Perhaps political scientists, historians and sociologists find the discussion of imperialism worthy of citation? Most intriguing, again, are the number of citations in psychology journals.

The Clergyman's Daughter, which recounts the ravages of scandal and the life of a social pariah, is one of Orwell's least discussed books. It has only garnered a handful of mentions in the more than twenty years we looked at, mostly in the field of literary studies. Like *The Clergyman's Daughter*, *Keep the Aspidistra Flying* is not heavily cited, garnering only thirty-four citations over this extended time period. Orwell's account of bourgeois life in England and the dangerous effects of money on human relationships appeals mostly to literary scholars and historians, although neither of these works are seen as major literary and scholarly contributions, if the citation patterns can be used as reputational measures.

The data helps us see which Orwell books different disciplines tend to read and cite most frequently. For example, sociologists cite *Road to Wigan Pier* and *Nineteen Eighty-Four* most frequently, although *Down and Out* also garnered a significant number of citations. Academics in the field of literary studies cite *Nineteen Eighty-Four* most heavily, although *Road to Wigan Pier*, *Homage to Catalonia*, and *Animal Farm* are also cited. Historians seem most interested in *Road to Wigan Pier*, with *Nineteen Eighty-Four* following closely. *Homage to Catalonia* and the *Lion and the Unicorn* were cited equally by historians. Political scientists cite *Nineteen Eighty-Four* most frequently, although *Homage to Catalonia* and *Road to Wigan Pier* have been cited significantly. Psychologists, once again, seem most interested in *Nineteen Eighty-Four* while *Road to Wigan Pier* and *Animal Farm* have been discussed significantly in this field. Philosophers and economists are mostly interested in *Nineteen Eighty-Four*, although the former have also discussed

Road to Wigan Pier to some extent. Anthropologists are most likely to cite *Nineteen Eighty-Four*, although *Animal Farm* and *Road to Wigan Pier* are also discussed in this discipline.

Beyond these patterns, some larger questions are worth asking. How did Orwell, without a university degree and lacking professional training in literary studies, exert such influence on peer-reviewed academic discussions in an age when the public intellectual is supposed to be obsolete? This involves general questions of how ideas travel across closed professional networks. Orwell clearly matters in the university today despite the fact that there is no 'Orwellian' school of theoretical criticism, no powerful networks of Orwell followers in control in the Modern Language Association, and he himself had no interest in academic politics. Orwell's influence is remarkable given that there do not exist any scholarly journals or academic newsletters devoted to Orwell nor are there any literary societies or scholarly associations of 'Orwell specialists'. This is possibly because the very prospect of such things would be anathema to Orwell, a viewpoint perhaps less common in these times dominated by academic career building. We know how important the building and maintaining of schools of thought is to academic life as well as how stifling this can be to intellectual dialogue and integrity.

Orwell citations in academic journals, of course, do not mean that he has a reputation as an academic. Citation counts are a notoriously slippery indicator of status, and Posner's methods have been widely criticised. It is clear, of course, that some of the citations to Orwell will be criticisms of his work done by scholars concerned *precisely* with maintaining professional boundaries and keeping Orwell's ideas and literary work out of academic debates. Orwell is often cited as something that is NOT the kind of thing literary critics, for example, should be doing today. In addition, in history for example, one is likely to get treatments of Orwell and his writings as the 'object' of study given his enormous influence on twentieth century politics, culture and ideas. Nonetheless, there is no question that books like *Nineteen Eighty-Four* and *Animal Farm*, among other of his contributions, are works that have entered into our general culture and then seep back into academic debates from outside. We know, of course, that Orwell's writings have entered the broad popular culture and the high school curriculum especially in the Anglo-American world. But the number and range of the Orwell citations suggests he is part of contemporary academic discussions in the university even though he is often rejected by academics. This is a common phenomenon since research programmes try to build an autonomous academic culture cut off from the broader society and the kind of amateur social criticism practised by Orwell.

Sociological Ambivalence and the Public Intellectual

The explanation for the contradiction between Orwell's non-academic status, which is widespread and rather remarkable, and his clear but uneven academic reception is sociological. It is too simple, however, to claim that the university is hostile to public intellectuals or social critics such as Orwell, as Edward Said suggests with his call for the 'amateur intellectual'. Academics are ultimately ambivalent about public intellectuals and are not simply hostile as the conventional wisdom suggests. This attitude is rooted in the institutional contradictions embedded in the very structures of the research university. Scholars are hired, tenured and rewarded in universities for original cutting edge research judged by their peers in increasingly specialised and technical academic areas. The occupation of professor, at least at elite institutions oriented to research, creates enormous incentives for narrowness, technical language and professional closure. At the same time, at least in the United States, this professional orientation to research productively is not, for the most part, undertaken in organisations such as think tanks/research centres designed to exclusively produce new knowledge and/or influence policy. The major site of academic research today is the research university, an organisational innovation created in the early nineteenth century in Germany and spread to and institutionalised in the United States, in particular, in the early twentieth century. Academics do specialised research evaluated by their peers, but they also teach students who very often value clarity and broad relevance in the classroom more than the specialised research programmes at the centre of disciplinary work. Academics are thus drawn to as well as pushed away from the kind of clarity of thought and writing that Orwell exemplified.

In addition, the very act of teaching pushes academics to try to relate to students at the intellectual level they are at, despite the tension between research and pedagogy built into the very occupation of university teacher. All this will be very different in applied programmes and in the natural sciences, but in the social sciences and the humanities university professors who care about teaching are always looking for intellectual reference points, common language and shared book knowledge. Few contemporary intellectual figures are as likely to help establish this shared starting point in the classroom as George Orwell. His writings on totalitarianism in *Nineteen Eighty-Four* and *Animal Farm*, his ethnographic observations of poverty and working class culture, his reflections on clarity and writing, and his contested but widespread stature as perhaps the premier public intellectual of the twentieth century brings him into our university classrooms even if the gatekeepers in graduate education in political science, sociology, anthropology and professional literary criticism might view him as less than scholarly.

There is an institutional level to all this. The work and writing of academic intellectuals is shaped by the institutional arrangements they are embedded in; the kind of broad public relevance and clear writing that Orwell represents is something universities value for various reasons. This is most obvious at public research universities, where relevance to the local community and national political establishment is mandated by direct political accountability. A public university that does not have professors who follow Orwell's instructions on 'Politics and the English Language', at least part of the time, would be an institution with little support in the local community. Universities create public relations units that try to arrange faculty speaking engagements in the local community. They expect faculty to be able to communicate as public intellectuals as well as specialised researchers. Even elite private institutions are accountable to the public in various ways. Since they are dependant on tuition paid by students, for example, elite private universities often hire faculty who appear on TV or write in popular venues in order to help them build and maintain high student enrolments not simply peer review status. Scholars who work in the Orwell mode of 'social critic' are attractive to universities, at least after they become well known, even if they do not fit the professional disciplinary profile.

Yet the issues of popular appeal cut both ways – Orwell tends to get relatively ignored in university curriculum *precisely* because of the appeal his work has in high schools and in the broader culture. While university professors are looking for common ground with undergraduate students in order to facilitate education, they are also concerned with maintaining status distinctions. The popularity that Orwell's books, particularly *Nineteen Eighty-Four* and *Animal Farm*, have in schools helps explain the relative neglect of these works in university.

Drawing on secondary school surveys, John Rodden in his *Scenes from Afterlife* (2003) presents evidence from the United States and Britain, showing that *Animal Farm* was found to be one of thirty literary works most read by students from the 1950s until the early 1960s. The book is on the 'junior high school canon' while *Nineteen Eighty-Four* has a 'different and less secure place in school canons' at more advanced levels as part of the 'senior high school canon' (Rodden, 2003). In British examinations, *Nineteen Eighty-Four* has been part of the A level examinations, but *Animal Farm* is used far more extensively, usually at O levels (Rodden, 2003). In the United States *Nineteen Eighty-Four* was often seen as too complex and long for junior high students, and the sex-scene is often viewed by parents as too controversial (Rodden, 2003). And it is sometimes taught as a failed novel, 'possessing insufficient literary merit' (Rodden, 2003:216) when discussed in A levels. By the time of university classes, however, the familiarity that students will have with Orwell's two most famous novels means that they will be consigned to classes in utopian novels or science fiction, if taught at all, leaving Orwell low down the academic status hierarchy even if, as I have shown, he is cited in the peer reviewed journals that few students will ever read (Rodden, 2003).

Orwell and the literary critics

Professionalism and politics

Even if Orwell's marginal but real influence in the academy has been under-emphasised, there is no question that his major contribution to contemporary cultural life has been as a 'literary public intellectual'. The driving force that has kept Orwell's name and writings in the attention space of readers has come from intellectuals in and around the important twentieth-century journals and magazines of opinion, particularly in the United States and Britain, such as *Partisan Review*, *Commentary*, *Dissent*, *The New Republic*, *The Nation* and *The Times Literary Supplement*. Written for the general educated public, these types of magazines provide an important space where elite journalists, novelists, poets, scientists, political reformers and academic social scientists and humanities scholars can discuss and debate broad issues of social and political importance. Intellectual magazines are inheritors of the public space of coffee shops and salons written about by proponents of the public sphere such as Coser, Habermas, and the revolutionary democratic political debate created by intellectuals during the French and American revolutions. Orwell himself wrote extensively in the British versions of these kinds of intellectual journals, and today those who most think that 'Orwell matters' tend to be found in the political networks and in the orbit of journals that continue this public intellectual tradition.

Literary scholars have always been central to this type of public intellectual life, and Orwell's major supporters among the intellectual elite have tended to be literary scholars like Lionel Trilling, Irving Howe, Philip Rahv and Isaac Rosenfeld. Indeed one could argue that Orwell was the central 'intellectual hero' or, what Trilling himself called a 'figure,' among twentieth century public intellectuals precisely because of his complicated sociological relationship to literary scholars.

There are obvious reasons why Orwell appealed to Trilling and Howe, as well as the circles of intellectuals around the important literary/intellectual journals. As Christopher Hitchens has argued, Orwell was centrally concerned with moral and political thinking on imperialism, fascism and communism, the three major political issues of the twentieth century. Orwell's reputation for decency, honesty and political commitment certainly drew young intellectuals to his work, inspiring generations of public intellectuals to take up the craft. And the image of Orwell (created by Trilling in his influential introduction to *Homage to Catalonia*) as a 'man of intelligence' not an intellectual genius, was particularly influential among literary scholars and political thinkers who defined themselves as writers for the public not simply the academic profession.

The bond between Orwell and such literary intellectuals as Lionel Trilling and Irving Howe goes far deeper, however, when one looks at this sociologically. Orwell is cited in academic journals today, but not to the same extent as professionalised theory scholars who shape contemporary debates in the humanities. Intellectuals like Orwell, Trilling and Howe have lost influence in the academic humanities taught in our universities over the past forty to fifty years since the specialisation and professionalisation processes that drive modern academic work tend to marginalise the 'man and woman of letters' oriented to broad cultural debate. General public intellectuals like Howe and Trilling often were employed in universities, but their intellectual orientation was formed in and around small intellectual journals not professionalised graduate programmes. Orwell was important to Trilling and Howe, for example, because he represented a type of intellectual discourse and a career trajectory that is difficult to sustain in a world dominated by research universities and the opportunities they open up for young scholars. Orwell is an intellectual hero for literary public intellectuals because he represents a 'world we have lost' as well as an inspiration for those who want to preserve a vibrant literary culture.

The literary critic Edward Said is a transitional figure in these debates. Trained in a specialised and highly traditional mode of literary criticism in English colonial education in Egypt and then at Princeton and Harvard, Said taught for decades in Trilling's English department at Columbia where the great books of Western literature were read and discussed. Politicised by the Israeli-Palestinian conflict and the political events of the late 1960s, Said eventually came to argue for the importance of the 'amateur' intellectual and literary critic, while writing essays in *The Nation* on opera and political polemics in various intellectual journals. Orwell was not one of Said's heroes, partly because of various political differences. Said was a far more outspoken critic of American foreign policy than Orwell's followers tended to be.

The Cold War era during which Orwell died, in fact, turns out to be central to understanding Orwell's reception in our universities. Lawrence H. Schwartz's *Creating Faulkner's Reputation* helps us understand Orwell's place in our culture by providing a comparative perspective that stresses the role of large-scale geo-politics in shaping intellectual reputations in the universities. The work of Orwell, like Faulkner himself, was promoted by Cold War politics since they both were liberal anti-communists championed, partly for this very reason, by Trilling and Howe (Schwartz, 1988). Rodden points out that Faulkner did subtly what Orwell did explicitly – they both played an important role in articulating a defence of the West against the threat posed by communism. As Rodden puts it, while Faulkner did this ideological work in elite cultural outlets, Orwell took the 'low' road, something that helps explain why Faulkner would retain intellectual status among elite literary critics in and around elite magazines and in universities, while Orwell would become a secondary school staple (Rodden, 2003). While Orwell does get cited in academic journals, on occasion, there are no literary journals, reviews or associations devoted to developing and promoting his perspectives, as is the case for writers who have entered the core canons of literary culture. This lack of institutional support for Orwell's work can be explained sociologically, as well as from a perspective that focuses on the nature and quality of his writings. What makes the frequency of the citations all the more remarkable is the fact that there are no 'organised lobbies' of professors to 'promote' him – unlike the case, say, for Yeats and especially C. S. Lewis, but also Shaw, Wells, Huxley, etc. etc. Orwell is the only major British writer of the last two centuries without such a lobby – an incredible phenomenon worthy of extended reflection.

Edward Said's relationship to Orwell illuminates many of the sociological dynamics. Writing in the post-Vietnam era with a very different perspective on American power than the view taken by Faulkner or Orwell, and with a different view on the Israeli-Palestinian conflict than Howe or Trilling, Said never became a supporter of Orwell within literary circles. Nonetheless, the irony here is that the type of work that Said did, with one foot in professionalised academic post-colonial studies and another in the general intellectual orientation that Orwell represented, suggests tensions that are deeply embedded in literary careers today. Orwell is important in our culture today because he did a genre of political public intellectual literary criticism that our research universities, think tanks and media saturated culture make difficult to sustain.

Orwell has been marginalised within our universities for a variety of sociological reasons. Professional status for literary criticism, alongside respect within the academy, depends on a specialised technical language that makes a distinction between the theoretical and methodological contributions scholars make to literary scholarship and the substantive insights about literature and political principles that were so important to Orwell, Trilling, Howe and Said. To write clearly like Orwell did, furthermore, undermines the very professional distinctions that academic disciplines and professions depend on in their professionalising processes. If everyone in the society can read and criticise novels as well as discuss contemporary political events and cultural trends in language understandable to the lay-person, then what provides the justification for specialised programmes, departments and PhD degrees in literary studies?

Since Orwell wrote explicitly about popular culture, as do contemporary cultural studies scholars, he is at the centre of a challenge to traditional academic divisions between professional and lay intellectual and political discourse and elite versus popular culture. John Rodden puts it well when he writes: 'probably no other writer's work has so decisively contributed to the development of popular culture studies as a formal domain of academic inquiry – and so widely penetrated the international imagination – that it qualifies as a substantial body of material for popular cultural analysis' (Rodden, 2003:3). One way to think about this irony is that cultural studies scholars have ignored Orwell's contributions to their own field by mistake or chance. In contrast, my view is that cultural studies scholars who today write about movies, popular music, Dr Phil and pro-wrestling do not see Orwell as one of the founders of their field *precisely* because that would undermine their professionalising project of establishing Cultural Studies as an elite theory-driven discipline within contemporary universities. Lionel Trilling, for example, once famously claimed that Orwell was such an important writer because it was such a relief that his keen insights came not from a genius but a plain-speaking, decent common man. Insights from a 'common man' may help promote the kind of democratic dialogue that public intellectuals like Trilling, Howe and Said, in their different ways, wanted to see in our common culture and intellectual life. Academic programmes, on the other hand, need 'brilliant' and certainly complex theories (like those promoted by Adorno, Derrida or Foucault) not 'plain speaking decency' to help establish professional credentials in modern research universities. Once again, Orwell's popular appeal undermines his professional status.

The present political climate in the United States brings together the issues of the conflict between broad intellectual culture and ideas and professional knowledge in new ways. There is a deep-seated culture war going on in the United States today between the political forces of Reagan/Bush Republicanism and the liberal New Deal/Neo-Liberal oriented political establishment of the Democratic Party. Cutting across as well as being implicated in this cultural divide, however, there is another division within American intellectual elites that is about the role of literary culture in modernity and its related institutions. While conservatives in American politics often defend both populism

and traditional elite culture, the American academic left is, it must be said, also deeply divided about the cultural politics of the literary academy.

These cultural wars have resulted in some strange bed-fellows when it comes to talking about Orwell and his legacy. Neo-conservative intellectuals like Norman Podhoretz would claim Orwell as an anti-Communist who would have supported Reagan's efforts to stand up to the evil empire of the Soviet Union while Irving Howe insisted that Orwell was a democratic socialist to the core. Both the conservative Podhoretz and socialist Howe, however, would have joined the liberal Lionel Trilling, the radical Edward Said and the Marxist Terry Eagleton in championing a focus on literature and writing that seems to be under siege today as cultural and post-colonial consolidate a 'theory' revolution in the contemporary humanities.

Orwell matters within our contemporary literary world because he provides a model for literary critics concerned with excessive professionalisation as well as for those who worry that clear and graceful language in our broader culture might be damaged by the 'high theory' that comes out of the contemporary critical humanities as well as by the 'sound-bite' and 'newspeak' culture created by modern media, think tanks and political campaigns. Unfortunately, however, the political polarisation that we have seen in American and global politics over the past twenty-five years has threatened the creation of a broad coalition of literary scholars who can unite on these general principles, while disagreeing on specifics such as the politics of the Middle East, racial and gender politics and the question of the welfare state. The political polarisation intensified by 9/11 and the war in Iraq makes it more difficult for literary scholars to unite around a broad commitment to literature, the central project for literary scholars today.

This is made easier, it should be said, by the fact that Soviet Communism has joined German Nazism as discredited and destroyed political and intellectual movements. Orwell got it right in opposing both Communism and Nazism in *Nineteen Eighty-Four* and *Animal Farm*, so with these issues behind us perhaps his example can inspire a new generation of young intellectuals to try to find a clear path to opposing both Western domination of the world and vicious anti-modern movements represented by radical Islamist parties and organisations. And while it is difficult, indeed impossible, to isolate the study of literature from the worldly concerns that Orwell, Trilling, Howe, and Said all put at the centre of their criticism, it might be possible to restore a civility to political debates among non-professional 'amateur' social criticism that could allow for a common stance against the excessive populism and professionalism that threatens the health and vitality of the academic humanities today. Without such a common front, Orwell may go down in history as one of the very 'last intellectuals' as Russell Jacoby once famously put it, destroyed not by the jack-boot of totalitarianism but by academic specialisation, literary careerism and cultural wars. These cultural wars put race, class, gender and religion at the centre of our attention, important issues to be sure, but political questions that should not crowd literature and an emphasis on good quality writing that should have its own place in our culture and in universities. Orwell is important for academics, intellectuals, students and our broader culture today, above all else, because of his politically engaged writing and the model he gives us for a literary criticism that matters.

Global public literary intellectuals?

Literary social critics for the twenty-first century will look very different than they did in the middle of the twentieth century, of course, and the 'Orwell' model for the engaged literary critic requires serious adaptation and revision if it is to be effective in engaging the imagination of young scholars and budding literary intellectuals. Orwell's maleness has been widely remarked upon, of course, and Said was not totally wrong in being sceptical of Orwell's relevance to the issues of race, representation and the 'other' so important in the contemporary critical humanities. What might the 'public literary intellectual' look like in this age of globalisation and the internet, at a time when Orwell's very English parochialism is no longer dominant nor desirable in our broader intellectual culture? It is clearly the case that the 'plain speaking' public intellectual of Orwell vintage has a particular resonance in the Anglo-American world. And Orwell's focus on the politics of the English language has to be expanded to include concern with and openness to different cultural, linguistic and political traditions.

Orwell himself was probably too deeply imbedded in his own time and place to give us a vision for a truly 'global public literary intellectual', and there is a danger of reading the context of our times unfairly back into Orwell's situation. The questions his example raises, however, are worth exploring and addressing in new ways today. The expansion of the research university in global directions will create more of the professionalism that will undermine the social space for Orwell-like intellectuals for some of the reasons we have outlined above. At the same time, the citation data we presented shows that ideas from the general intellectual world do enter academic debates and discussions, even in this age of academia as Jacoby once put it. The Orwells of the future will emerge because politics, literature and good sense matter, and are essential for democratic debate and vibrant cultural life.

These new Orwells will be far more feminist oriented than Orwell himself was, and they will certainly not be exclusively white and English as the forces of globalisation create the possibilities for a truly world culture and public sphere. In addition, global public literary intellectuals for the twenty-first century will have to be far more media savvy and far less tied to the pace of mid-twentieth century intellectual journals and quarterlies as was Orwell. The internet, blog technology, television and celebrity culture have created the need for different types of public intellectuals, as the models represented by Chomsky and Orwell give way to Hitchens, Zizek and Paglia. The public intellectuals of the future who will shape intellectual debate beyond their life times, however, like Orwell himself, will be politically complex and principled. Whatever these literary public intellectuals of the future look like, they will almost certainly draw on the inspiration of Orwell's clear thinking and writing, and his commitment to a life of the mind engaged in the public cultural and political issues of the day outside of the narrow confines of the professionalised academy.

The institutional perspective on the sociology of public intellectuals I have stressed here has its merits, but the case of Orwell raises questions beyond sociology. Orwell's influence spread throughout the world and across academic disciplines not because of networks of academic supporters or journals designed to promote his work. Nor was Orwell's personal charisma or relationship with powerful mentors or political figures central in explaining his extraordinary influence over fifty years after his death. Orwell's writings help draw individuals into the world and the tradition of the public literary intellectual, one by one, and by the force of the work and the example (Rodden, 2003). Universities, publishing, media and the institutional basis of the life of the mind have changed dramatically over the past 100 years, but the Orwell tradition will continue into our new century transformed by new realities but motivated and energised by his concern with writing, ideas, clarity of thought, literary judgement and political principles.

NOTES

1. Posner's data is culled from a search of three Lexis-Nexis databases – Major Newspapers, Magazine Stories (Combined), and Transcripts (of Television and Radio Shows) – in July 2000. For scholarly citations, Posner relies on Science Citation Index, Social Sciences Citations Index, and the Arts and Humanities Citation Index. His internet list is a result of a search of www.Google.com. Although Posner's methodology has many problems (he himself admits this), his data is useful for a first approximation of the influence of Orwell as a public intellectual.

2. My data are culled from a search of three ISI databases: the Social Sciences Citation Index, Science Citation Index Expanded, and the Arts & Humanities Citation Index performed in December 2004. I did not perform what sociologists call

content analysis – that is, going through and analysing how Orwell is discussed. Thus, this method does not discern between a brief mention and a complete article on Orwell, praise or criticism. Even more importantly, this measure only counts formal citations of Orwell's work, not mentions of his ideas or name in the text of an article without a citation, something that could be traced and measured now with new technology. While I am aware that this methodology has its limitations, it does show how Posner's categorisation of Orwell's academic reputation as 'not applicable' is incorrect and suggest directions for further research.

3. This is, of course, an imperfect measure since we are using the categories established by the Web of Science and I am not 'controlling' for the number of total journals in each discipline or the average citation rate in each field. Moreover, the coverage of the Social Science and the Humanities Citations Indexes is imperfect, misses some journals and has been increasing over the years so we cannot compare change over time with any reliability. This chart does not tell a story of the decline of Orwell's influence since generally citation patterns do tend to have a 'half-life' of sorts, especially if one is not a canonised thinker. There are, moreover, more journals covered in the Social Science Citation Index in 1996–2003 than there were in 1976–2003, and the third set of years in the chart shown is for seven years not ten. This data gives only a rough idea of citation patterns not a systematic account of change over time.

4. These data was culled from the same database search of citations between 1976–2003, and are broken down into the various fields provided by the database: literary studies, history, sociology, political science, anthropology, multi-disciplinary and non-specialised humanities and social science. As I have already mentioned, the methodology is not perfect, and the disciplinary categories overlap.

5. My data cannot discern between the specific essay 'Shooting an Elephant' and various essays that are collected in *Shooting an Elephant and Other Essays* (1950).

14

JOHN RODDEN

Orwell for today's reader:
an open letter

Dear George,

Until you entered my life, I vaguely imagined I would become a professor much like those whom I had admired as an undergraduate and as a graduate student, a specialist in Wordsworth's *Prelude* or a scholar who had mastered the minutiae of literary modernism. Your work and legacy have served as my introduction to intellectual life, indeed my passport to contemporary cultural history.

I am often asked what it was that drew me to you. After all, I've been reading and pondering your work for a long time. Indeed, I've written hundreds of pages about your writings, and I've returned to them again during the editing for this Cambridge Companion to your work. The answer that I find myself giving is that you inspired me – because you lived what you wrote and you wrote out of the depths of your experience.

As I delved more deeply into your life and work, I also discovered a few surprising personal links between us. In fact, my father worked as a day labourer just two miles away from the Gloucestershire working-class hospital in Scotland in which you convalesced. His peasant father in County Donegal, Ireland felt sympathy with Irish nationalists (like Sean O'Casey, whom you reviled) and flirted with communism. Certainly you would have castigated my grandfather as a knee-jerk socialist and an Irish revolutionary agitator. (And what about me? Would you, George Orwell, have liked me? I'm a vegetarian, a sandal-wearing religious believer, an Irishman, a Catholic. The odds are against it!)

You also led me to numerous discoveries. Thanks to you, I have met so many interesting people. The portrait that I have painted of you in my books is not altogether flattering, but you wouldn't want that, would you? I do hope that it conveys your courage, your steadfastness, your passion, your faith in a better future, and above all, your intelligence and intellectual integrity. To demonstrate my gratitude, I periodically come to the defence of your reputation.

Now, in this final reckoning, let me share directly how you have influenced me. My own case is less important in itself than for what it represents about the changing condition of intellectual life in the half-century since your death.

I

How does one become a writer, or indeed (to use an old-fashioned phrase), a man or woman of letters today? Or, for that matter – to use a newfangled term – a 'public intellectual'?

It's not possible in quite the way that it used to be for thinking persons of your generation. The culture of Anglo-American intellectual life has altered permanently and irrevocably from the post-Second World War era of your day – the age of the intellectual coteries, little magazines, and highbrow literary quarterlies. Those institutions formed literary journalists, intellectuals, and even men and women of letters like you a half-century ago.

Today they don't. Nor does any other literary institution or group or setting. And nothing since has replaced them – not universities, not think tanks, not Internet chat rooms. No wonder that no intellectual since then has replaced you either.

How does a serious reader with aspirations to contribute to cultural life become an 'intellectual' nowadays? *Is* it actually possible, in the age of academe, to become an engaged critic? A political writer? A man or woman of letters? Indeed: an 'American Scholar', in the broad, Emersonian sense?

No graduate programmes exist to develop such a being; graduate education in the humanities fosters specialists. No creative writing workshops cultivate intellectual breadth and diversity – in fact, nonfiction is typically excluded altogether from creative writing programmes. 'Journalism school' is not the place – and certainly not law school. The think tanks are oriented toward policymaking, social science research, or ideological agendas – and typically unreceptive to younger writers.

Younger people today have been shaped by a system of mass higher education, not the world of books and little magazines. The university has expanded, and corporate journalism has become omnipresent, absorbing all these people who in an earlier age might have aimed a little higher. A number of intellectual magazines still thrive today, in and out of the academy, but none bring together a group in quite the way that *Horizon* or *Partisan Review* once did.

So where does one go, now that the little magazines and the London and New York intellectual scenes are largely dead and gone? That was the dilemma that Russell Jacoby's *The Last Intellectuals: American Life in the Age of Academe* meditated on two decades ago. Jacoby had no answers then. And, if anything, the institutions and settings that once fostered intellectual life are even fewer and weaker in our own time. Since the rise of theory in the literary academy in the late 1980s, academe is arguably even more inhospitable to an intellectual vocation. (The concept of the 'public' intellectual has emerged in reaction against academic specialisation and jargon, but some intellectuals have reacted against the term itself, worrying that the adjective 'public' has overwhelmed the noun 'intellectual'.)

So how is it done today?

I submit that it can still be done the old way: writer to writer. That's the way you did it, George, and *that* approach can still be taken today. The old way is the self-appointed literary apprenticeship. One looks for a model, one enters the Tradition. It is a tradition of writers and intellectuals who developed public voices. And one listens so keenly and resonates so deeply to the pitch and passion of those compelling voices that one internalises them. One 'ingests' one's literary models. One learns their language – their accent, their rhythms, their intonation. One does all this not in order to slavishly imitate them, but rather to grow in and through them toward one's own unique voice and vision.

Furthermore, I submit that the old way of mentoring is crucial, more indispensable today than ever to the intellectual calling. It is necessary to establish and maintain a connection with the tradition of thinkers, both dead and alive. For the vocation of a writer is about something more than a career, a profession, or a job. It is indeed a calling – the calling of 'the word'. Not merely in the sense of becoming a wordsmith but rather an author in the old sense (L. *auctores*, an authority). And all authority comes with corresponding responsibility.

The relationship with one's self-selected literary authorities eventually develops so far that they become even more than one's teachers, more even than one's mentors. One 'adopts' them as members of one's intellectual – and even spiritual – family. They become elder brothers and sisters.

Indeed, the directive to learn – and 'unlearn' – lessons from an intellectual big brother or sister aims to self-legislate a programme for the epidemic of orphaned, would-be intellectuals. Yes, this is actually a big brother and sister programme for intellectually hungry boys and girls – precisely because there are no graduate, or journalism, or law schools – or writing programmes – that can parent them into sufficient intellectual maturity to become public voices.

II

Of course, as we all know, there are big brothers – and Big Brothers. I real-ise that the latter, upper-cased phrase immediately evokes images of corrupt tyranny rather than caring tutelage. Fair enough. But there are Bad Big Broth-ers and benevolent big brothers. It's oppressive when 'Big Brother is watching you'. But we could also imagine how the final line in *Nineteen Eighty-Four* – if lifted from the novel and let stand alone – could refer to a benevolent big brother: 'He loved big brother' – 'loved' because of the gifts given, gifts that many intellectuals, on the Right and Left and Centre, have acknowledged receiving from you, George Orwell. And that is why intellectuals across the ideological spectrum have exalted you as their 'intellectual hero'.

Now I know something about big brothers because I am the oldest in a family of four boys and have heard a lot about big brothers – both benev-olent and not-so-benevolent. Admittedly: a big brother can be a royal pain. (That was never the case in our family, of course.) But one thing that all big brothers, both bad and benevolent, have in common: it seems as if they're always with you. Unlike the father, one doesn't expect them to die off in some not-so-distant future. Maybe that's why you, George, chose 'Big Brother' – rather than 'Big Daddy' – as your image of terror. For all of the Freudian frenzy about the male's hidden urge for parricide, the plain fact is that fear of the father can wane for quite practical reasons – simply because one day you know you'll be stronger than the 'old man'. He'll weaken and die. One day you'll probably even pity him. But that's not the case if the 'old man' is only a year or two older than you. He is *always* going to be there.

Yet a benevolent big brother can also be a great gift. Here too, I speak from experience because you, George Orwell, have been just that kind of intellectual big brother for me.

I'm not at all sure you would approve me as your 'younger brother', let alone be proud about it. But after living in your presence for twenty years and authoring five books about your work and legacy, I've definitely forged a bond with your ghost – you've become a central presence in my intellectual and even personal life. ('So how's life with George?' my friends periodically ask me.)

'George Orwell' has never been a scholarly topic or an academic specialty for me; even since the day I read *Animal Farm* as a tenth-grader, I've felt a certain kinship with you. It seemed natural to teach university courses such as 'The Utopian and Anti-Utopian Imagination' organised around your work, and then to write a dissertation about your legacy. It seemed natural because – as I ultimately came to understand and to accept – I was really engaged in veiled autobiography. Through my studies of your heritage, I was, in fact, claiming it. And I was also talking about my own imaginative flights and fears. Yes, your legacy was part of my inheritance. (In fact, I've often spoken with such passion about your work in my university course on utopias that, when I mentioned years ago to an undergraduate student of mine that I intended to write an essay with the title 'My Life with George Orwell,' he asked me: 'Was George Orwell really your roommate in college? I heard that he was'.)

What did you impart to me? What do you still have to say to young people today, more than a half-century after publication of your last book, *Nineteen Eighty-Four*, and your death?

Repeatedly I've asked that question – I've put it not just to myself and my friends, I've even posed it to your friends and colleagues. In fact, during the 1980s I interviewed several of your old friends for my first book – as well as many intellectuals in the following generation who had been influenced by you – and in turn who influenced me.

All that has been part of my intellectual coming-of-age, indeed of an unfolding, half-conscious programme to discover my vocation by acquiring a personal visa to the world of my intellectual fathers and mothers.

III

Before going on, I ought to elaborate on the circumstances of my 'coming-of-age' – and where I have arrived, politically and culturally, since gaining intellectual maturity. In *The Politics of Literary Reputation* (1989), I described myself as a 'post-Vatican II Catholic liberal', but I doubt a 'Catholic liberal' would pass muster with you any more readily than did Graham Greene (your 'Catholic fellow-traveller'), let alone Catholic conservatives such as Evelyn Waugh and Christopher Hollis.

Yes, as I surmised earlier, I don't think you, George, however sympathetic you sought to be, would cotton to my Catholic faith, even though I'm an Irish-American 'cradle Catholic' (and not one of your hated English converts – like those three writers).

Yet, although 'liberal' characterises my politics better than any other term, the 'L word' is not a central part of my identity. I believe that, even as one embraces a political tradition, one should acknowledge that conservatism, liberalism and radicalism overlap in important ways. All three traditions value tradition, liberty and equality – though they prioritise them differently.

In saying this, I am speaking very personally. Each of the great political traditions attracts and has influenced me precisely because it affirms a fundamental commitment to metaphysical values. I am indebted to them all. So I suggest: Yes, let us honour their profound differences and resist any impulse to collapse them into a hodgepodge. But need we invariably see them as mutually hostile? I think not.

I realise that all this may seem confused or eccentric. But I am not interested in wrangling over the correct terminology for my current political outlook. I do believe a substantial aspect of it is properly termed 'nineteenth-century liberalism', but my political outlook also possesses elements of 'cultural conservatism' and even 'socialism', g owing to a strand of populist, rustic, backward-looking English radicalism that you shared with Cobbett, Morris, and other contrarian populists and Tory radicals.

Like theirs, mine is an eclectic radicalism. But the label does not overly concern me. What I do know is that I subscribe to an egalitarian, anti-elitist politics at odds with traditional Conservatism – and also to an anti-progressive, tradition-minded politics quite resonant with cultural conservatism. I distrust elites – whether in the form of aristocratic castes or Leninist vanguards. Like both you and Chesterton, both of whose thought also eluded political labels, I share a belief in the emotional sustenance of small property, a distaste for industrialism, an antagonism to monopolistic practices, and a faith in the common sense of common people (like my immigrant, working-class Irish parents).

I have long discerned these features as part of your intellectual physiognomy too – what Conor Cruise O'Brien once called your 'Tory growl'. Indeed, both Chesterton and you remind me of a simple truth: Radicalism need not mean progressivism, and a repudiation of Marxism need not imply acceptance of social injustice.

I am also a cultural conservative – as, I think, you were (your love of popular culture, including penny postcards and boys' weekly newspapers notwithstanding). For me, the value of cultural conservatism is precisely its will to conserve – not just high 'culture' in the narrow sense, but all that sublimely uplifts and nurtures life. It is a practical philosophy that wisely acknowledges human limits. It starts with an acceptance of the conditions of Reality – yes, the conditions, but not the outcome. I stress this, because the not-infrequent conservative acquiescence to injustice is unacceptable to me. A 'decent' conservatism still battles injustice, but it acknowledges that most human beings need a stable environment and the ownership of property – to know, to see, and to handle something, however small, that is their own. (Neoconservatism, in its championing of progress, business conglomerates, and capitalism, does not prize such values.)

My admiration for you endures. I am still inspired by your moral courage and intellectual integrity. And yet, unlike you, I am not a socialist: I am a social democrat. I am wary of fixing my gaze on dazzling communitarian ideals that are beyond me and my fellow citizens. Better to honour 'where people are' in their lives – and to legislate from there – rather than to mesmerise them with a vision that is far beyond their moral reach.

IV

So then: What have you, George Orwell, my intellectual big brother, taught me? What I have learned – or unlearned – from your work and example?

I should stress that a large gap exists between what I've learned and how well I practice it. Your intellectual courage and clarity of mind were extraordinary – not to mention your literary achievement. But you were also blessedly 'ordinary', as many of your admirers have marvelled – and it's a perception of you as 'an extraordinary ordinary man' that gives me the temerity even to proceed to enumerate my debts to you, cognizant that any such list can be misconstrued as an attempt to police your legacy. Or worse: as an act of self-nomination to don your mantle – just the sort of body-snatching and grave-robbing of you I've decried in two full-length studies.

So much for my personal disclaimer. Let me frame my answer to my two earlier questions via your most famous essay. In 'Politics and the English Language' (1945), you gave six rules for 'good writing' in the sense of prose style. And perhaps we could give six similar rules for 'good writing' and 'good thinking' in the sense of intellectual integrity, which would represent the very opposite of Oceania *goodthink*. So let me share these six 'unlessons' derived from your example, which I might entitle 'Politics and the Literary Intelligentsia'.

1. *Unlearn Groupthink*. Don't ride along with the intellectual herd. Refuse to accede to coterie politics. Become instead a truly 'freelance' writer. Risk becoming the conscience of your reference group, indeed a public conscience. Look to your own failings, your own self-righteous anger and intolerance.

To be an intellectual is to embrace the vocation of a critic. Even American neoconservatives, who are typically uncritical of the major power centres in culture, are nonetheless critics. They are critics of the intellectual culture, rather than the larger culture. They are critics of their own reference group of intellectuals.

You exemplified a writer independent of all coteries. Such a writer is sceptical of all ideologies and isms. You stayed on speaking terms with many of your ideological enemies, respecting your differences with them and agreeing to disagree.

Unfortunately, this very seldom happens in contemporary intellectual life or even in academe. A dissent is overblown into a betrayal; horrendous disagreement provokes ostracism, even exile. As you once observed, in an inescapably ideological age, a dissenter within the ranks seems to get tagged with all the positions of opposition.

2. *Unlearn treating the glitterati as more than equal than others.* Resist the bewitching attractions of court patronage and courtly politicos. Keep instead a wary distance from power.

You had no truck with ideology and –isms. You insisted on seeing what is 'in front of your nose' and said that the test of intellectual honesty was to speak out against Stalin. (You were rather uninterested in the crimes of Hitler because Hitler was beyond the pale, an obvious fascist on the other side. You were far more concerned with the behaviour of Stalin.)

The 'critical intellectual', ever since the Dreyfus case, keeps a keen eye on all power centres – and especially on his own vulnerabilities to its seductions. The critical intellectual cannot be flattered or bought. He or she is a prophet outside the city walls, not a high priest representing the status quo. (You once remarked caustically on those 'socialists who are patted on the head by a duke and are lost forever to the Labour Party'.)

You practiced what you preached about relating at a distance to power, as your bracing criticism of Nye Bevan, even after the Labour Party came to power in 1945, made clear. (You were careful to say that you were a supporter, not a member, of the Labour Party.)

3. *Unlearn simplistic scepticism.* Renounce the alluring, merely oppositional role of critic and sceptic. Commit also to a constructive vision. Commit wholeheartedly yet not uncritically. Be not just a critic and a conscience. Be both a sceptic and a dreamer, a realist and an idealist. Let us remain responsive to what George Gissing referred to as 'the intelligence of the heart'.

Your criticism was directed at socialists, not socialism. You mercilessly assaulted their lies and their orthodoxies. (You once remarked that the worst thing about socialism was socialists.) You criticised from within the Left, and that is why you became known as the conscience of the Left.

Yes, you believed in socialism. You were not just its loyal critic. You wrote *Animal Farm* in order to create a myth that would fight the false myth of Russia as a socialist country. But we must not get lost in our ideals or escape into a dangerous Utopianism or into inhumane abstractions. Yes, we must value principles, but more important is an acceptance of realities: not to get carried away by abstract reason or by ideals, and to gain a balanced wisdom, the realism of maturity.

Your positive reception by the neoconservatives is evidence that you ran the risk of being misunderstood and claimed by the opposing side. You may have been an excessively scrupulous conscience, but you flayed the Left in order to strengthen it, not to weaken it or abandon it.

4. *Unlearn politicising the personal and personalising the political.* Break the intelligentsia's lazy, knee-jerk habit of lining up people in categories. Power is not everything. In addition to a politics, there is also an ethics, an esthetics, an erotics of life and literature. Yes, the personal is political – but the personal is also not *just* political. The personal is also ethical, aesthetic, erotic – and so much more. Attend to the level and domain of enquiry at issue, in order to see the extent to which politics is a conditioning or determining factor in any particular case. Here again, dialogue with political adversaries – staying open to rethinking, keeping the conversation alive, respecting differences and agreeing to disagree – is a mark of the healthy capacity both to honour and to distinguish the political and the personal.

This unlesson honours the voice of experience. It acknowledges that intellectual integrity rests on the concrete, the individual, the particular.

5. *Unlearn Elitespeak and its Newspeak idioms.* Avoid addressing primarily the cultural elite – and avoid the self-referential allusions and jargon that usually accompany such practices. Address instead the informed layperson, the literate public – not merely the literary intelligentsia.

This unlesson addresses the question of language. Writing to be read by the informed layperson and the literate public, rather than merely for a clique or group of specialists, is a choice. To prize accessible writing is to open oneself to the charge of simple-mindedness or 'bourgeois liberal empiricism'. Accessible writing means avoiding specialised vocabulary and academic jargon. It means writing 'prose like a windowpane'.

6. *Break any of these rules, rather than do something that violates intellectual integrity.* This directly echoes your sixth rule in 'Politics and the English Language', George, whereby you concluded that, however valuable your previous advice, no rules for good writing exist. There are only rules to minimise bad writing. The English language, like all languages, indeed like the richness and complexity of life – admits of no rule-making. And so, with your example, I too can urge: Treat all of the foregoing unlessons as ad hoc. Treat all of the foregoing 'rules' as prisms not isms.

Let me also summarise now the lessons that I have learned from you, what six 'rules' you've taught me – by precept and example. And here let me speak quite personally:

- You tempered my will to systematise and gave me a respect and love for the concrete particular.
- You emboldened me to speak out, to make a commitment and to abide by it.
- Your example fortified me to sustain a process of rigorous self-questioning, to hold my own side to the highest possible standard.

- You showed me how important it is to live what one writes. In practical terms, this meant a concentration on friendship and on lived experience.
- You vouchsafed me a vision of my 'best self' one that is truly realistic, not just calculating or pragmatic or willful.
- You taught me to write in an accessible manner and not to embrace elitism or 'specialness', not to insist on being 'superior' by taking the moral high ground and remaining self-righteous, as if only I myself know 'the Right Way'.

V

And what did you, George, my intellectual big brother, *not* teach me?

In the end, you did not teach me 'the Way' to become an intellectual. You simply modelled *one* way to grow intellectually. For instance, you did not see – quite possibly because you did not live beyond mid-century and witness the full development of trends under way in your own day – the importance of race, gender and class. You did not live to see the rise of social movements such as feminism, multiculturalism, and other forms of radicalism that have come to dominate academic and intellectual life. As a result, you can – unfairly, I think – seem dated.

In these and other ways, I must grant your considerable limitations and shortcomings. Still, one weakness to which you did not succumb was the lure of System. You, George Orwell, recognised the limitations of logic and method. You had no System or Grand Theory. The passion for a System can slip into dogma. You help inoculate one to resist that.

You also show us that it is possible to act even when the timing seems premature or our knowledge seems inadequate: 'I know enough to act'. That's what you did. To know that emboldens one. One can learn by doing – as you did in *Down and Out in Paris and London*, in *The Road to Wigan Pier*, in *Homage to Catalonia*.

And that is something else you have taught me, however poorly I practice it: intellectual courage. You exemplified the willingness to risk going outside one's specialisation, to risk failure. Having 'failed' so dramatically and completely in prep school – or so you thought – you, Eric Blair, became willing to risk failure for the rest of your life.

For all that, I thank you. Yes, my emphasis in this essay has not been on your limitations but rather on your inspirational power. This emphasis is legitimate; it does not entail whitewashing or lionising you, but acknowledging a debt and a legacy.

VI

So that's my testimonial – or manifesto. I believe that one way to grow intellectually is, as it were, to 'adopt a big brother or big sister' – and thereby enter the intellectual tradition by entering his or her work. To do so self-consciously, by selecting a model of how to do it: that is a slow yet time-tested and proven way.

But it is not a matter of simply entering their writing. One ought to see their written work in the context of their daily lives and thereby gain an understanding of the larger world of the writer – beyond his or her art – and also the role of artistic and intellectual activity in that life. All this is pursued not in order to slavishly imitate that life, but to embrace its strengths and understand its weaknesses – as a way of building one's own strengths and growing beyond one's own weaknesses.

To adopt an intellectual big brother or big sister means that we, their readers and would-be heirs, must take the initiative. The potential for an impassioned, powerful response is always there, because the work is there, and it remains available to us.

15

ERIKA GOTTLIEB

George Orwell: a bibliographic essay

After decades of financial struggle as the author of four naturalistic novels, three critically acclaimed but politically controversial documentaries, and a body of literary essays and journalism, suddenly Orwell emerged as a major writer of international repute with two satires, the political allegory of *Animal Farm* in 1945, and the dystopian satire *Nineteen Eighty-Four*, published in 1949, a few months before his death. A wide array of critical reviews by Golo Mann, Lionel Trilling, Arthur Koestler, V. S. Pritchett and Bertrand Russell among others – some of them also taking the shape of obituaries – identified his last novel as an outstanding achievement. In his 2003 *Scenes from an Afterlife: the Legacy of George Orwell*, John Rodden points out that after his early death, Orwell's life became a legend still vital and alive all over the world today, an observation echoing the one made by Jenni Calder in what Gunter Grass called, aptly, the Orwell decade of the 1980s. Orwell's last two novels, Calder states, are not only part of our literary tradition and heritage, but [also] have entered our mythology *(Animal Farm* and *Nineteen Eighty-Four: Open Guides to Literature*, 1987). But figures in mythology are not necessarily beyond political controversy. Providing an encyclopedic view of the controversies in Orwell's reception up to the mid-1980s, in *The Politics of Literary Reputation: The Making and Claiming of St George Orwell* (1989) Rodden outlines not only a picture gallery of Orwell's widely different critical portrayals as The rebel, The common man, The prophet and The saint, but also the battles among the body snatchers, critics of the most diverse political persuasion, who argue that if Orwell, the man who claimed to fight for democratic socialism and against totalitarianism, were alive today, he would be on their side. During the plethora of Orwell conferences resounding over continents in 1984, the range and volume of critical voices – mainly admiring, but often also quite hostile – demonstrate that by then the 'fault-lines' for the eruption of critical debate have been clearly drawn.

In his 1982 *A George Orwell Companion: A Guide to the Novels, Documentaries and Essays* John Hammond deems Orwell 'one of the most significant writers of the twentieth century', and in his first-rate biography, *Orwell: Wintry Conscience of a Generation* (2000), Jeffrey Meyers declares Orwell 'the most popular English writer of our time' who 'had succeeded in revealing the truth to European and American intellectuals who'd been sympathetic to the Soviet system'. Carefully balancing biographical fact and textual analysis, Ian Slater claims that Orwell's work will 'endure – because ultimately his attack is not directed so much toward a political system as upon a state of mind' (*Orwell: The Road to Airstrip One*, 1984), and in his discussion of his 'new find' of Orwell letters and memoranda relating to the two years Orwell worked for the BBC, W. J. West declares Orwell 'one of the best-known English writers of the twentieth century and . . . *Animal Farm* and *Nineteen Eighty-Four* [as] master works of their era' (*The Larger Evils. Nineteen Eighty-Four: the Truth Behind the Satire* 1992).

Nevertheless, the very works that created Orwell's sudden and still powerful international reputation also became the focus of severe, often vicious criticism. In *George Orwell, a Political Life* (1993) Stephen Ingle explores Orwell's legacy to British Socialism, pointing out that 'few writers on politics have left behind a more ambiguous legacy than George Orwell'. There is no doubt, for example, that Orwell's essays commanded increasing and well-deserved attention in the past 20 years, but often the critic's praise of the essays also implies some kind of a reservation about the last novel. Thus, when Peter Davison, editor of the magnificent work of scholarship, *The Complete Works of George Orwell* in 20 volumes, concludes that, Orwell 'has been instrumental in broadening and redefining concepts of culture' and 'his influence in so doing is still felt and it will continue', he also adds, 'especially through his essays' (*George Orwell: A Literary Life* 1996). Also, when Gordon Bowker declares him 'one of the greatest writers of the twentieth century . . . still widely read and greatly admired', he also states that 'as a novelist Orwell had his shortcomings . . . As an essayist he was supreme' (*Inside George Orwell*, 2003).

In fact, in spite of its reputation as one of the most influential works of the twentieth century, *Nineteen Eighty-Four* has been considered a 'flawed masterpiece' by many critics – even by Bernard Crick, whose *Orwell: a Life*, published in 1980, is probably still the most comprehensive and factually reliable biography of Orwell. In agreement with George Woodcock (whose *The Crystal Spirit* [1982]) was considered for a long time as the definitive critical work on Orwell), Crick suggests that due to the flaws undermining *Nineteen Eighty-Four*, *Animal Farm* should be regarded as Orwell's crowning achievement. The widely accepted notion that Orwell's most famous work is a flawed masterpiece is usually associated with the author's alleged despair, expressed by the breakdown of Winston Smith, the central character in the novel. Few critics raise the question why despair does not undermine the uncontested genius of Kafka or Swift, or go further to explore whether the defeat of a protagonist in a dystopian satire does indeed express the author's apathy or inertia we usually associate with a state of despair.

In the 1970s not only Winston Smith, but also Orwell is 'psychoanalysed' by depth psychology. In the mid-1950s Anthony West argues that the dying Orwell's terminal despair in *Nineteen Eighty-Four* should be traced back to the 'hidden wound' of his school years. West (still echoed by Michael Shelden's *Orwell: An Authorized Biography* as late as 1991) does not consider that 'Such Such Were the Joys', Orwell's essay on his school years at St Cyprian, was written when Orwell was already deep at work on *Nineteen Eighty-Four*. Is it not more likely that Orwell projects his adult hatred of dictatorship on his school principals retroactively, than that his childhood suffering was responsible for his political judgement about German and Soviet totalitarian systems in the 1930s and 1940s? The thought-provoking Freudian explorations in depth psychology by Gerald Fiderer, Marcus Smith, Paul Roazan, and by Richard Smyer's *Primal Dream and Primal Crime: Orwell's Development as a Psychological Novelist* (1979), analyse what they see as Orwell's terminal despair expressed in Winston's breakdown in Room 101 in terms of his Oedipus Complex, his wish to return to the womb, sadomasochism, homosexuality and paranoia. None of them contemplate Orwell's point that since the totalitarian regime is capable of identifying the particular 'Achilles heel' in any personality, defeat in Room 101 is inevitable for each and every individual (hence the torture chamber as the central institution of the Inquisition, the Gestapo and the KGB). It is only in the mid-1980s that critical emphasis shifts from the psycho-pathology of Winston – or Orwell – to the pathology characteristic of totalitarian dictatorship, as in Mason Harris's 'From History to Psychological Grotesque: the Politics of Sado-masochism in *Nineteen Eighty-Four*' and Erika Gottlieb's 'Room 101 Revisited: the Reconciliation of Political and Psychological Dimensions in Orwell's *Nineteen Eighty-Four*'.[1]

Although the 1970s passion for subjecting Winston – in essence his author – to Freudian psychoanalysis has, understandably, subsided by now, many of the terms introduced by critics of the psychological persuasion – such as hysteria, sado-masochism and paranoia, for example – slipped, almost unnoticed, into the vocabulary of Orwell's recent biographers. Thus, in his carefully researched biography Gordon Bowker casually mentions that 'those who criticized Orwell had no idea how strongly he felt [about the power of the Stalinist Left in England], how powerful was his paranoia'. Yet, Christopher Hitchens (*Orwell in Spain*), D. J. Taylor (*Orwell*) and Bowker himself make excellent use of the KGB files unearthed in the 1990s that show that Orwell had good reason to fear that he was on the 'hitlist' of the Stalinists when he fought in the POUM in Spain; that he was considered by Moscow as a 'rabid Trotskyist', fated, most likely, to be eliminated at a rigged trial had the communists stayed in power in Spain. From the KGB files it is also clear that Orwell was followed by Comintern agents not only while in Spain, but also after his return to London; Peter Smolka, surreptitious Stalinist agent at the BBC, played an important part in suppressing the publication of *Animal Farm*. As W. J. West points out, Orwell's *Nineteen Eighty-Four* 'criticised for generations by communist intellectuals as being an exaggerated fantasy by a terminally ill man, proved to be a precisely accurate account of a bureaucratic totalitarian state'. In other words, by now it is quite clear that Orwell's antagonism to Soviet terror, to the Stalinist Left in England and to their control of much of British literary life was not irrational, that is, not based on what Bowker refers to as 'paranoia' or a persecution complex.

Another interesting example of the somewhat too ready use of psychological terms introduced in the 1970s is in the otherwise excellent biography of Jeffrey Meyers, who after a lifetime of serious Orwell scholarship still argues for Orwell's 'masochistic', self-punishing attitude that often verged on the suicidal throughout his literary career, particularly when, at the end of his life, he rejected the doctors' suggestion to 'leave the bleak island of Jura and to get a typist in London for *Nineteen Eighty-Four*'. As for Orwell's earlier life choices, Rodden raises the question whether 'Orwell's socialist convictions play no role in his life decision', while W. J. West, Shelden and Bowker point out the genuine attractions of Jura over London in 1948. They also ask whether the idyllic landscape of the Golden Country is not, at least to some extent, inspired by the landscape in front of Orwell when he was writing the novel, and also suggest that it was not his death wish, but the memory of Eileen, and Eileen's desire for a world far away from London, that may have influenced Orwell's choice of Jura.

Another significant direction of critical enquiry introduced fairly early into the Orwell debate, deals with Orwell's despair as a spiritual-religious dilemma, for example in *The Fugitive from the Camp of Victory* (1961) by Richard Rees, both a political ally and a personal friend of Orwell. Patrick Reilly in *George Orwell: the Age's Adversary* (1986) suggests that in reading Orwell, 'the dilemma of man's ontological significance, sharpened to anguish by the death of god and the revocation of eternity, may suddenly ambush us', as if Orwell's mind was 'forever circling it, ready by any moment to swoop up this abiding preoccupation' – a note also echoing Christopher Small's notion of Orwell's despair in *The Road to Miniluv* (1975). Among the studies exploring Orwell's religious-spiritual vision of the world it is only Valerie Simms's 'A Reconsideration of Orwell's 1984: the Moral Implications of Despair' (1973–74) that raises the question whether Orwell's dark political announcements, inspired by the darkness of historical reality, were not already there in his essays years, even decades before his last novel.

But the notion of terminal, suicidal despair that contributes to the verdict that *Nineteen Eighty-Four* must be a flawed masterpiece, if not even a failed novel, is even more significant among the political critics (since their number is, probably, a great deal larger). There is no doubt that even during the 'Orwell decade' critics not in sympathy with Orwell's politics accuse his last book of aesthetic shortcomings. In his *George Orwell: L'Engagement* (1984) Gilbert Bonifas talks about an 'immeasurable pessimism' that distorts Orwell's vision at the end, and therefore chooses *The Road to Wigan Pier* as the peak of his achievement. In his *Orwell and the Politics of Despair* (1988), Alok Rai argues that the last novel is flawed aesthetically by Orwell's 'paranoid imagination' and Cold War 'hysteria'. In her extremely influential Feminist critique, *The Orwell Mystique: A Study in Male Ideology (1984)*, Daphne Patai argues that 'suppressing recognition of women's oppression and ignoring the issue of patriarchy lock Orwell into an insoluble double bind, and the inability to express this contradiction and then think it through undermines his work'.

Although at the Centenary Conference on George Orwell held at Wellesley College in 2003, Patai significantly modifies this verdict, the voices of political hostility camouflaged as aesthetic criticism are not an isolated phenomenon. Why, for example, someone of the reputation of Harold Bloom would accept the editorship of essays on *Nineteen Eighty-Four* and on *Animal Farm*, two works he obviously disliked (or maybe by the 1980s or 1990s only imperfectly remembered) is a question hard to answer. But editor he became of *George Orwell's 1984: Modern Critical Interpretations* (1987), arguing that 'the aesthetic badness of 1984 is palpable enough', since Orwell 'lacked nearly all the gifts necessary for the writer of narrative fiction'. He echoes here Q. D. Leavis's 1940 view that 'nature did not intend [Mr Orwell] to be a novelist', a verdict rather harsh even for its time, that is before Orwell's fictional breakthrough in the satires of *Animal Farm* and *Nineteen Eighty-Four*. In his Preface to the *Notes on Animal Farm*, a collection of critical essays published in Contemporary Literary Views (1999), Bloom simply ignores that the animal fable happens to be a satire on Stalin's USSR and that it was 'of the utmost importance to [Orwell] that people in western Europe see the Soviet regime for what it was' (v.3, 458). Instead, Bloom declares that Orwell was 'a liberal moralist . . . grimly preoccupied with preserving a few old-fashioned virtues while fearing that the technological future would only enhance human depravity' – a strange and, I fear, not particularly helpful pronouncement about Orwell and his targets in *Animal Farm*. How much more useful for the student or the general reader is Jenni Calder's *Open Guide to Animal Farm* (1987), and more recently, John Rodden's *Understanding Animal Farm. A Student Casebook of Issues, Sources and Historical Documents* (1999), including documents by and about Trotsky, Lenin and Stalin, among others, in order to help the reader explore Orwell's unmistakable satirical allusions to the political figures targeted.

There is no doubt that terms introduced by some of the hostile verdicts are slipping into general parlance. When Leslie Fiedler in his 1984 lectures borrows well-established terms about Orwell's 'cardboard characters', this line is also taken over by Michael Radford, director of the 1984 film version of Orwell's *Nineteen Eighty-Four*; in the *New York Times* Radford declares that 'Orwell's book is a political essay with a melodrama attached and some cardboard minor characters. What I tried to do is make it real'. Taking this condescending (if not openly hostile) tone even further, Neil Sinyard praises Radford for 'cutting through the novel's 'pamphleteering' and making more of the dream atmosphere of the novel than Orwell did' (*Filming Literature*, 1986).

But probably the most influential line of political attack camouflaged as aesthetic criticism was introduced by Raymond Williams, who blames *Nineteen Eighty-Four* for creating 'the conditions for defeat and despair' for millions. Williams wilfully and consistently misreads Orwell's anti-Stalinism as anti-Socialism and thereby sets the tone for much of the New Left's hostility to Orwell. In the words of Christopher Hitchens, even in our days it is hard to believe the 'sheer ill will and bad faith and intellectual confusion [that] appear to ignite spontaneously when Orwell's name is mentioned in some quarters' (*Why Orwell Matters*, 2003), while John Rodden in *The Politics of Literary Reputation* offers a probing analysis of the harsher and harsher charges Williams levels against Orwell according to the different political stages in Williams's own political journey between the 1950s and the 1970s. Hitchens reminds us that Williams, who 'introduced two generations of English readers to the idea of "cultural studies", was 'member of the Communist generation of the 1930s and 1940s [who became] one of the germinal figures of the New Left'. In his immensely influential book, *Culture and Society*, published in 1958, Williams declares the total effect of Orwell's work 'in an effect of paradox. He was a humane man who communicated an extreme inhuman terror, a man committed to decency who actualized a distinctive squalor'. As Hitchens points out, 'what Williams means to imply, but is not brave enough to say, is that Orwell "invented" the picture of totalitarian collectivism'.

The best answer to this innuendo of Williams is, of course, in the many political, historical studies and memoirs Orwell had a chance to read and review in his time, not to mention later testimonies of writers like Milan Simecka and Czeslav Milos who felt amazed that Orwell 'who never lived in Russia should have so keen a perception into its life'. In case Williams was not satisfied with the veracity of personal accounts, he must have been familiar with later highly acclaimed studies analysing Nazi and Stalinist forms of terror, such as Hannah Arendt's *The Origins of Totalitarianism* (1951) and Carl Friedrich and Zbigniev Brzezinsky's *Totalitarian Dictatorship and Autocracy* (1956), scholarly confirmations that Orwell's original 'anatomy' of totalitarianism was an accurate diagnosis of reality and not the fantasmagorical 'invention' of an author in the throes of terminal despair.

In fact, it is interesting to look at the Orwell handbooks or collections of critical essays over the years to demonstrate what a clear equation Orwell's political opponents draw between Orwell's alleged despair and his alleged aesthetic incompetence as a novelist. In his 1969 *The Making of George Orwell: An Essay in Literary History*, Keith Aldritt declares that Orwell 'obviously had neither the intricate sensibility nor the creative energy of the true novelist', and in his last novel he is sinking 'into the most precipitous declension of despair'. In the 1971 *Twentieth Century Interpretation of 1984: A Collection of Critical Essays*, editor Samuel Hynes aims to represent the spectrum of Orwell criticism by including such favourable essays as those by Irving Howe, Lionel Trilling and Alex Zwerdling, together with one of the most influential of hostile essays, Isaac Deutscher's 'The Mysticism of Cruelty' (originally written in 1955).

Deutscher, also author of 'The Ex-communist's Conscience', assumes, incorrectly, that Orwell was a disillusioned ex-Stalinist and therefore temperamentally unable to offer what Deutscher would have considered an appropriate view about the future of Socialism. Therefore Deutscher declares Orwell's last novel simply a harmful 'cry from the abyss of despair, making millions vent their anger and despair on the giant Bogy-cum Scapegoat of Stalin's USSR'.

In the 1974 *Collection of Critical Essays* (in Twentieth Century Views) the choice of criticism is dictated even more clearly by the hostile editorial hand of Williams himself. Here Stephen Greenblatt's 'Orwell as Satirist' elaborates on Anthony West's and Deutscher's lines about terminal despair, suggesting that 'the black pessimism of this book may be, in part, explained by the fact that Orwell's wife died suddenly in 1945, that his own health was deteriorating, . . . but the mood of suicidal despair which pervades *Nineteen Eighty-Four* seems even more to be the result of Orwell's conclusion that he had explored all the so-called solutions of man's misery and found [that]. . . . here is absolutely nothing that can stop the monstrous progress'.

In effect, Orwell's political views, as expressed in his essays and journalism at the time he was writing his last novel, were far from 'suicidal despair' or the conviction that the 'monstrous progress' of totalitarianism was unstoppable. Orwell's intention to destroy the 'Soviet myth' does not signify disillusionment with the Socialist ideal. On the contrary, he makes clear that it is precisely in the interests of the 'revival of the Socialist movement' in the West that one has to destroy the 'belief that Russia is a Socialist country' (v.3, 458). Goldstein's Book suggests that if totalitarianism takes over the Western world, this takeover will not come from being conquered by the outside (in 1984 the three power-blocks of Oceania, Eurasia and Eastasia are in perfect equilibrium) but from the wrong choice made by the Leftist intellectual who fails to see the falsehood of the Soviet mythos, believing that Russia is a Socialist country to be respected and emulated. We would do well to remember, however, that when the satirist warns his Adversary against making the wrong choice, he implies that there is a right choice available as well, that of creating a society with 'economic security without concentration camps', that is, the choice 'to make democratic Socialism work' (v.4, 370).

One of the reasons for the 'Orwell Conundrum' – the reams of critical attacks against a work that is not only one of the most popular novels of the century, but also the centre of an entire Orwell industry in criticism – has to do with the question of genre. According to Irving Howe, 'To ask what kind of book *1984* is may seem a strange, even pedantic question. After all, you might say, millions of people have read the book and appreciated it well enough without troubling their heads about fine points of genre'. Yet, many of the critics' 'complaints have really to do with genres or misunderstanding of genres; they reflect a failure to grasp the kind of fiction Orwell was writing and what could legitimately be expected from it' ('*1984*: Enigmas of Power' in *1984 Revisited*, ed. Irving Howe, 1983). Jeffrey Meyers, for example, states that 'the fundamental problem is that Orwell breaks the conventions of both literary forms that shape the novel, realism and utopian romance, and deliberately disappoints the reader's expectations'.

Indeed, Orwell admits that his last novel is a mixed genre. As a naturalistic novel (v.4, 378) in the mode of psychological realism, the novel makes its appeal to the readers on the basis of our almost unconditional identification with the central character. At the same time, it is also intended as a fantasy

ERIKA GOTTLIEB

of the future (v.4, 378; 536), what we call today dystopian satire. As such, Orwell tells us, it is a parody – a word he uses as a synonym for satire – about the splitting up of the world by the superpowers (v.4, 520), the effect of the atom bomb on the divided world, and the perversions of a centralised economy (v.4, 564). But more important than any of these individual targets, it is a parody of the intellectual implications of totalitarianism, of 'the totalitarian mentality' (v.4, 520; 564). Hence the complexity of the genre, a composite Orwell defines 'in a sense a fantasy, but in the form of the naturalistic novel. That is what makes it a difficult job' (v.4, 378). In spite of the novel's tremendous impact in the past fifty years, few critics have asked the question why Orwell felt it was necessary to go ahead with the 'difficult job' of combining political allegory and psychological verisimilitude. Yet the dystopian satire could not warn us against allowing the 'worst of all possible worlds' of totalitarianism coming to power without demonstrating that the greatest political disaster created by that regime is psychological: it is the irrevocable disintegration of the individual psyche.

The mixture of genres is indeed decisive in explaining the overall effects of the novel. There is no doubt that Winston reaches a tragic end and the psychological dimension of the naturalistic novel makes us identify with him. Yet, in the overall structure of the book as dystopian satire, we are also asked to examine Winston's fate from the intellectual distance created by Goldstein's Book in the middle of the novel and by the Appendix of Newspeak at the end. 'What happened had to happen' is the enlightenment reached at the end of tragedy. Enlightenment here comes as a result of, after the catastrophe. In satire our enlightenment consists of another kind of catharsis, and I suggest it consists of the recognition that, frozen into the time-frame of the Ideal Readers to whom the satire was addressed in 1948, we are still before the catastrophe and hence in the possession of freedom to avert it. When asked to read Goldstein's Book and the Dictionary of Newspeak, dealing with the past of the 1940s and the future of 2050 respectively, we are reminded that Winston's moving story taking place in 1984 has not happened yet – and it does not have to happen. Unlike Winston, we still have the freedom to shape the future according to our intelligence and free choice.[2]

According to Irving Howe, accepting the novel as a mixture of genres 'may train us to avoid false expectations', and as Valerie Meyers also points out, in *Nineteen Eighty-Four*, 'Orwell's polemic purposes led him to combine genres and styles in a daring and original way. His attack on totalitarian systems is far more complex than in *Animal Farm*, blending realism, parody . . . and satire' (*George Orwell* in Modern novelists series, 1991). As she also warns us, we should be aware that *Nineteen Eighty-Four* 'does not belong

198

to that category of art which offers consolation. It reveals [Orwell's} . . . imaginative sympathy with the millions of the persecuted and murdered in the name of absolutist ideologies in the twentieth century . . . closer in spirit to Franz Kafka's fables or to Alexander Solzhenitsyn's tales of the Soviet prison camps than to other English novels' (139).

Response to Orwell's last novel was indeed remarkable in Russia and in the Soviet bloc.[3] In fact, Orwell's dystopian fiction about Oceania with the one-party system, personality cult, rigged trials, the rewriting of history, and Doublethink is astonishingly similar to 'realistic descriptions' of many a genuinely dystopic society in the Soviet Bloc at the time. (In his *Scenes from an Afterlife* John Rodden singles out the GDR to show this resemblance in convincing detail.) If reading Orwell's last novel in the West worked, in effect, as a rallying cry not to succumb to the totalitarian mentality in the future, reading the book in the Soviet Bloc (or anywhere in the world where people live(d) under government-imposed terror) worked as a rallying cry for changing the totalitarian regime in existence. As Hitchens suggests, 'We commonly use the term "Orwellian" in one of two ways. To describe a state of affairs as "Orwellian" is to imply crushing tyranny and fear of conformism. To describe a piece of writing as "Orwellian" is to recognize that human resistance to these terrors is unquenchable'. "Orwellian" then means the desire to change, not to acquiesce in despair and apathy. This has been seen by many a reader. As Anthony Burgess puts it: 'Orwell's *Nineteen Eighty-Four* is one of the few dystopian visions to have changed man's habits of thought. It is possible to say that the ghastly future Orwell foretells will not come about, simply because he foretold it: we have been warned'. In the words of William Steinhoff: 'literature and the world since [*Nineteen Eighty-Four*] have been different; it changed the world'.[4]

In spite of some influential hostile voices (or their unexamined vestiges) still lingering in contemporary Orwell studies, we should not really be surprised that in the BBC's *The History of Britain* series, Simon Schama frames his television programme on the Second World War between the portraits of two Winstons whom he singles out as the most memorable representatives of resistance to totalitarianism: one is Winston Churchill; the other, Orwell's Winston Smith.

NOTES

All quotations from Orwell's essays are taken from the four-volume *Collected Essays, Journalism and Letters of George Orwell*, ed. Sonia Orwell and Ian Angus (Harmondsworth: Penguin, 1970). Volume and page numbers are provided in parentheses, e.g. (v. 4, 564).

1. Both essays in *George Orwell: A Reassessment*, ed. P. Buitenhuis and I. Nadel (London: Macmillan, 1988).
2. Erika Gottlieb, *The Orwell Conundrum: A Cry of Despair or Faith in the Spirit of Man?* (Ottawa: Carleton University Press, 1992). Distributed by McGill-Queen's University Press.
3. See, for example, Hungarian György Dalo's 1985: *Tortenelmi Jelentes* [1985: Historical Report] (Budapest: Uj Geniusz, 1984); Russian Abram Tertz's (Sinyiavski's) *The Trial Begins*, trans. George Dennis (Berkeley: California University Press, 1982); or Vladimir Voinovich's *Moscow 2042*, trans. Richard Lourie (New York: Harcourt Brace Jovanovich, 1984).
4. William Steinhoff, *George Orwell and the Origins of 1984* (Ann Arbor: University of Michigan Press, 1975).

16

CHRISTOPHER HITCHENS
Why Orwell still matters

As I was beginning to write this Afterword, I received two invitations, both of them from London, in the space of two days. The first came from the BBC's 'Open Book' radio programme, which forwards readers' queries and difficulties to supposed 'experts', and invites them to act as 'radio doctors' giving advice to patients. Here was what my own patient complained of, in email form:

> I have always wanted to read *Nineteen Eighty-Four* by George Orwell. I have tried and tried but get lost very quickly and haven't managed to have gotten past chapter 3. I have difficulty picturing the scenes described in the book. I have never had so much difficulty with a book, and it would be a big achievement if I could read, understand and love the book. I believe it is a brilliant piece of literature and feel I am missing out. I have tried to track down the film which I thought might help.

My second invitation was from the Frontline Club, a group of war and foreign correspondents who meet to discuss new books and films in their general area of interest. A new documentary had been made, about 'Orwellian' manipulation of the media in the United States, and the invitation closed with the ominous proposition that '1984' might not be 'just a date in the future'.

It was much easier to respond to the second of these than to the first. I simply sent a laconic email, suggesting that they take another editorial look at that closing line, while privately marvelling that the novel itself somehow retains its capacity to be futuristic. To the first query, I had no idea what to suggest. In particular, I wondered how any one would have any difficulty 'picturing' the scenes in the first three chapters which, it must be agreed by even the sternest critic, are rather vividly 'pictured' by the author himself. But it was touching to see how much the reader wanted to master the book, and how much he or she believed in its importance. (One of the things that would most have astonished Orwell, had he lived, would have been the immortalising of his book as a compulsory 'set text' in schools. I have found, in teaching the book at college and graduate level on numberless occasions, that it is one of the few such works that is not spoiled for younger readers in this way.)

A sample of problems, then. A slight but common misuse of the word 'Orwellian' in an everyday discussion of the manipulation of news, an unintended tribute to the continuing power of his most famous novel, and a confession of total failure by somebody who could not even tackle it as a thriller. About once a week, I come across the first distortion. A White House attempt to 'spin' the story is revealed, or someone is pulled to one side in a 'Homeland Security' search at an airport, and it's *Nineteen Eighty-Four* all over again. It takes a bit of breath to point out that in Orwell's dystopia the state *is* the mass media, and vice versa, and that the citizens of Airstrip One do not have the right to go to the airport of their choice, or choose between airlines, or indeed to move anywhere they are not directed. The supposedly Orwellian attempts to influence the press, and the mingled incompetence and intrusiveness of the anti-terrorist system, are more reminiscent of a banana republic, with the occasional admitted touch of Franz Kafka. The official enemies of the state, from the Taliban through Saddam Hussein to the Kim Jong Il cult in North Korea, do indeed have very advanced ideas of how absolute the power of the state over the individual should become, but it can take even more breath, when speaking in polite circles, to point out this very evident fact.

Undertaking to defend Orwell's legacy, during and after his centennial year, involves one in much the same difficulty of estimating, in each case, from exactly what it is that one is defending him. Reviewing my book *Why Orwell Matters* in a most generous way, the conservative social analyst David Brooks argued that I could indeed have saved a lot of the sort of breath I mentioned above, since the battles and quarrels in which Orwell took part are now quite irrelevant to us. All that was left was a tribute to a certain kind of integrity and truth-telling. Publishing an entire book attacking both Orwell and myself in the same year, *The Betrayal of Dissent: Beyond Orwell, Hitchens, and the New American Century*, Scott Lucas rested his case on Orwell's surrender of principles in his own time, and my similar surrender in our own. Morris Dickstein politely reproved me for having written that Orwell, who usually allowed himself about one joke per novel, had not included a single one in *Nineteen Eighty-Four*. (He cited the biography, fabricated by Winston Smith in the course of his duties at the Ministry of Truth, of a certain Comrade Ogilvy. . .).

I very much wanted to agree with Mr Brooks, if only because my own book had striven to make the same point about intellectual courage as a virtue for its own sake. Yet I know very well that I would be melancholic if the day ever came when the names of Andres Nin, and Nikolai Bukharin, Victor Serge, Arthur Koestler, Dwight Macdonald and others were ashes in the memory-hole of history. Thus, in a contradictory fashion, I almost preferred the amazing party-line illiteracy of Scott Lucas, in whose cortex these supposedly ancient and arcane disputes are still, at least partly at any rate, vivid and present. We do not absolutely have to know, when we relish the prose and poetry of Orwell's favourites such as Pope or Swift or Milton, who were the targets and the duellists of their own day. But who can deny that such knowledge furnishes an extra dimension to that relish? In much the same way, who cares for the opinion of an atheist who has never read the Bible, or of a Creationist who has not bothered to grasp the points made by Darwin? As William Empson used to emphasise, there is an absolute need for an understanding of the context in which writers lived, and in which writing took place. There is also another imperative: that the spoken word and the written word must never become too much separated.

Thus, to take just a small instance from contemporary life and criticism, the decision of those who imagine that they are practising 'literary theory': the decision, that is, to adopt a mode of discourse that is virtually private on the page and quite impossible to keep up in ordinary speech, may arouse our suspicion of its authenticity not because of its supposedly superior 'difficulty' (it is in fact a relatively simple language to decode) but because it seems to desire an existence apart from the common tongue, in which it must be said that its practitioners do not excel.

This dispute has a potent historical analogue in the struggle to have the Bible translated into plain English: a struggle that along with other struggles eventually acquired the general name of Protestantism. I would surmise that Orwell was an atheist, but I could be much more sure of saying that he was a Protestant atheist. For him, the battle to have the psalms and prophets and parables available to the common people ('understanded of the people', as the Thirty-Nine articles of the Church of England put it, as an appendix to Thomas Cranmer's *Book of Common Prayer*) was a victory over a class of tyrannical priests who had masked their arbitrary but shaky authority in Latin. The existence of a doubly secret yet treacherous text, a possession of both the 'resistance' and the Inner Party in *Ninety Eighty-Four*, is a metaphor clearly drawn from that story. So is the existence of 'Newspeak': a tongue in which concepts of freedom cannot even be formulated, let alone expressed. For all his suspicion of America, Orwell gives Thomas Jefferson's preamble to the Declaration, in his 'Dictionary of Newspeak', as an example of what might be impossible to think or utter under the totalitarian linguistic order.

Then again, I am not so certain that we have quite managed to leave the age of ideology behind us. The young British essayist Michael Gove, recently elected to the House of Commons as a (somewhat neo) Conservative, may be the last person ever to have been converted to socialism by Orwell, during his school days in Scotland. But in those regions of the world where the state retains not just the ambition but the power to enslave the citizen, Orwell's work continues to be relevant in what one might call its original form. I was reading an article about a female Chinese 'blogger' recently: one of those who have begun a movement that will certainly outlast the Chinese Communist Party. She had first commenced to think for herself, she told the interviewer, when reading a banned copy of *Animal Farm*. (The book itself is still banned in China, though an enterprising group has succeeded in publicly performing it as an opera: an event I should very much like to have attended.) In Zimbabwe, beggared and terrorised by the Mugabe regime, the chief opposition newspaper brought revenge upon itself by publishing a cartoon of the leader as Napoleon the pig, and by serialising *Animal Farm* without comment. (Even this would be impossible in the Islamic world, where the novel is still banned because of the presence of so many pigs – even wicked ones – in its pages.) The attention paid to the three states of Iran, Iraq and North Korea, as a consequence of President Bush's speech on the 'axis of evil', has reminded us that the absolute state, with its supreme, ubiquitous leader and its cowed, scarcity-dominated population, is a real presence in our own lives as well. Many reporters in Saddam's Baghdad were compelled to use the imagery of *Nineteen Eighty-Four* to convey a sense of the atmosphere: on my own visit to North Korea I had no choice but to speculate that the Kim Il Sung state, founded at about the same time as the publication of *Nineteen Eighty-Four*, might actually have employed the novel as a blueprint in designing its system of total surveillance and regimentation, and endless, hermetic misery.

Orwell, however, was more than a foe of totalitarianism and totalitarians. He was a critic of the human species. He understood – this must have been partly the result of his experience as a colonial police officer – that while slavery is hateful, servility is contemptible. It is not only intellectuals who make excuses for power and become its fawners and valets. Many people fear freedom and wish to be relieved of its responsibilities. In the early stages of dictatorship, many of the 'spontaneous mass demonstrations' in its favour are exactly that. People derive pleasure from informing on their fellow-citizens. Nor can it be doubted that there is a sexual element – at any rate a sublimated sado-masochism – in the cult-worship of torturers and murders. A mediocre person can derive a vicarious thrill from the cruelties practiced by his 'Leader': I have met half-starved and frightened Iraqis who were still ready to yell praises for Saddam, the man who had thoughtfully televised for them the effect of his Scud missiles. The will to command is useless without the corresponding will to obey.

When I wrote my little book on Orwell for his centennial year in 2003, I had – to my great shame and embarrassment – not read Victor Klemperer's diaries. The first two of these three volumes begin in 1933 and end in 1945, and record every single day in the twelve years' existence of the Thousand Year Reich. The third book recounts Klemperer's experience as a citizen of East Germany after the war, ending with his death in 1959. I can't summarise the extraordinary effect of this work except by saying that, for the later part of Orwell's life, and obviously quite unknown to him, there actually was a Winston Smith, keeping a life-threatening private journal in the very belly of the totalitarian beast. And it's all there: the increasing strangulation of the private life, the hysterical speeches and grotesque uniformed youth movements; the militarisation of news bulletins and the gruesome standardised food; the hourly expectation of the knock on the door and the ghastly end. Klemperer was a Protestant convert from Judaism and was married to a Protestant woman: his wife – who could have saved herself by leaving him, but chose not to – was a more consistent ally than Winston's Julia, and made Klemperer's life and private resistance worthwhile. At this point, it would be nice to record that Klemperer also formulated a dictionary of Newspeak. And so he did! He made continuous notes for a future anthology called LTI: *Lingua Tertii Imperii* or 'Language of the Third Reich'. (It was actually published in post-war Germany and had a considerable effect on the generation of 1968.) He noticed the absurd boastfulness of the press and radio, the ridiculous claims of high production at home and of continuous war victory on faraway fronts, and the euphemisms and slogans by which murder and torture were explained away.

Having opted for East Germany after 1945, in the optimistic belief that it was the more de-Nazified side, Klemperer soon realised his mistake and resumed his journal. Once again, we get the texture of life under an oppressive collectivism, less terrifying this time but almost as stultifying. Everything we now know about the Stasi state was recorded in detail by this survivor of Hitler. I began to wonder, given Klemperer's interest in developments in the West, if he had ever heard of Orwell or been able to get hold of a *samizdat* edition of any of his books. But here I was disappointed: the news seems never to have penetrated to him. The nearest to a hint comes in an entry on a 'cultural conference' in West Germany, which Klemperer follows second hand and through the filter of state propaganda. He tells his diary that he is interested in what he's learned of a speech by a certain Arthur Koestler . . .

In some ways the most arresting element in Klemperer's diaries of the Nazi years is a detail that would be impossible to confect. He and his wife were cat-lovers (his wife especially so) and possessed a fairly ordinary but affectionate tomcat. There came a point where, with pedantic sadism, the authorities forbade Klemperer to make donations to the German cat-lover's organization, or to receive subscription copies of the magazine *German Feline*. This magazine had in any case become unreadable because of its solemn promotion of the 'Aryan cat' over other affected 'breeds'. Nor did the insanity cease. As time went by, it became a matter of policy to prevent Aryan cats from residing in Jewish or even part-Jewish homes. By the time that the Allies were bombing Germany in daylight, the Nazi party could still spare functionaries to go from door to door to enforce this order, to collect cats that lived in inappropriate houses, and to have them. . . taken to gas chambers. Thus the Klemperers were deprived of their sole companion, the tomcat Muschl.

In its depiction of the remorseless destruction of the private life, this thread of Klemperer's work exceeds even the moment when Winston Smith's lovely paperweight is smashed by the Thought Police, revealing the piece of coral within the glass as a pathetic shard. There were some things that even Orwell might not have guessed, or invented, about the workings of totalitarianism. But it is a tribute to him, all the same, that when we come across such episodes we are automatically put in mind of him. It's for this reason that I dissent from Morris Dickstein's view that the story of Comrade Ogilvy counts as a joke:

> At the age of three Comrade Ogilvy had refused all toys except a drum, a sub-machine gun and a model helicopter. At six – a year early, by a special relaxation of the rules – he had joined the Spies; at nine he had been a troop leader. At eleven he had denounced his uncle to the Thought Police after overhearing a conversation which appeared to him to have criminal tendencies. At seventeen he had been a district organizer of the Junior Anti-Sex League. At nineteen he had designed a hand-grenade which had been adopted by the Ministry of Peace and which, at its first trial, had killed thirty-one Eurasian prisoners at one burst.

Do I have to explain the historical (and admittedly satirical) elements of this story to my students? Yes I do. But did I expect in my own lifetime to witness ethnic cleansing taking place in Europe, or to see mass graves dug up in Iraq and discover that some of the victims had been used for experiments in poison weapons? Not when I first read about Comrade Ogilvy I didn't.

I should also like to add some of Big Brother's own comments, as fabricated by Winston Smith, on Comrade Ogilvy's character:

He was a total abstainer and a non-smoker, had no recreations except a daily hour in the gymnasium, and had taken a vow of celibacy, believing marriage and the care of a family to be incompatible with a twenty-four-hour-a-day devotion to duty.

Orwell's own sexual life may have been somewhat distraught, but he had an insight into the relationship between sexual and political repression, and the sketch above cannot but make us think of the debased asceticism that animated Mohammed Atta and his fellow fanatics: at once highly pure and extremely defiled. This is, one might say, no joke.

The game of WWGOD – What Would George Orwell Do? – is in some ways over. I think it certainly terminated with his centenary, and probably well before that. In a debate with Norman Podhoretz about Orwell's probable attitude to the war in Vietnam, which I began having in 1984, I could concede that Podhoretz had certain obvious things, such as social-democratic opposition to Communism, on his side. But since Orwell had never had any illusions in Communism to lose, and since he detested colonial rule in Asia and would have been bound to notice the continuity between American policy and the French empire, I think I can marshal more evidence on mine. Emma Larkin's book, *Secret Histories: Finding George Orwell in a Burmese Teashop*, published twenty years later in 2004, traces another contradictory observation made by Orwell, to the effect that as bad as the British empire was, it might well come to seem benign compared to some of its successors. (Her journey through the horror and wretchedness of today's 'Myanmar' includes a meeting with an old savant who refers to Orwell as 'the prophet' of what was to come when General Ne Win seized power in 1952 and imposed a hermetic and terrifying rule of quasi-Buddhist and quasi-Stalinist absolutism.) The striking thing is therefore this: Orwell would have had something to say in either event, or about either outcome. This was not because he tried to have it both ways, but because he was invariably on the side of elementary humanity against all 'experiments' on the human subject. It was not a matter of what he thought but of *how* he thought, which in turn is the explanation of why he still matters, and always will.

FURTHER READING

Atkins, John, *George Orwell: A Literary Study*. London: Calder and Boyars, 1954.

Bluemel, K., 'St George and the Holocaust', *Literature Interpretation Theory*, 14 (2004).

Bowker, Gordon, *George Orwell*. London: Little Brown, 2003.

Bowker, Gordon, *Inside George Orwell*. New York: Palgrave Press, 2003.

Brander, Laurence, *George Orwell*. London: Longman Green, 1954.

Branson, Noreen and Margot Heinemann, *Britain in the Nineteen Thirties*. New York: Praeger, 1971.

Brown, Gordon, *Maxton*. Edinburgh and London: Mainstream Publishing, 2002.

Calder, Angus, *The People's War: Britain 1939–45*. New York: Ace, 1972.

Collini, Stefan, 'The Grocer's Children: The Lives and Afterlives of George Orwell', *Times Literary Supplement*, 20 June 2003.

Collins, Randall, *The Sociology of Philosophies: A Global Theory of Intellectual Change*. Cambridge, MA.: Belknap Press of Harvard University Press, 1998.

Connolly, Cyril, *Enemies of Promise*. London: Routledge, 1938.

Crick, Bernard, *George Orwell: A Life*. London: Secker and Warburg, 1980.

Crick, Bernard and Audrey, Coppard, *George Orwell Remembered*. London: Ariel Books, 1984.

Cronkite, Walter Preface to *Nineteen Eighty-Four*. New York: Harcourt Brace Jovanovich, 1983.

Davison, Peter (ed.), *The Complete Works of George Orwell*. London: Secker and Warburg, 2000.

Davison, Peter, *George Orwell: A Literary Life*. New York: St Martin's Press, 1996.

Eagleton, Terry, 'Reach-Me-Down Romantic', *London Review of Books*, 25:12, 19 June 2003.

Emerson, Ralph Waldo, 'The American Scholar', 1837, rpt. *Essays and Lectures*, ed. Joel Porte, New York: Library of America, 1983, 53–71.

Fyvel, T. R., *George Orwell: A Personal Memoir*. London: Macmillan, 1982.

Gollancz, Victor (ed.), *The Betrayal of the Left: An Examination and Refutation of Communist Policy*. London: Gollancz, 1941.

Gross, Miriam (ed.), *The World of George Orwell*. London: Weidenfeld and Nicolson, 1971.

Havighurst, Alfred F., *Britain in Transition: The Twentieth Century*, 4th ed. Chicago: University of Chicago Press, 1985.

Hennessy, Peter, *Never Again: Britain, 1945–1951*. New York: Pantheon, 1993.

Hitchens, Christopher, *Why Orwell Matters*. New York: Basic Books, 2002.

Hollis, Christopher, *A Study of George Orwell*. London: Hollis and Carter, 1956.

Howe, Irving, 'George Orwell: "As the Bones Know"', rpt. *Decline of the New*. New York: Horizon, 1970, 269–79.

Katz, Wendy, 'Imperialism and Patriotism: Orwell's Dilemma in 1940', *Modernist Studies: Literature and Culture*, 3 (1979), 99–105.

Kogan, Steve, 'In Celebration of George Orwell on the Fiftieth Anniversary of "Politics and the English Language"', *Academic Questions* (Winter 1996–1997), 15–29.

Lucas, Scott, *Orwell*, London: Haus Publishing, 2003.

Lucian, *1920: Dips into the Near Future*. London: Headley Bros., 1918.

Lutman, Stephen, 'Orwell's Patriotism', *Journal of Contemporary History*, 2/2 (1967), 149–58.

Marwick, Arthur, *The Deluge: British Society and the First World War*. New York: W.W. Norton, 1970.

Meyers, Jeffrey, *Orwell: The Wintry Conscience of a Generation*. New York/London: Norton, 2000.

Nadel, Ira Bruce, *Biography: Fiction, Fact and Form*. London: Macmillan, 1984.

New, M., 'Orwell and Antisemitism: Toward 1984', *Modern Fiction*, 21, 1 (1975).

Newsinger, John, *Orwell's Politics*. New York: St Martin's Press, 1999.

Orwell, George, *The Collected Essays, Journalism and Letters of George Orwell*, ed. Sonia Orwell and Ian Angus. New York: Harcourt, Brace & World, 1968.

Orwell, George, *1984*. San Diego: Harcourt Brace Jovanovich, 1977.

Orwell, George, *Animal Farm*. New York: Harcourt, Brace and Co., 1946.

Orwell, George, *Burmese Days*. Harmondsworth, Middlesex: Penguin Books Ltd., 1949.

Orwell, George, *A Clergyman's Daughter*. Harmondsworth, England: Penguin Books Ltd., 1969.

Orwell, George, *Coming Up for Air*. Harmondsworth: Penguin Books, 1970.

Orwell, George, *Down and Out in Paris and London*. New York: Harcourt, Brace and World Inc., 1961.

Orwell, George, *England Your England, and Other Essays*. London: Secker & Warburg, 1953.

Orwell, George, *The Lion and the Unicorn: Socialism and the English Genius*. Searchlight Books; no. 1. London: Secker & Warburg, 1941.

Orwell, George, *Homage to Catalonia*. London: Secker & Warburg, 1954.

Orwell, George, *Keep the Aspidistra Flying*. Harmondsworth, England: Penguin Books Ltd., 1970.

Orwell, George, *The Road to Wigan Pier*. Harmondsworth, Middlesex: Penguin Books Ltd., 1974.

Orwell, George, *Shooting an Elephant, and Other Essays*. London: Secker & Warburg, 1950.

Orwell, George, *Coming Up for Air*. New York: Harcourt, Brace & World, 1950.

Orwell, George, *Collected Essays, Journalism, and Letters*, 4 vols., ed. Sonia Orwell and Ian Angus, New York: Harcourt Brace, 1968.

Orwell, George, *Essays*. ed. John Carey, New York: Knopf, 2002.

Posner, Richard A., *Public Intellectuals: A Study of Decline*. Cambridge, MA: Harvard University Press, 2001.

Rees, Richard, *George Orwell: A Fugitive from the Camp of Justice*. London: Secker & Warburg, 1961.

Rodden, John and Thomas Cushman (eds.), George Orwell Into the Twenty-First Century. Boulder, CO: Paradigm, 2004.

Rodden, John, *The Politics of Literary Reputation: The Making and Claiming of 'St George' Orwell*. NewYork/Oxford: Oxford University Press, 1989.

Rodden, John, *Scenes From An Afterlife: The Legacy of George Orwell*. Wilmington, Delaware: ISI Books, 2003.

Rodden, John (ed.), *Understanding Orwell's* Animal Farm *in Historical Context*. Westport, CT: Greenwood Press, 1999.

Rose, Jonathan, *The Intellectual Life of the British Working Classes*. New Haven and London: Yale University Press, 2001.

Rose, Jonathan (ed.), *The Revised Orwell*. East Lansing, MI: Michigan State University Press, 1992.

Rossi, John, 'George Orwell's Conception of Patriotism', *Modern Age*, XLII, no. 2 (Spring 2001), 128–32.

Schwartz, Lawrence, *Creating Faulkner's Reputation: The Politics of Modern Literary Criticism*. Knoxville: University of Tennessee Press, 1988.

Shelden, Michael, *Orwell: The Authorized Biography*. London: Heinemann, 1991.

Spurling, Hilary, *The Girl from the Fiction Department*. London: Hamish Hamilton, 2002.

Stansky, Peter and Abrahams, William, *The Unknown Orwell*. London: Constable, 1972.

Stansky, Peter and Abrahams, William, *Orwell: The Transformation*. London: Constable, 1979.

Stevenson, John, *British Society 1914–45*. Harmondsworth: Penguin, 1984.

Symons, Julian, 'Orwell: A Reminiscence'. *London Magazine* 3 (September 1963), 35–49.

Taylor, D. J., *Orwell: The Life*. London: Chatto and Windus, 2003.

Tyrell, Martin, 'The Politics of George Orwell (1903–1950): From Tory Anarchism to National Socialism and More Than Half Way Back', *Cultural Notes*, no. 36 (1997).

Wadhams, Stephen, *Remembering George Orwell*. Harmondsworth: Penguin, 1984.

Walton, D., 'George Orwell and Antisemitism', *Patterns of Prejudice*, 16, 1 (1982).

Westbrook, R., 'The Responsibility of Peoples: Dwight Macdonald and the Holocaust', *Holocaust Studies Annual* 1. Florida: Greenwood, 1983.

Williams, Raymond, *George Orwell*. Englewood Cliffs: Prentice Hall, 1974.

Woodcock, George, *The Crystal Spirit*. London: Jonathan Cape, 1967.

Young, John Wesley, *Totalitarian Language*. Charlottesville, VA: University of Virginia Press, 1991.

Zwerdling, Alex, *Orwell and the Left*. New Haven: Yale University Press, 1974.

INDEX

Cambridge Companions to...

AUTHORS

TOPICS